THE
CUTTER

THE CUTTER

Billy Henderson

In dedication for the following who inspired me:

Betty Jo Petty
Laura Botsford
Gary Goode

Chapter 1

On a cold raw Friday morning in the early spring of 1950, James and Earlene Parks and their three children loaded their meager possessions into a '46 Ford truck and homemade trailer. They were moving from a poor hill farm in Conway County, Arkansas, to Silver Leaf Farms in central Lonoke County, Arkansas. James, Earlene, and the two smaller children crowded into the small cab of the truck; Penny, the oldest, found a little nook in the bed of the truck and hunkered down.

James and Earlene lived through the depression as sharecroppers in the hills of Conway, County. They married young full of hopes and plans for their new life together. The depression years had been hard on James and Earlene. Penny was born during that terrible time and almost starved to death. Earlene, because of her poor diet and lack of food, could not produce enough breast milk to sustain Penny. She came very close to dying. The Parks were always on the move trying to find a better place and a better life for their family.

Penny has turned 17. Her name is Penelope but she prefers to be called Penny, a name given to her by her grandmother who lived with them after her husband died. Granny was Earlene's mother. She used to read to the children from the Bible, and instilled in them that God loves them as much as he loves the richest people on earth. She taught them to never feel ashamed, to be happy, and to make the best of the lot they had drawn in life. Granny died last year but her words of encouragement, strength and pride stay with them always.

They arrived at the Silver Leaf Farm late afternoon. It had been a long hard trip, with two flat tires and the truck overheating twice. They checked in at the farm headquarters where they met the foreman, McKenzie. McKenzie had found them while scouting around rural areas visiting local Masonic lodges and cafes' looking for a young man with good mechanic and farm hand skills. He is pleased with the Parks family and thought they would fit in very well with Silver Leaf Farms. McKenzie showed them to their new home. Being late, they unloaded the cow and staked her on a grassy spot near the house and hastily unloaded the truck.

"It looks like a real nice place, doesn't it Earlene?" said James who is looking forward to providing a better life for his family.

"Yes, it does. We are going to be very happy here," Earlene enthusiastically replied. She had a happy outlook throughout their marriage and always made the best of every day with what they had to work with. She is a petite little woman with a big heart, patient, hard-working and seldom complained or blamed anyone for their hard times. "Life is what you make it," is her motto.

"I have a good feeling about this move," James said.

"You did good James to come here; things are going to be alright," said Earlene.

Earlene and Penny had cooked and packed enough food for a couple of days. After a prayer of thanks for their new beginning and safe trip they had a quick dinner of bologna sandwiches. They made beds and crashed for the night; all worn out from the hard trip.

The next day they explored their new surroundings. The house has five rooms and a medium-sized kitchen with a pantry. There were no curtains for the windows or rugs on the floors. The wallpaper is in good condition but was tacked to the wall with round-headed tacks. It is a thick heavy grade and would stop the cold wind from blowing through the cracks. The house did have electricity and a septic tank; something the Parks had never had in their life. There is a porch running the full width of the house with a porch swing.

The house faced the east on a dusty road just off a bayou; not good but livable. The house place had a small barn, a hog pen, a chicken house, a smoke house and enough room for a garden. There is no pasture for the milk cow so each day they staked the cow out on the ditch banks where old Bessie had plenty of grass.

On Monday after their trip there are no clean clothes for the kids to wear to school. It took a couple of days to get their clothes washed and ironed and sewn up. With so few clothes there had been many missed days of school.

On Wednesday, Earlene designated Penny to go with the younger children and enroll them in school, their third one that year. It is a short walk to the bus stop to catch the bus. James Jr., is Thirteen years old going into the seventh grade. He is tall for his age and kind of shy. He had been held back a year because of all the days missed. Missy is a girl with bright eyes and a cute mischievous smile. She is going into the sixth grade and also had been held back a year. Penny is in the eleventh, and managed to keep an average grade despite all the moving and missed days. When they arrived in the school office she met with the Principal who asked a lot of questions about her family.

"I'd like to welcome you and your family to the school Penelope," Principal Watkins said and added, "Are you settling into your new place?"

"Yes, we like it so much better than the old house. We have indoor plumbing, electricity and a room just for me and my sister! We love it; you can call me Penny, that's what most folks call me." Penny is friendly, honest and spoke her mind. "I am wondering if there is some food you brought with you until McKenzie starts paying your dad." Mrs. Watkins asked.

"Mama and I put up some canned food from last year and have a dozen or more jars left and Missy and I made some bread just yesterday. Daddy fried up some bologna last night and we ate it with biscuits this morning," Penny plainly told her.

"I hope you will feel at home here and if there is anything I can do, just let me know," Principal Watkins said. She could tell by her conversation with Penny that they didn't have much but what they did have they were proud of. The lady, as it turned out, is a Baptist Minister's wife. She put the word out about the family and their needs.

The next week the Pastor and a few of the church members delivered several packages to the Parks family. One package contained clothes— mostly used—but clean and ironed, for the entire family. There is a large food package, which the family needed badly. The last package contained curtains for each window in the house and the hardware to hang them. The Pastor and members visited with the Parks family, ministered to them and warmly invited them to church next Sunday.

The Parks did not know the Hacketts; in fact, they knew little about them except that they had been hired and now work for them. This is a God-send coming to Silver Leaf they were feeling like a huge load had been lifted, they settled into the routine life of a share cropping family on the Silver Leaf Farm.

The farm is a large farm, maybe the biggest in the county. It consisted of about 400 acres of cotton, with an 80 acre pecan grove, and enough corn and hay for the livestock. Several hundred acres of pasture provided for the grazing cattle. Hogs were also raised. The farm employed 20 families, and a house is assigned to each family. There were large barns and large trees that lined the roadways through the farm headquarters providing shade in the summer and fall. During the 1890's, when cotton prices had dropped drastically, the Hackett family planted a large grove of pecan trees and to this day sell them to people and candy companies.

On a warm breezy summer day when the farm families were in the field chopping cotton, Penny is left to fix the noon meal and have it on the table at 12:00. Penny is sitting on the front porch swing shelling peas for the family's dinner letting her mind wander far away. She did not hear a young man ride up behind her on a horse. The horse spied Penny and nickered loudly. It startled her and she let out a yelp, getting his attention. Riding up the yard to the front porch, he introduced himself as Smith Hackett. She told him her name is Penny Parks.

She is wearing a pair of cut off pants and a t-shirt tied up leaving her mid riff exposed; typical dress for the times. Smith observed a very blonde girl with a tanned complexion, arms muscled, her belly absent of any fat with stomach muscles very evident; all from the hard work in the fields. Her hands were rough, but her complexion is smooth and her green eyes were bright and sparkling. Her teeth were white and well-tended. Smith, in his mind, had never seen a more gorgeous girl.

They talked for a while, lost in each other's conversation; not only is Penny pretty, Smith noticed, but she has a happy and outgoing personality, as well. Soon she realized the time has flown by. She stated that she must hurry and get the peas shelled and cooked before the noon lunch hour. Smith, being a gentleman, volunteered to help. In moments, they were sitting side by side on the swing. Almost immediately Penny noticed that Smith had never shelled peas before. She laughed at him and showed him how. Smith didn't tell Penny he is the Hackett's grandson.

As Smith rode off, he could not help wondering how a girl like Penny could find herself in this kind of situation. Smith would not forget Penny and looked forward to the next time they met. Penny was thinking about the very handsome young man with sandy colored hair, medium height and the perfect smile. She is hoping to see him again.

HB and Ruth Hackett are the sole owners of Silver Leaf Farms. They have one son, Mark; his wife's name is Mary. Mark and Mary are the parents of Smith. The farm came to HB through his parents and grandparents, who were actually some of the early settlers of the county. HB has a vision about the future of the farm. Times were changing from the horse and mule days to modern farm mechanization. Many of the workers on the Silver Leaf were getting older and probably would not be replaced when they retired.

Back in the winter, HB sent his farm manager McKenzie out to recruit some younger help. He is looking for workers that had the ability to adapt to the new ways of farming. This is how he found James Parks through his scouting a round in some of the area cafe's and lodges which was the practice then, no computers or emails, just plain old word of mouth. And, after he did some background checking, he offered the Parks family a job on the farm. They are a good family he had a good judge of character and they were a hard-working family.

Ruth Hackett, considered by all to be very bright, had come to the farm as a young girl much the same as the Parks family. Because of her background she became the support person for the sharecropper families. McKenzie is the farm foreman. He has lived on the Silver Leaf for over twenty years. It is his job to manage the farm and take care of any disputes that might arise with the farm labor. Sometimes he would get them out of jail, if there is a good reason. McKenzie could be seen carrying a heavy stick, about as long as a walking cane. Most of the field people called him "Stick Man," but not to his face. McKenzie is a good man who knew farming and how to treat people but when necessary, he could be a bucketful of hornets.

It had been a long-standing tradition for the Hackett family to have a 4th of July party for all the families employed on the farm, as well as friends that lived in the area. Cotton was mostly "laid by," which meant the cotton had grown to the point it shaded the ground and is beginning to set blooms; no more plowing and only spot hoeing to catch any escaping weeds. Ruth Hackett is the promoter and organizer for the event.

The day before the party she invited all the older teens to help with the decorations and table setting. There were excellent cooks on the farm and she recruited them to prepare the food. The menu consisted of fish, barbecue, burgers and hot dogs, along with vegetables grown on the farm. Watermelons were planted to be ready for the party. There were plenty of cold drinks iced down in big galvanized tubs; desserts prepared by the ladies on the farm and homemade ice cream topped off the menu. The party had a festive atmosphere, with music from some of the farm's workers. Dancing is allowed, but at that time blacks were not allowed to dance with the whites; just a fact of life for the times and most people were just accustomed to it.

During the preparations for the party Smith showed up to help. Ms. Hackett put Smith and Penny in charge of the decorations but kept them under her watchful eye. Penny was a little bashful at first, but got over it quickly. In a few minutes they were laughing and teasing each other. Penny is dressed in shorts, a shirt that matched her pretty eyes, and an old pair of tennis shoes with no socks. Her tanned, firm body and her happy personality were definitely assets that did not go unnoticed by Smith who took to her a little more each time he saw her.

As they were decorating the Silver Leaf Farm sign, Penny is on the ladder that Smith is holding for safety. As she reached to put up the final piece, Smith saw she might be in trouble. He was about to yell as the ladder and Penny came tumbling down. Smith was ready; he reached for her and caught her well enough to break her fall. Smith stumbled and fell right on top of Penny. "Are you hurt?" Smith anxiously asked her. She started to laugh and said, "Please get off me and help me up." Smith is pleased he had kept her from hurting herself and Penny is happy that he had risked getting hurt to save her.

After the decorations were finished, the helpers sat around one of the tables McKenzie and his crew had set up for the party. They had a good time talking and telling stories about themselves the cooking is to start later today so Penny thought she'd better get on back soon.

Smith asked Penny if he could drive her home and she accepted. It is not dark yet, so they walked down to the bayou for a while.

Afterwards, Penny asked Smith to sit in the porch swing with her. They sat on the swing and visited about an hour. It was dark by then and the full moon is hanging over the bayou like a big biscuit; a good omen, Penny thought. They had a good talk and made plans for the next day. Penny is so happy. After Smith left, Penny started making preparations and helped her Mama bake a chocolate cake.

In the morning she got ready for the party. She had filed her fingernails the night before just keeping them long enough to look nice, but not too long. She now polished them a pretty pink shade. Her mom favored the red shades; Missy just used the clear polish on hers. Penny and her sister both wore pedal pushers. Their mom had bought them for the Fourth of July party. She had thought of this ahead of time, and set aside money for the girls. She knew they would both want to look nice that day and her girls would in their new outfits that she had saved weeks for.

Penny knew the Hackett's' had invited a few family friends in the area to the party, so there would be more boys and girls coming. Of course Smith would be there. Penny had this in mind as she curled her hair. She didn't want her blonde hair too tightly curled; just enough to lift it up and make it look like a nice hair-do for all the kids to notice. She decided to wear a barrette in one side. She had that barrette for a long time. It is gold with a little butterfly on it. Penny didn't need much make-up. But she used just enough she thought. Penny's pedal pushers were white. She wore a light yellow top, button-up, which her mom had made for this event. She had also made one for Missy. Missy is wearing her bright red pedal pushers with a pink top. Penny put lotion on her hands and legs. That was another thing their mom taught them they should keep lotion on after taking a bath from working in the fields.

Mrs. Parks did seem to have a few good ideas, although Penny thought most people over teen-age years weren't up-to-date with their thinking. Penny had a thin pair of white bobby socks to wear with her white tennis shoes. She wanted to be as cool as possible.

After getting dressed, Penny looked inside her old jewelry box, containing notes from friends from school, some bobby pins, other hair accessories, a couple of old rings; a special one from Momma that she had been told the clear set is a real diamond. It is a tiny but Penny liked it. It is set in a gold color. The other one is a cheap thing that didn't look like gold on parts of it any more. Penny decided to wear the diamond ring. It would match the gold in her barrette, the part of her earrings that held her little pearls, and a small gold chain bracelet that had a little heart dangling from it. It still looked good. The gold wasn't real but is still shined and the pearl gleamed.

Now, all she needed to do is help Missy get ready. She didn't want to be embarrassed by a sister that might not look so great. Penny had Missy sit down, and she braided each side of her long brown hair. First, she brushed it all out, and then made two braids with the top part, and after that, brushed the rest up to the crown of Missy's head and made it all into a long thick braid. She put a rubber band at the end, and covered that with a red ribbon her mom had in her sewing box. Missy didn't want any make-up or jewelry on but she sported her white tennis shoes that she had polished up with canvas white polish, they looked all new again and she was ready for the party.

James Jr. wore some cut-off pants with a light blue shirt he usually wore to Sunday school. He also wore tennis shoes, instead of his work shoes. Momma had cut his hair and daddy's the night before. She had to make him comb it. He is old enough to want the girls to look his way, although he wasn't about to get too interested in girls right now. He is too busy helping his dad in the fields and the yard, and going hunting and fishing.

Dad wore his Sunday going-to-church clothes. Momma made him put on some of that face cream the lady selling cosmetics told her would help his skin on his face. She had bought some men's lotion for hands at the dime store. She knew he and the boy needed that. As for Momma, she didn't look so bad for an old woman.

Penny tried to think, how old is her Momma now—forty? She had braided her hair, which is kind of in-between the colors of her daughter's hair. It is a light brown sandy blonde color that is beginning to get some kind of gray in it. She wore her gold wedding band. She decided not to take her purse along, and hid it in the laundry basket in case somebody decided to break in. After getting ready to go, she had James Jr. take the pies she had baked to the truck. He placed them in a box in the bed of the truck for holding things. The Parks family is looking real good as they got into the old pick-up truck and headed to the party.

Chapter 2

✼ ✼ ✼ ✼ ✼

The farm headquarters is a short drive to where the party is set up. James found a good parking place under a big oak tree, a real shady spot. It is a hot Delta day, as expected. They got the cake and pie out of the truck and placed them on the table for desserts, then found a good place for the family to sit. James Jr. immediately headed for the cold drinks and picked up a big strawberry soda, as did Missy. They sat talking and watching the people arrive. They were anxious to know who won the cornbread cooking contest. It had been the most talked about event on the Silver Leaf; everybody is guessing. Smith saw Penny and sneaked up behind her and "goosed" her in the ribs. Penny let out a big scream. She saw it was Smith and they all had a good laugh. Penny asked Smith to join them, which he did.

They all had a good visit. Smith and James talked quite a bit; he found James to be a very intelligent man despite of his lack of education. He was a good hire for the Farm. Smith is glad McKenzie found him. Smith visited with Earlene, Missy and James Jr. too. They all liked Smith; a nice young man with a good head on his shoulder and not one to take life too seriously.

The line for the meal was forming and Smith excused himself to go find his family. HB asked Buttons to bless the meal. Buttons had come to the farm as a young black man and now at the age of 70 being there round 50 years he is a loved and treasured family member to the Hackett's. Afterwards, he announced the winners of the cornbread cooking contest. There were ten entries and the judging is done by a well-known black chef. The pans had been numbered so he had no way of knowing whose cornbread he is judging.

The final verdict declared "pan number six" as the winner. Pan number six belonged to Bub Dixon, an older employee who lost his wife to cancer several years ago. That came as a big surprise to the crowd but all gave him a standing ovation. Ruth Hackett presented the prize: $25.00 and a trophy. Bub tearfully thanked the Hacketts and all present. Bub missed his wife who had taught him how to make cornbread, but he felt her presence that Fourth of July day. After the judging, the entries were set out on a table for all to sample.

The Hacketts, HB and Ruth, with their son Mark and his wife Mary, went table to table visiting with each family. There were some folks Mark had grown up with and were about the same age. They had a lot in common; they had hunted and fished together and had played some mischievous pranks. They had a good time talking about growing up on the farm. When they came around to the Parks family they introduced the Parks family to Mark and Mary. They were quite interested, as they had heard about Penny and Smith. Ruth asked Smith to escort Penny to their table after they finished eating. It is a good meal, the cold drinks were cold and sweet, and the cake and ice cream were out of this world. Penny could not remember when she had homemade ice cream and cake, especially all you could eat.

A little later Smith asked Penny to come with him to the Hackett table. Once there, Penny sat by Ruth and Smith sat by his mom. Mark and Mary had private concerns about their son getting interested in a sharecropper's daughter. They wanted to know more about Penny. She told them about how she met Smith. She told it in such a way that everyone had a good laugh. Mary asked about how she liked living on the farm and what her future plans were. Penny just replied she looked forward to making her own way once she finished high school. She also said she is not going to marry a field hand and get trapped in a poor way of life. Penny dropped it there and went about talking about how much she liked to work in the house for Ms. Hackett. She giggled some as she talked and the Hacketts all noticed how at ease she is, displaying her happy and outgoing personality.

Ruth asked Penny if she would go with her the next day to Little Rock for the 4th of July sales, adding she needed someone to help with the packages. Penny said, "I would be happy to go." Ruth said, "Fine! I will pick you up in the morning at seven o'clock."

By that time the music had started, Smith asked Penny to dance with him. Penny had some experience at dancing so she told Smith, "OK. I will do the best I can." The music is not too fast, but kind of upbeat. The Hackett family had a good time watching them dance. They noticed Penny is keeping up with Smith and he had taken dancing lessons. After a while other boys asked Penny to dance; she looked at Smith and he nodded ok. Then all the boys started lining up and Penny had to turn them down, saying she is too tired. Smith is glad and a little bit jealous.

As the party wound down, Smith asked Penny if she would go with him to town and visit some of his friends or maybe go to a movie. Penny said "sure, but you have to come with me while I ask my mom and dad." She got permission but was told not to stay out late. Smith assured them he would have her back by ten o'clock. Smith and Penny went to tell his mom and dad what they were planning. They could see why their son is interested in Penny. They were impressed with her looks and outgoing nature, as well as her sparkling green eyes. That really scared them; they were concerned that Smith might get married before he finished college. They hadn't planned for their son to marry a sharecropper's daughter. However, they remembered that Mark's mother Ruth Smith came to the farm same way that Penny did as a sharecropper's daughter. Her maiden name was Smith, which is where Smith got his name. All they could do is to pray for the right outcome.

As Smith and Penny drove off to town and just before they reached the highway Penny told Smith to stop the car. Smith said, "Why Penny?" She said, "Smith, stop and kiss me or take me back to the party." Smith almost ran the car in the ditch getting it stopped so fast. Penny didn't say a word as she moved over next to Smith. It is a long passionate kiss, good for both of them. Smith had wanted to do this since they first met but was afraid to try. That was their first kiss, certainly not the last. From then on when they were on a date, Penny sat next to Smith. Smith felt like the king of the world.

They did visit some of Smith's friends and they played pool and had a good time visiting. All his friends were now Penny's friends too. Before Smith drove into Penny's yard he stopped the car and hugged Penny and kissed her again and again. Penny is a happy girl. She said, "Take me to the house. Mother and Daddy will be waiting." Smith said. "Penny, I want you to know you are the first girl I have ever really been in love with." Penny replied, "Smith, I know you are the grandson of the Hacketts and I am a sharecropper's daughter. Before I tell you I am in love with you, I want to tell you that I expect to be treated as an equal." Smith responded, "I never thought of it any other way." Penny replied with a very serious tone in her voice, "Smith you are the delight of my life. Of course I love you, and will never love anyone the way I love you, no matter what future plans you may have."

The next morning Ruth, true to her word, picked Penny up and headed to Little Rock and Penny was full of herself. She is a happy girl Ruth noticed. Ruth asked how she thought the party went. Penny replied "Ms Ruth, it was a great time for me and my family! Everyone seemed to have a great time." Ruth had to ask, "What did you and Smith do after the party"? Penny didn't hesitate. She told Ruth about her conversation with Smith. In fact she told her everything, including the part about being treated as an equal and Smith's response. Ruth smiled lightly and said, "Congratulations!

Love is a wonderful thing." She remembered her conversation with HB many years ago. It was almost word for word.

Ruth drove her new Cadillac down Main Street and parked in a parking lot on Fifth and Main, not far from the major department stores in Little Rock. She had been coming here for years. As they shopped, Ruth would point out which stores carried the best brands of clothes. She told Penny that after they had shopped they would stop at McClellans and take a break. Penny is inspired, she watched as Ruth shopped for clothes for her husband and herself, and learned a lot. Ruth asked Penny if she needed anything. Penny replied, "I really do need some underwear and a couple of bras, if I have enough money. I have been saving up for clothes for a while." Ruth told her to wait until they got to Pfiefers or Blass. At the time, Pfiefers had a reputation of having the best brands of clothes.

When they arrived, Ruth took Penny to the ladies department. There was a good sale, and Penny is able to get just what she wanted. With the money left over, so she bought underwear for her mother, and Missy and James. Afterwards Ruth took Penny by the ladies clothes and said, "Penny, because you have been so good to come and work in the house for me and to come here with me today, I want to buy you a couple of outfits." Penny said no at first, but she could see Ruth was not going to take no for an answer. They picked out several outfits which Penny tried on. Penny looked like a beauty queen in each one. The store clerks couldn't keep from staring; Ruth is proud of Penny. Two outfits were selected by Penny and Ruth. There is a good sale, and Ruth saved some money; in fact, she saved so much money she bought Penny a good pair of shoes.

By the time they reached McClellans, they were both hungry. They went in and had a cold fountain drink and a snack. After resting awhile they continued shopping. Finally Ruth said "I think we have done enough for today. Let's go home." There were lots of packages which they put in shopping bags. Both were loaded down and Penny made sure she carried the heaviest ones. It is a long walk back to the car. Ruth is tired and so was Penny. Ruth told Penny, "If you don't mind I am going to ask Smith to teach you how to drive in the city. I need someone to help with the driving. When he is busy I can help you. Do you have a driver's license?" Penny said "I'm sorry, Ms. Ruth I don't." "We can take care of that," Ms. Ruth responded. Penny is a little nervous about driving a new Cadillac car that cost lots of money, but she knew it was time to learn how to drive.

On the way out of Little Rock, Ruth stopped at a Bar-B-Q place and bought enough BBQ for HB and her for dinner. She knew Smith would be there tomorrow so, she bought enough for him too. She also bought a sack full of BBQ sandwiches for the Parks; BBQ sauce was included. They were wrapped in foil so they would stay warm. They smelled so good. When they drove in the yard at the Silver Leaf; Penny and Ruth unloaded the packages. Ruth then drove Penny home. Penny, with tears in her eyes, said to Ruth, "Oh, Ms. Ruth, thank you so much for letting me go with you and thank you so much for the clothes!" She hugged Ruth and said, "Ms. Ruth, I love you so much." Then Ruth had tears in her eyes too. Missy and James Jr. came out to see if Penny had brought them something. When Ruth got home she said to HB, "Over the years I have seen lots of people come and go on this farm, but none has ever captured my heart the way Penny Parks has."

The next day it is back to the real world. Earlene, Penny, Missy, and James Jr. were in the field pulling escaped weeds out of the cotton. They didn't see McKenzie walking towards them. As he got closer James Jr. spotted him and alerted his mother. They stopped and waited for McKenzie to approach them. McKenzie spoke to them and said he had some good news for them. "First, let me say I have already spoken to James and I wanted to talk to you in person. I also want to say this has been in the works for some time and no one knew about this but HB and me. Now the good news: We want you Penny to take the job in the farm headquarters office. We need someone to learn all of the record keeping practices. To start you will be the designated errand person. You need to learn to drive and get a driver's license. We have someone in mind to teach you. It will be a good salary. We want you to start in the morning at 7:30. Just come to the office and I will be there to get you started," McKenzie said.

"Earlene, you and your entire family are good help. James is a good asset to this farm and has been promoted, effective the first of the month. He will be in charge of the farm shop and he will supervise three men. He will make a nice salary. Good enough that you can be a stay at home mom if you want. Missy and James Jr. can continue in the field if they choose to. Now here is the good part. Every five years or so, we try to build a new house for farm help. One is under construction now and will be finished in a month or so. Best part of that is it's a three bedroom half brick home with two bathrooms with good heating and air conditioning, and a garage. We pay all utilities. Stop by and look at it. I am sure you will like it. Also, you will be asked to pick out the curtains and the floors you like. You can have carpet if you want. Oh, I forgot to tell you! There is a new washer and dryer included," McKenzie said and went on some more. "Now we know you don't have furniture for a new home.

HB asked me to tell you that they were redecorating their house and almost all of their furniture will be moved out. If you want, it will be for sale at a cheap price. He will work with you. You won't have to pay anything until you are ready, then the payments will be very low. As you know Penny, it is very good furniture. Do you have questions?" Earlene looked at Penny, they stared at one another then all of a sudden Earlene and Penny broke down crying. It is a hard sobbing cry, with big tears flowing down their faces. They had been so very poor all their life and had no real hope of digging out of that hole. Then they both sat down in the dirt and continued crying so hard they were shaking. Missy and James J. were crying too. Penny said to McKenzie in between sobs, "I will never be able to thank you and Mr. Hackett enough."

"Look, this is not a gift; it is something you all have earned. Just be happy and continue with your life. We hope you are on the Silver Leaf for a very long time. Now Penny I suspect you need to get home and get your office clothes together. Your field hand days are officially over. HB said if you needed new clothes the farm would pay for them and he would ask Ms. Ruth to help you find them. I almost forgot, after you learn to drive you will be Ms. Ruth's personal driver." McKenzie replied. Earlene asked McKenzie if it would be alright to take Penny home and help her get her things together. "I am too excited to finish the day," McKenzie said that is a good idea. It took all the Parks family, including James, a while to get used to the good news.

On their way home from the field they walked silently, all trying to make sense out of what McKenzie had told them. As good as it all sounded, it took the Parks family by surprise and out of their comfort zone. They were use to the hard work and the simple life. Now, they were unsure and hoping they would not let the Hacketts down.

When they reached home, they stowed their hoes under the porch by the doorsteps, same as always. Penny is wondering if it is really the last time she would need a hoe for field work. She went directly to her closet and pulled out all the clothes that might be suitable for working in the farm office as well as for school.

The clothes Ruth Hackett bought her would not go into that pile. They were for church and special events, like on a date with Smith. When they were all sorted out it was obvious there were not enough clothes to fit Penny's needs. She put her head down and started to cry for the second time today. Penny has a strong will and does not cry easily, but all her emotions were piling up on her. Earlene knew what Penny is thinking. She took Penny in her arms and told her not to worry. Penny was still sobbing and said, "Mama I can't go to Miss Ruth and ask her to help me get the clothes that I need. I need clothes for work and for school and for being with Smith. Mama, what am I going to do?" "Sit down and listen to me," Earlene said. She looked into Penny's eyes and said, "Penny, before mother's death she told me a day will come that will change all our lives."

She handed me a purse that contained all the money she and Papa had put back in savings, plus the money from the sale of the farm and farm tools they had accumulated. Earlene is the only surviving child. There had been a son and two daughters that died at birth or soon after.

"We have the money hidden away in a safe place and not in a bank. Now Penny listen to me, we love you very much. We watched you suffer from sickness after you were born. We thought we had lost you but you were a fighter and that is what got you through. We watched you work in the fields from the time you were six years old, never complaining. Now it is our turn to give back. Your daddy and I have talked about this day. We knew it was coming too just as mother said it would."

"This coming Saturday we will all go to town and you can pick out the clothes you will need for work and school. We will buy for Missy and James Jr. too. We have to consider you three are still growing so we will adjust for that. You will need the best and the most. We will pick out good clothes; you will never have to be ashamed of your appearance. We will buy some material and ask Miss Russell to make special outfits for you and Missy." Penny replied, "But Mother what about you and Daddy? He will need clothes suitable for a farm supervisor and you will need things for the new house." "We will be just fine," Earlene replied. 'There is enough money to get what we need and there will be money left. Plus we have saved some of our own money. We will be okay with the new house, too. Penny, ease your mind and be happy."

Penny went to the porch and sat in the porch swing by herself, thinking about what she needed to do. Penny is tough, both mentally and physically; she had the grit and "spit" necessary to get her through the hard times. Penny is known to possess a "sweet spirit." She only needed clothes until Saturday when they were to go to town. She laid out enough for that. The clothes were certainly not fancy but they were good enough. Penny is feeling a bit better about her future.

When her dad came home they all talked about what McKenzie had told them. Earlene told James she had told the kids about the money and promised them they'd all go to town Saturday to get new clothes and material. James is happy and proud of his family. Then he addressed the family. "Your mother is right to tell you about the money. We will go to town Saturday as she said. "Penny," James continued, "if you can, ask McKenzie which stores carry the best and biggest assortment of clothing and shoes." Penny, Missy and James Jr. were very surprised to learn the family had money to spend.

Chapter 3

The next morning, Penny bathed and fixed her hair and dressed in the best of the everyday clothes. After that she presented herself to her mother and said, "Mom, what do you think? Do I look okay?" Earlene assured her she looked perfect. "I made you a lunch; you will need it." Penny then faced her new career with a walk to the farm office, which is a little less than a quarter-mile away.

She waited at the office door for McKenzie. He arrived a few minutes later. "Come in Penny and I will show you around. First, there are two full-time employees working here. The main supervisor is Sue Weems. Both she and I will assign your work. The other employee is Martha Smith. Don't hesitate to ask questions. Sue has worked here about as long as I have and she knows everything about this farm. Martha has been for three years now."

"HB and Ruth have acquired more land this past year most of it in timber. The Silver Leaf Farm maintains a large cattle herd. We breed quality cows and breeding bulls. Silver Leaf farm has a reputation as one of the top cattle breeding operations in the south. HB also breeds and raises Quarter horses, but Cutting Horses is his main hobby. Smith will show what that is all about. Do you like horses Penny?"

"Well I don't know" Penny replied. "I have always liked to watch them in the movies but I have never been on one."

"Smith loves horses and is a good hand with them. I am sure he will have you on one soon. Here is your work station," McKenzie told her. It is a small area in the back corner of the main office next to his office. Pointing to a desk with two office machines, he said, "This is your desk. We will teach you about the machines."

McKenzie went on to show Penny HB's office. It is beautiful, with a huge desk made of fine wood, and carpet on the floor. There were pictures on the wall of the family. His dad and mother's picture were at the center, and there is an aerial map of the farm. On the opposite wall there were pictures of his champion horses and a trophy case to display trophies they had won.

McKenzie went on to say, "When they inherited the farm it was large for the time. Since then they accumulated more land as it came available. They will add more when it comes up for sale, if it is good productive land. Eventually they will sell the timber off the land they acquired this year."

"About 80% of the crop land can be irrigated. That is important. HB has invested heavily in irrigation wells and power units."

McKenzie continued, "You know about the pecan trees, and I told you about the cotton gin we are opening this fall. It will gin all the Hackett cotton and the cotton for as many of the neighbors who choose to bring it here."

"One thing to understand, farming on the Silver Leaf is big business and a big responsibility for every employee. You are taking on a huge responsibility Penny, but we know you can handle it. You will have plenty of time to learn your job. We believe you possess the leadership qualities that will take you a long way in life, if you apply yourself. Come in to my office and have a seat," he said with a welcoming smile.

By that time Sue and Martha had arrived. "Close the door please, Penny. I need to go over your duties then I will introduce you to Sue and Martha. First let's talk about your pay. We are offering you a dollar fifty an hour. That's good pay. In the fall or about Christmas time, HB gives each employee a bonus based on how well the crops fared. Sometimes it is quite good. The office help works eight-hour days except in the fall, when they may work 12 to 14 hour days. When school starts, we want you to come in as much as you can after school. Don't worry if you have something else to do. You are not required to come in."

"When harvest starts, we will ask you to help as much as you can. We expect your attendance and promptness. Please do not go into HB's office unless he asks you to. If you need to see him, come to me first. Any questions so far?"

Penny said, "This is so new I don't have questions about the job at this time." Penny went on to say, "Daddy and Mother are taking us to buy clothes this Saturday and they told me to ask you where the best place is to go for clothes." McKenzie told her that the best place is in Stuttgart, about twenty miles away, but worth the trip. "Go down Main Street to Mansours Department store and ask for Ms. Daughtery," he said. "She is my wife's sister. Tell her you are from the Silver Leaf Farm and she will take good care of your family."

McKenzie continued, "There is one more thing we need to talk about, and that's Smith. We have asked Smith to show you all the land including the cattle and horse operations. You need to have a full picture of the farm in your mind. He will introduce you to the farm help. We need you to learn to drive, as we have to have a designated "gofer," in other words an errand person. Smith will teach you on Tuesday and Thursday afternoons when he is available. I know all this is new to you, but don't get discouraged if you think it is a bit much. We will get you up to speed by fall. You may be called on to show visitors around the farm. This farm uses the most modern equipment and applies all the latest acceptable farm practices. There are lots of farmers and Agriculture people who will visit the farm to see our operation. We will accommodate them if we can. Now, come on out and meet Sue and Martha."

McKenzie and Penny walked out of his office. "Come on over girls," he called to Sue and Martha. "I want you to meet your new helper. You may already know her. Her name is Penny Parks, James and Earlene's oldest. We need an extra hand in the office especially since we have more land to keep records on. Penny assured me she is eager and ready to learn and I know she is a hard worker."

"One more thing, Penny is dating Smith. I want to get this out in the open. Be assured that is not going to affect her job and she will receive no special treatment. Treat her with the same kindness and respect you would any new worker. "Any questions?" Sue spoke up and said, "Welcome Penny! I am sure you will like working here. Some days we are very busy and some days it gets kinda slow. If you need to ask a question, feel free." Martha also welcomed Penny.

Sue is dressed in slacks and a blue blouse, while Martha dressed in blue jeans and cowboy boots and a western belt with a silver buckle. For some reason, that impressed Penny. McKenzie asked Penny if she had anything to say. Penny thought a minute and said, "I want to tell you I am willing to take on any task assigned to me. I will work as hard as I can to succeed at the job. I know I will need help. I promise I will carry my share of the load, and I thank you for being so kind."

"One more thing I need to say," McKenzie replied. "You will be involved in keeping records about farm business. It is important that you do not discuss farm business with anyone outside this office, not even your family." "Okay, he continued, "If you are ready, I am assigning you to Sue and Betty to start your training.

Sue asked, "How old are you Penny?" "I am 17 but will be 18 on September 18th. I will be in the 11th grade this fall," Penny replied. "You look to be a little older for your age," Sue said. "First thing, Penny is to clean your work area and get the feel for sitting behind a desk. You will spend a lot of time there." After Penny had her work station organized, she reported to Sue and asked if it is clean enough.

Penny managed to stay busy until things began to slow down about four o'clock. Sue called Martha and Penny over and they sat around Sue's desk and talked, not so much about work but mostly about their families. Sue looks to be in her mid to late 50's, and has a slender build. Her personality is outgoing and seems to have lots of energy. It is easy to see how Sue was selected for her job. She and her husband live in Lonoke, where he manages the John Deere dealership. They have two grown children. John, her son, is the oldest and is a doctor in Little Rock. He is married and has two girls, 9 and 12 years of age. Sue's daughter Bobbie is married, and she and her husband own a Ford auto dealership in Lonoke. They also have two children, a boy, 16, and a girl, 14. Sue has all their pictures proudly displayed on her desk.

Martha appears to be her early 30's. Her husband works on the Silver Leaf as a cowboy. He oversees the cattle operation. Martha moved to the farm after she was married. She was raised in England, AR. They met at a community dance there. Martha told Penny they did not have any kids yet but she is hopeful she would before she got too old. Martha said she likes to ride horses and help her husband work the cattle when she can. Martha told Penny, "Maybe Smith will get you interested in horses and we can ride together. The farm has lots of horses." Penny replied, "That sounds interesting I will ask Smith about it. I think I would like that."

They continued to talk. Penny told them what her life was like before moving to the Silver Leaf Farm. It was a good visit, then Sue said, "We have done enough today let's go home. Let's put the books up for the night." "Penny," she said, "each night before leaving we put all the ledgers in the fireproof safe in McKenzie's office. "Sue showed her the safe. "It is huge. In case of fire the records will not be lost."

"Penny I hope you aren't too confused about your new job, you will be just fine," Sue said. "Oh, by the way we have some papers to fill out concerning your employment here. We will do that in the morning," she continued. With that they gathered up their personal belongings, walked out the door, and said their goodbyes again. Penny started walking home. Both Sue and Martha offered her a ride home but Penny declined, saying she needed the exercise. When Penny arrived home, Earlene is waiting at the front door. "Tell me what you did today? Who works in the office? Are they nice? What will you be doing?"

Penny said she enjoyed what she was doing and liked Sue and Martha. She went on to tell her, "Smith is going to teach me how to drive. McKenzie set aside Tuesday and Thursday afternoons for that if Smith is available. I am looking forward to it, and to seeing Smith. It seems like a month since I last saw him."

The next morning, Wednesday, Penny is waiting at the door when Sue arrived. They greeted each other, and Sue told Penny, "We will fill out the papers I told you about yesterday. As soon as I get settled in I will call you over." Penny went to her desk. She and Martha spoke, then Martha got busy with some papers she was working on. Sue had given Penny some old ledgers to look at to get her familiar with the record keeping system.

After 30 minutes had passed, Sue called Penny over to complete her paper work for the job. She told Penny she would have to sign in at the beginning of each day and sign out at quitting time. She showed Penny the time sheets and how to fill them out. "Payday is on Friday so your week will begin on Friday morning and will end the next Thursday at quitting time," Sue said. "You will find we keep records of everything on the farm. We record each dollar spent and what it is spent on, in addition to keeping records for all money coming into the farm. HB is thorough; he reviews the records very close."

"In the spring before tax time HB will have an accountant to come in and audit our records so it is important to pay attention to what you are doing, and question anything you are not sure of. At the end of the month, either McKenzie or I will take the records to the accountant in town."

Sue then explained the phone system in the office and how the phones were to be used. There were two phones in the office. "If I am available, I will answer it," Sue said. "If not, then Martha will answer it. If Martha isn't available, then you will have to answer the phone, Penny." Sue went on to show Penny the phone log on her desk, saying the directions were self-explanatory. "We don't want an important call to get lost. If it is for McKenzie, there is a buzzer on the phone that will let him know to answer the phone."

Penny asked Sue, "Will I be paid by check or cash?" Sue replied, "We pay-day labor by the day. Salaried labor like Martha and I are paid by check every two weeks. You will be paid Friday by check. If you want we can cash it here." Penny is satisfied with that answer.

Penny went to her desk and resumed reviewing ledgers. They all stopped about mid-morning and took a break. There were cold drinks in the refrigerator and a hot plate for coffee. Sometimes Sue or Martha would bring cookies or a cake to share. Penny will bring a cake when her time comes around.

At noon Smith walked in the door and spoke to Sue, saying he is there to see Penny and set up the driving lesson the next day. Penny blushed a little when she saw Smith but didn't dare stop what she was doing. Sue grinned at Penny and told Smith to go on over and talk to her. Smith went about asking Penny how she liked her job. Since it is noon, Penny asked Smith to come outside with her.

Penny took her lunch with her and they went to a bench under a shade tree. While she ate, Penny and Smith caught up with each other. "It seems like forever since I last saw you. I missed you so much," she said. Smith told Penny how he had missed her. They finally got around to talking about the driving lesson. Smith told her he would come for her in an old open-topped jeep. "Penny, it will be a dusty and dirty ride—so dress accordingly." "I have been dusty and dirty all my life," Penny responded. "I am so pleased I am going to spend the afternoon with you."

Smith and Penny were enjoying each other's company but it is time to go back to work. Smith went to Sue and told her he would be picking Penny up the next day at noon for her driving lesson. Sue is aware of that. Penny finished the day and took her time walking home. She is humming a tune as she walked. Then Smith drove up in the jeep. "This is the chariot that will come for you tomorrow. Hop in and let's ride around a while." Penny is happy to oblige him.

Penny inspected the old jeep. Already she figured it to be a rough ride. No matter, as long as she is with Smith. As soon as he could, Smith pulled off the road at the edge of some bushes and leaned over to kiss Penny. Penny kissed him back. Smith said, "I have missed you! I am glad I will get to spend the afternoon with you tomorrow." "Me too," Penny replied. They rode slowly around the bayou in the shady part of the road. Penny told Smith it is time for her to be home; mother will be worried. When they reached the house Penny said, "I have been talking to Martha and she says she rides horses and helps her husband with the cattle. Do you think I could ride one of the horses sometime?" Smith is glad to hear that. "Sure you can! Tomorrow we will drive by the horse barn and introduce you to Martha's husband, Ronnie. Granddad hires a full-time horse trainer to ride the horses and trains them on cattle. I love riding horses and working the cattle. Matter of fact, this fall we are going to have a cutting horse show here at the arena. I am going to show the horse I was riding when I first met you." Penny is anxious to see the horses.

Earlene is waiting on the porch, as Penny expected. Smith walked Penny to the house. Earlene and Smith spoke. "Ms. Earlene, don't fix any lunch for Penny tomorrow, I am bringing our lunch and we will find a good place for a picnic." That was the first Penny had heard that, but she is glad. Penny asked Smith to sit on the porch with her. The swing is in a shady spot and a breeze is blowing; it felt good. After Smith left, Earlene and Penny were talking about what she would wear the next day. About that time Missy came out of the house and wanted to hear about what is going on with Penny and Smith. Missy had begun to notice the boys, too.

The next morning Penny put on her "driving" clothes but still wanted to look good for Smith. She took a ball cap with her to wear while driving or riding in the jeep. As she reached the office, McKenzie is there. He asked about her job and how she liked it. "Are you and Smith going for a driving lesson this afternoon?" he asked.

Penny replied "Yes sir, Smith came by yesterday and said he would be here at noon to get me." McKenzie said. "Good, enjoy the ride." Sue came in and she and McKenzie talked about farm business. Martha spoke, then went directly to her desk and continued her work. Penny went to her desk and started looking at papers Sue had laid on her desk. She got the idea that it might be good to take notes and save them in a notebook. She went to Sue and asked to borrow pencil and paper. Sue accommodated her, agreeing that it is a good idea.

It was a little hard to concentrate on the ledgers and papers she was reviewing. Penny was glad when break time came. Sue is on the phone, so Martha and Penny got them a drink from the fridge and sat in the break area visiting. Penny found Martha a very interesting person. She liked talking about riding horses and working cattle. Martha said she had been a "tomboy" all her life. She liked the outdoors and going hunting in the fall. She and her husband have two bird dogs and they hunt quail when the season is in and they have a day off.

Finally Smith drove up in the Jeep. He came in and spoke to Sue and Martha then asked Penny if she is ready to go. Penny got her hat and a shirt to keep some of the dust off. Smith told Penny he would drive them to a place to have their lunch. Smith picked a place with giant trees on the edge of a small lake. It is a beautiful spot, and they selected a place under a tree that had a canopy of limbs and leaves. There is no grass to speak of, so no danger of an uninvited snake or something else maybe worse. Smith got the lunch basket out of the jeep; spread a tablecloth on the ground and Penny took the food and placed it on the cloth. "Smith, did you fix all this?" Smith laughed and said, "If I said I did you would not believe me! No Granny Ruth fixed it." It is a satisfying meal: tuna sandwiches, chips, ice tea and cake.

Chapter 4

After lunch was done they loaded the lunch basket in the jeep. "I am going to get the jeep turned around and headed in the direction we want to go." Penny is anxious to get started. "Okay, Penny here we go; let's change places."

"This is a standard transmission so you will have to shift. Let's practice before we get started. First let me show you where Neutral is. This means when you stop you can shift to neutral and it won't go, but remember—if it is on a hill, it can coast. There is no emergency brake so keep your foot on the brake if you are parked on an incline." They went thru the gears until Penny is comfortable with it. Smith showed her the clutch and the break, and explained how to use them.

Penny had driven her dad's truck some, so she is familiar with driving. She started the jeep, pushed in the clutch and shifted to low gear. As she tried to move forward, the jeep "jumped" and the engine went dead. Penny laughed and was embarrassed. Smith told her it was okay. "Let's try again." He showed her how to push in the accelerator. It took a few tries but then Penny got it right. It was easy from then on. Smith pointed the direction to go and Penny maneuvered the jeep in that direction. She moved along slowly for a while then slowly accelerated to a comfortable speed.

"Okay Penny, relax; you are doing fine." After a while Smith told Penny to stop. "Let off the accelerator and push in the clutch as you push in the brake. Not too hard come to a slow stop". When the jeep was stopped Smith told Penny to put the jeep in neutral and climb out of the jeep and walk around it.

"Now get back in. We are going to back up." Penny and Smith spent some time in reverse, but before long Penny had that down too. The driving lesson continued with Penny driving on the farm roads. After a while Smith told Penny to turn left on the next road. She slowed down and maneuvered the jeep around the turn. Penny is now feeling good about being able to drive. They were coming up on the community store. Smith said "Let's pull in to the store and have a cold drink." He showed Penny where to park. She eased in to the parking place and turned off the motor.

They went in and spoke to Mr. Beavers the store manager. Everyone called him Mr. Britt. Smith told Mr. Britt that Penny is driving him around the farm. Then they got a cold drink out of the drink box and sat on the front porch in the shade and talked.

Penny told Smith about the trip coming up on Saturday to Stuttgart to buy clothes. Smith could tell Penny is excited about the trip. "Good for you. School will be starting soon." Before she thought, Penny said, "My birthday is coming up soon and clothes will be my present from Mama and Dad." This took Smith by surprise. He hadn't thought about Penny having a birthday.

"How stupid of me not to know when Penny's birthday is," Smith thought. He apologized to Penny for not knowing. Penny wished she hadn't said anything. "It's next month, September, 18. I will be 17 years old." "Congratulations," Smith said. "We will have a special date on that day."

After they were finished, Smith told Penny to turn right on the next road. "Now we are going to the horse barn." The main barn is huge, lots of stalls for the horses and lots of hay in the loft. The horses were beautiful, Penny thought. The horse trainer was riding a horse in the arena. Smith called him over and introduced him to

Penny. "His name is Billy Rosewell." Rosewell is an older gentleman who had a reputation for being really good with the horses. Smith told Billy, "Penny wants to learn how to ride horses and we will be coming over for lessons."

Billy and Penny hit it off really well. Billy said, "Penny we have a few broncs to ride." Penny said, "Billy, don't get me hurt the first day!" Billy laughed, "Don't worry; we will put you on ol' Bones—a pretty paint horse. He is older and gentle and likes pretty girls. Penny laughed, she felt comfortable with Billy. Martha's husband was out in the pasture tending to some sick calves so Penny didn't get to meet him.

Smith showed her to the stall where he kept his horse. Penny said, "He is beautiful. He is a "he," isn't he? Smith said, "Yes, he is a "he." He is a gelding; that is a male horse that has been "fixed." "When can we go riding?" Penny asked. "Well we can come over after you get off work, or on weekends," said Smith. Then Penny said, "I will like that. Smith, we should be getting back to work. It will be quitting time soon and I need to sign out for the day. I get paid tomorrow."

Penny drove them back to the office and parked near the front door. Smith asked Penny for a date on the next Friday night to take her to supper at the City café, then to a movie. When Penny walked into the office, Sue and Martha wanted to hear all the details. Penny told them about her embarrassment about driving and they all had a good laugh. The trio walked out the door together, and Penny headed for home. Smith was waiting and drove Penny home in his vehicle. They left the jeep parked at the office.

Next day is Friday and payday. Penny is glad the week is about over. She is looking forward to shopping for clothes in Stuttgart. Sue gave Penny some real payroll sheets to add up and check. She was a little nervous at first and had to ask Sue about some of the entries on the ledger. She got finished about noon and took them to Sue to look over. Finally Sue said they were correct. "Good work, Penny."

After lunch Sue came over and handed Penny an envelope—her check for the week. Sue told Penny to open it and she would explain the withholding for Social Security, which wasn't much. Penny is getting paid for 32 hours times $1.50 an hour = $48.00 minus $1.96 = $46.14. Penny is pleased with that. She could buy herself a pair of blue jeans and a belt. Penny has to help support the family, so she will give most of what is left to her mother. Sue said to Penny, "I got a call from Smith. He said if you don't mind walking over to Miss Ruth's house, he will drive you home.

After closing time Penny made the short walk to Ms. Ruth's where she and Smith were waiting. Ruth had a cold drink and some chips ready for Penny. Ruth wanted to know all about Penny's job, how she liked it and what she was doing. Penny told Ruth she is going to Stuttgart the next day to buy some clothes. Penny is a happy girl. Smith asked if she needed to go home before their date. Penny said, "Yes, I sure don't want to go out with you as nasty as I am." Smith drove Penny home and waited at Ruth's until she is ready to go. Smith and Penny are growing closer. Both find they have most things in common and that helps their relationship.

In about an hour Smith drove up to Penny's in his car and they headed for town. At the Café they met some friends and they all had supper together. The movie was very good. Penny is so glad to be with Smith. She loved him so much. After the movie they drove around town a while, then headed back to Penny's house. Smith is spending the night at his Granny's. After he pulled off the main road, Smith pulled into a wooded place and stopped. He and Penny kissed and hugged. Smith almost went too far but controlled himself.

Smith asked Penny to go to church with him Sunday and then have lunch with him and his family at the Country Club. Penny asked if Ms. Ruth would be there. Smith said he didn't know for sure, but she and Granddad might be. Penny thought would feel more comfortable if Ruth was there. Penny accepted the invitation but is a little nervous about it. Smith said, "If you want, you could bring a swimsuit and we could swim in the pool." Penny nixed that idea.

It is getting late and Penny had to get ready for the trip to Stuttgart. Smith walked her to the door and said "Penny, I love you." Penny gave him a big kiss and said, "Smith, I love you too. I can't stand the thought of losing you." Saturday morning the family had breakfast and they all were happy to get to buy some good "store-bought" clothes. Missy is so excited; she is growing up and knew the importance of good clothes. Around nine o'clock, after breakfast, James, Earlene and Penny got in the cab of the truck. James had made a cover over part of the truck bed and a place for Missy and James Jr.

It is a good chance for Penny to spend some time with her mom and dad.

So far they hadn't mentioned the new house. They were still in doubt that something that good would come to pass. They talked about Penny's job, and James told them what he would be doing. He said the farm is furnishing him a new truck to use as a service truck, but he could drive it home at night and use it for personal business also.

Soon they were in Stuttgart. The saw the Main Street sign and turned south. Earlene said, "Watch for Mansours Department Store." A few blocks later they all saw it at the same time. James eased the truck into a good parking place and they all got out of the truck. Earlene and Penny dusted off Missy and James Jr., and straightened their clothes.

They entered the store and asked for Ms. Daughtery. The clerk asked," Can I help you find something?" "No thanks," James replied. "We will wait until Miss Daughtery is finished."

After a bit Miss Daughtery came over and said, "Hello, you must be the Parks family. McKenzie told me you would be coming in today. You must be Earlene; you're Penny, and Missy, and James Jr., and James Sr." "Very good," Earlene replied. "McKenzie did a good job describing us."

"Where do we start, Earlene?" Miss Daughtery asked. "We want to purchase some clothes for school and every day wear. Let's start with the girls. They will take the most time." Miss Daughtery led them back to the ladies' department. It is a big, nice store with lots of clothes. Earlene is pleased McKenzie had told them about the store, it was everything and more than they had hoped for.

Missy is so pleased! She tried on dresses and slacks and blouses, and picked out underwear. Penny did the same and looked at the western style blue jeans. As they were shopping James told them he is going across the street to the car dealer. Earlene picked out some clothes for James Jr. and bought some a bit big on him because he is growing so fast. By school time they would be a good fit.

When Penny got a chance she asked Ms. Daughtery about the blue jeans and a belt. Penny tried on a few pair. Ms. Daughtery pointed out the ones that most women wear. She also bought a nice belt. Penny bought some nice clothes for work and school and for everyday wear.

Before long the entire family is fixed up, including Earlene—but not James. "Where is James? He should be back by now." Earlene went ahead and bought him some work clothes and a pair of good work boots. Finally James came in and tried on the boots. He told Earlene to meet him at the front door. Miss Daughtery was sorting the clothes out and figuring up the bill. Soon Earlene was back and they checked over the clothes and shoes. They all got exactly what they wanted. It is such a good feeling to get to buy new clothes, especially to get to pick out what they wanted.

Finally the bill is ready. Ms. Daughtery went over each item to make sure nothing was missed. Ms. Daughtery said the bill came to $232.23 and then noted that the store gives all employees on the Silver Leaf farm a 10% discount leaving a total of $209.01. Earlene is surprised. She thought the bill was going to be much more.

They gathered up the sacks and boxes and went to the front door where James is waiting. Missy said, "Where is the truck?" James said, "We don't own a truck anymore, just an almost new car." He pointed it out. It is so pretty they all screamed at the same time. They couldn't wait to get in it and ride home. The car is a Chevrolet that is a year old. The owner had a problem with it and traded it in on another one. James was able to get a good deal on it mostly because he worked for HB Hackett.

The car still had that wonderful new car smell. They were all so happy and the drive home was like a dream. Slowly the Parks family is getting away from the poor sharecropper image and more to a working family that is making a decent living and looking forward to the future. On their way out of town they stopped at a good restaurant and had lunch.

The ride home in the new car was like riding on a cloud, no more riding in the back of a nasty old truck. Once they arrived at home they unloaded the car and unpacked the new clothes. They took each garment, laid it out and carefully took all the tags off. Earlene told them to save the tags in case they had to be returned. They had tried on all the clothes at the store, but she wanted to be safe, just in case they weren't pleased with the clothes once they got them home.

Penny is wishing Smith would drive by but they had no date for that night. About thirty minutes later Penny got her wish: Smith came driving up in his car. He came to the door and Penny is so glad to see him. She showed him the new car and told Smith, "as soon as I learn to drive better, I will take you for a ride." Smith liked that thought. Smith then said to Penny he needed to talk to her about a very important matter. Penny said, "Do you want to talk here?" Smith said, "I think it will better if we went for a ride." Penny could tell by the concerned look on Smith's face this is not going to be good news. They drove to the horse barn and Smith parked in a shady place near the arena.

"Penny, I have something that I hate to tell you. My Parents are sending me to a military school for my senior year. Be assured they are not trying to split us up. My dad went to a military school his senior year and he thought it taught him things such as leadership and discipline, plus they have tutors to help with the courses. That will help when I go to college. I really have no choice. I told them I wasn't ready to be sent off away from home but they said my application had been accepted. I will be leaving the third of September." Penny dropped her head and sat silently for a few minutes. She said, "I knew you were too good to be true. I knew I was going to lose you, but I didn't expect it so soon."

"It hurts me as much as it does you; maybe more," Smith said. "The school is in Missouri so I will be coming home as much as I can, especially holidays. I love you Penny, but we both have a lot of growing up to do. You are the only girl I have ever loved. We have grown close this summer and, believe me, this is not just a summer fling."

Penny opened the door of the car and stepped out. Smith could tell Penny is very disappointed. After a while Smith got out of the car and put his arms around Penny. She started to cry. It seems she has been crying a lot lately. Smith asked if she would ride to town with him, mainly just to be together. "Yes, anything to be with you," she said. They drove by Penny's house to tell them where she is going. Earlene could tell Penny is upset but didn't say anything to her about it. She knew Penny would tell her when she is ready.

They drove to town not saying much to each other. Penny sat as close to Smith as she could. "Smith, what am I going to do? I will miss you so very much. I know you will be seeing other girls and I am so jealous already." Smith went on to tell Penny, "Please don't make it any harder, I am just as hurt as you are but we have to overcome all of it. I promise I will write every chance I get and I expect you to do the same."

On the way home Smith said, "Remember we are going to church in the morning then eat lunch with my parents at the Country Club." Penny is a little nervous about it but didn't say anything. Smith said, "I will pick you up at 10:30. Church starts at 11:00." Smith stopped the car in the usual place so he could hold Penny in his arms. She held on not saying a word. Her mind is still spinning from the news Smith is leaving. Penny is sad; it is hard for Smith too.

Next morning before Penny started getting ready for church she told her mother about Smith leaving for military school. Earlene tried to make Penny feel better but she just didn't have the words for that. Penny cleaned up and dressed to wait for Smith. She is wearing one her new outfits. It is nice and the first time Penny has worn it. When she was dressed and ready she asked her mom to give her the "once over" to make sure everything is in the right place. Earlene said, "Penny, you are so beautiful. Try to relax and have a good time; do not let Smith's mom and dad see you sad."

After a while Smith drove up and walked to the door. "He is so handsome!" Penny thought. On the way to church Penny tried to be in a better mood. The church service went well and helped Penny deal with her disappointment. Smith and Penny followed his parents to the Country Club. The meal is buffet style. Before they got in line, Smith's mother and dad complimented Penny on how good she looks. They were friendly but Penny has a feeling they have never accepted her as Smith's girlfriend. That thought is hurtful to Penny, and she hoped she is wrong.

As they got in line, Smith went first to make Penny feel more comfortable. It was a very good meal. Finally Mary, Smith's mother, brought up the subject of Smith going off to school. They looked as if they were uncomfortable talking about it. Penny just said, "I want what will be best for Smith, just as you do." Smith is holding Penny's hand under the table. Finally Penny spoke up and told his parents, "Mr. and Ms. Hackett, I want to tell you that I love Smith. This is not just a summer fling. I know we both have lots of growing up to do but I will do everything I can to hold on to what we have now." Penny was matter-of-fact, and Smith's parents nodded and told her that, "Growing up is not always an easy thing to do, but life moves forward and things have a way of working things out."

"Let's move outside by the pool," Mark Hackett suggested. They found a shady spot out of hearing range from anyone else. To make things worse, three girls about Penny's age walked by and made the comment "Smith, is that your sharecropper girlfriend?" They giggled and hurried off. Mark and Mary didn't say a word. Smith is mad and started to say something to them, but Penny interrupted. "I will handle this. Please excuse me." She caught up to the girls near the swimming pool. Mark and Mary didn't know what to expect, but Smith knew the girls didn't know who they were making fun of. Penny backed the girls up to the swimming pool fence. They had no place to run. Penny thought the Hacketts were thinking there would be a fight and they were embarrassed. No one knows to this day what Penny told them. She then walked back to the Hacketts and said, "I am sorry for that. I hope you are not too embarrassed." They only said, "Penny, we are so sorry too. Penny replied, "Please don't worry about it. I knew this was coming sooner or later."

In about ten minutes, as they were getting ready to leave, the three girls came up and apologized to Penny, then to Smith, and then to Mr. and Mrs. Hackett. They assure them they didn't mean what they said and asked Penny to accept their apology, which she did. She then hugged each one of the girls and said, "I am sorry, too."

That did get Mark and Mary's attention. They saw firsthand that Penny can take care of herself in a dignified way. The Hackett's didn't say it, but they were proud of their sons' girlfriend who handled things with diplomacy. Smith felt really bad that he didn't stand up for Penny. Penny noticed that too and gave his hand a squeeze of loving appreciation.

Chapter 5

Penny had an almost sleepless night. The love of her life is leaving for Military School for his high school senior year and then four years of college after that. She is thinking there is no way they could hold on to each other.

She dressed for work and met McKenzie at the front door. "Penny, Ms Ruth wants to see you so go on over there. Hope nothing is wrong," Penny said. "Smith is leaving for Military school, it probably has something to do with that. "Penny walked over to Ms. Ruth's; she is use to going in the back door that led to the kitchen. Ruth asked Penny to come in and offered her a chair at the kitchen table. She asked Penny if she wanted a cup of coffee or something to eat. Penny declined.

"I know you have been told about Smith leaving for school and Mary told me about the incident at the Country Club yesterday. I am so sorry for you both. I want you to know I went through the same thing with HB. People thought I was not good enough for him. It is very hurtful but HB stood up for me each time someone made such a comment. "Penny, it's not the end of the world, life goes on. I know Smith hates to leave as much as you hate to see him go."

"Things have a way of working out. You both are young and need to meet other people and have new experiences. You will hurt for a while but gradually things will get better." Penny said, "Ms Ruth, it is a sad experience for me. I love Smith and I think he loves me. I knew the time was coming that he would be leaving but I guess I will never be ready when the time comes." Ruth said, "Penny you are welcome here anytime. I want you to come visit; I don't want to see you hurting." Penny thanked Ruth and said, "Ms Ruth I love you, you have been so kind to me and you know how I feel but I will try not to let it show."

"Any news I get from Mark and Mary about Smith I will pass on to you. I will help you deal with it." With that Ruth stood up and said, "I don't want to keep you from work." Tearfully Penny stood up and hugged Ruth and said, "thank you so much for your understanding." With that Penny walked slowly back to the office. Sue and Martha both spoke. They already knew what is going on. In a bit Sue brought Penny some time sheets to figure up. She said, "Penny I know Smith is leaving and I can imagine what you are feeling. If you need to talk please feel free to come to me."

Penny settled in and concentrated on the time sheets, she knows there is no room for error. She kept her mind busy then at noon as she is stopping for lunch Smith walked in and asked Sue if it is ok to see Penny. They walked outside and sat in the shade as Penny ate her lunch. "Penny, I still plan on teaching you to drive. Tomorrow I will bring the pickup truck and you can drive to town. You are ready for that?" Penny said. "That's great Smith; one afternoon after work can you take me by the horse barn and let me ride a horse?" Maybe I will get into that after you leave." Maybe that will help keep my mind off missing you so much."

Smith said, "We can go this afternoon after the driving lesson. I will like that and hope you get to loving horses as much as I do." After Penny finished lunch they walked behind the office and down the shady part of the long driveway. Smith guided Penny in behind a clump of trees where they hugged each other. After a bit it is getting close to work time and Smith came in the office with Penny to let Sue know he would be coming for Penny at noon the next day. He then walked over to Penny's desk and told her not to bring a lunch they would eat in town.

The next morning on Tuesday, Penny is waiting as usual at the office door waiting for McKenzie or Sue to unlock the door. It is Sue that came first and let them in. Sue questioned Penny about Smith but didn't push very hard for information. She didn't have to Penny told her everything she knew about Smith leaving. "He is leaving in two weeks but he is going to continue with the driving lessons until then." Martha arrived about that time and Penny told her about her plans to ride a horse that afternoon after work. Sue brought more work for Penny, enough to keep her mind occupied until lunch. About lunch time Penny had finished her work and handed it to Sue who would check it out and correct it if needed.

At noon Smith is waiting outside the office in a pickup truck. Penny is going to get some highway driving and then drive in town. Smith opened the driver's side door and helped Penny adjust the driver's seat to make her comfortable. Once ready to go Smith leaned over and gave her a kiss. "That is for good luck." The shift is not on the floor like in the jeep, it is on the steering column. Smith took some time to let Penny practice shifting before they started. That made Penny a little nervous she didn't want to get embarrassed again. Smith told her to be calm and start the truck which she did.

She didn't give quite enough gas and it died on her. "OK, push the clutch in and restart it, this time a little more on the gas. Slowly let out on the clutch and give it some gas." Penny got the hang of it and they slowly backed out of the parking place. Now push in the clutch then mash the brake pedal softly so it won't come to a hard stop." Penny didn't get it perfect but good enough. Smith told her, "OK Penny, push in the clutch and put the gear in the reverse position. Now give it some gas so it won't die on you, not much so it will move slowly when you back up." She did not give it enough but the more driving she did the easier it got."

She started out on the highway very slow and Smith told her to give it more gas, but not too much. After a bit she had it up 30 miles an hour and Smith said that is fast enough for the first time. There is a stop sign ahead and she would have to bring the truck to a full stop. When they got there Smith told her to slow down and ease in on the brake a bit. "Now push in the clutch and ease it to a stop close to the stop sign." Penny is nervous about that maneuver but did just fine. "Ok Penny make a left turn and keep to the right. There will be more traffic on this highway so you might increase the speed to 40 miles an hour."

Penny gradually got it to 40 miles an hour Smith could tell she is a little tense. He told her to relax and started carrying on a conversation with her. This helped. As they came to town Smith said to slow down to 25 that is the speed limit here. "Be aware that vehicles may stop in front of you with out warning so you have to be quick on the clutch and brake," Smith said. "The City Café is just a head so roll down your window and put your arm now straight out the window. That signals a left turn. OK, now ease into that parking space just passed the black pickup." Penny eased up on the gas and applied the brake to slow her down and shifted gears to be sure the truck didn't stall out. 'You made it good for you!" Penny said, "This has really made me nervous." Smith reassured her, "The more you do it the easier it gets kinda like riding a bicycle."

They went in and ate. Smith spoke to some of the people he knew and found them a booth next to the front window. Lunch was good and they sat and visited a while after they had finished eating. Penny is glad to have a rest. "We will ride around town a while to get some practice." They were in the small town of England which made the driving easier. After a while Penny became more relaxed Smith alerted her to some of the things to be aware of. "Some intersections don't have a stop sign so you have to slow down and see if anyone is coming. She soon found out as an older gentleman pulled out in front of them and Penny had to come to a quick stop. The driving lesson continued for another hour, finally Smith told Penny to start back to the farm. "Penny, when we get there drive straight to the barn and Billy and I will give you your first riding lesson." In about thirty minutes Penny pulled up to the barn.

Billy, the horse trainer, was working a horse in the arena. Smith waved at Billy telling him to come over. Smith said to Billy, "Here we are for Penny's riding lesson." Smith had already told Billy they would be coming by. "Ok, she is all yours," Billy told Penny to come into the arena. "This is your horse for the day Penny this is Ol' Bones." "He is pretty Billy." "Yes, he is and a kind and gentle animal. He is a Paint horse. You can tell by the color it looks like someone threw a bucket of paint on him. We will get to that later." Billy spent the next half hour going over the riding gear and the do's and don'ts when dealing with any horse. "You will hear this from me many times, it's important."

Finally Billy told Penny how to mount up in the saddle. He had to give her a little boost. "Ok now dismount and remount." He talked her through that. "Now Penny take the reins and give him a little kick in the side. I know it is your first time so take your time and try not to be nervous, a horse can sense that." Finally Penny is walking around the arena on Ol Bones. Billy instructed Penny on how to sit in the saddle. Smith watched as Penny rode around. He thought Penny really looked good sitting on a horse. Penny rode the horse until it is time top go. Billy told Penny, "To come over anytime and ride. The more you ride the easier it gets. What we are trying to achieve now is to get you a riding balance. That takes some time but necessary. Pretty soon you will be riding a cutting horse." Penny thanked Billy and said, "It was a really big thrill to get on that horse." She petted Ol Bones and hated to let him go.

She drove back to her house as it was past quitting time. Earlene and Missy were watching as Penny drove up into the yard. Penny and Smith sat in the truck and talked and made plans for the rest of the week. Then, Penny and Smith sat on the porch swing for a while. Finally Smith said it's time for him to go. They made plans for a date for the next night, which is Wednesday. Penny is still sad

Smith is leaving but had come to accept it. She knows she has to move on with her life.

The next morning McKenzie was opening the door as Penny walked up. "Good morning Penny! How did the driving lesson go?" he asked. "Fine," Penny said. She told him what they did, and also told him about going horseback riding. McKenzie said, "Good for you, Penny. Feel free to ride any time you like. Billy will help you anytime he can. He is a very good person and a heck of a horse trainer."

Penny moved in to her desk and waited for Sue who came in a few minutes later. Sue always gets everything lined out for the day. Penny is falling into a routine at work. So far she hasn't made any errors on the work she has been assigned. She is beginning to get the hang of her new job. At the morning break she told Martha about riding a horse. They talked about horses the entire break period. Sue is busy on the phone as usual.

Next night, Wednesday, Smith and Penny went out to eat and drove around and talked. Neither of them was in the mood for a movie. Smith drove Penny in her yard promptly at 10:00. The goodnight kisses were long and passionate. Penny told Smith she had to go in the house.

In no time it seemed it was time for another driving lesson. Smith arrived promptly a noon and they took off on another lesson in the same vehicle. Smith brought a student's driving manual for Penny to study to get ready for a driving test to get her license. They drove to Lonoke which is north of them. Penny drove a little faster, being careful as she rounded the curves. Smith knew the town well and knew where they should go. Everything went smoothly and they drove back to the horse barn to ride Ol' Bones.

Smith showed Penny the proper way to brush a horse. Smith said no one wants to ride a dirty, dusty horse. Penny liked to rub her hands on Ol' Bones; seemed like it made her feel better. Smith showed her how to saddle a horse and then he went and got his horse out of his stall. Penny waited until Smith's horse was saddled. Penny asked, "what's his name?' Smith replied, "He has a long registered name but we call him Red. He is a good horse." They rode around the arena a while then Smith said, "Lets ride down a turn row." Smith opened the gate and told Penny "kick him up; make him come through the gate." Penny is a little nervous but remembered what Billy said about being nervous. The horse can sense it and it makes him nervous too. Penny relaxed and rode up even with Smith so they could talk.

Smith told her about the school he is going to and about what he would be doing. Penny felt better about it. After a while Smith said, "OK, Penny let's kick them up to a slow trot. It took her a while but soon Ol' Bones was in a trot. Penny said, "Smith this is so rough I can't do it very long." Penny was bouncing all over the horse. Smith got them back in a walk and said I did this to show how rough Ol' Bones is, but there is a way around that. Remind Billy to show you how to ride a horse in a trot. They continued their riding for another thirty minutes, Smith said, "That is enough for today. Let's go unsaddle them and put them back in the barn." Penny wanted to unsaddle Ol' Bones. It took her a few minutes but got him unsaddled. She petted him and talked to him. She knew she and Ol' Bones would become good friends.

They got in the truck and kissed and hugged a while. Then Penny drove them to her house. They visited some more and Smith said, "Penny there is a dance at the country Club tomorrow night. It is for teenagers and I would like you to go with me." "I don't know, Smith. Remember what happened last Sunday." "I know," Smith said. "And I am so sorry I didn't speak up sooner." "Smith, I told you the first night we kissed that I intended to be treated as equal and I still mean that. I will fight anybody that treats me bad."

"Penny, I guarantee nothing will happen. Let's go and have a good time." "How do I dress? Is it a dress-up affair?" Penny asked. Smith said, "heck no! I am wearing jeans and some shoes comfortable for dancing. You wear what you want, but wear comfortable shoes. You will do lots of dancing." "Sounds good to me," Penny replied.

Next day is Friday—pay day—and Penny will have in 40 hours. She thought her check ought to be about $55, which is really good money for the times. She would give some to her mother and put the rest in her little "savings account." No one knew where Penny kept her money. After work, Penny walked to see Ms. Ruth. Penny knocked on the back door and Ruth told Penny to come into the kitchen. "Ms. Ruth, Smith invited me to a dance at the country club tonight and I need advice on good manners for that."

Ruth said, "Penny, smile and speak to everyone you are around. Smith will introduce to some of the people. Just smile and give a greeting like, 'nice to meet you,' or 'good to meet you,' or something like that. If they offer to shake hands go ahead and do it. I doubt they will, but some might. You can offer to shake hands if you want. Just play it by ear. There will be punch and snack food on the table. Just do what everyone else is doing. You will be fine. Be sure you dance and mix with the crowd. I promise you they will like you."

"Thanks Ms. Ruth. I am going to wear one of the outfits you bought for me. You know the one with the pants and bright green shirt?" "Yes, that will be perfect, it will match your pretty eyes." "Ok, I am going to go start getting ready. Smith will be here in about an hour," Penny said. Ruth was reassuring. "Penny, have fun and just be yourself. Don't worry about what other people think." "I will tell you about it sometime next week. By the way I should be getting my driver's license maybe next week," Penny said with much excitement. "Good, then you can drive me around!" Ruth replied, laughing.

Chapter 6

Penny hurried home, bathed, and washed her hair. She used the fan to help get it dry. Earlene helped her put some pin curls in her hair. Earlene enjoyed helping Penny get dressed. Penny is thrilled to be going to the dance. Penny dressed in her special outfit. The pants were thin and cool and looked expensive. The shirt is bright green. Penny used the cologne she bought at Stuttgart. She wore a matching ribbon around her neck. This was the style when her mother was a teenager. It might not be fashionable now, but it did look good on Penny. It pulled the color of her shirt and her eyes and her hair together. Finally she put on her new shoes. She was just putting the final touches on when Smith drove up. Earlene said to Penny, "You look darling. I hope you have a real good time."

Missy let Smith in and when he saw Penny he said, "WOW! Penny you look great! You will be the prettiest one at the party." On the way to town, Penny sat as close to Smith as she could. Same as always, when they are on a date. Smith is in a good mood and told Penny they would have a good time. "Remember, I get the first dance." "I would not dance with anyone else until we have danced together." Penny replied.

They drove into the parking lot and got a good place near a street light. They held hands as they walked up to the door. Penny whispered, "Don't run off and leave me." The party had a live band and was chaperoned by some of the parents. Smith introduced Penny and they talked a bit. They moved on in to the dance hall where chairs and tables were set up around the dance floor. There is a big table for the punch and snacks. It was decorated with a table cloth and flowers. Smith walked around and introduced Penny to those he knew. They spoke to all his friends. Everyone was in a happy mood. Smith told Penny, "Let's go get some punch and cookies or something."

They got their punch and something to snack on then moved around to find a good seat. Some of Smith's friends, some that Penny had met a few months ago, waved at them and asked them to sit with them. This made Penny a little more at ease. They chatted about what they had done this summer. Penny brought up Smith leaving for military school.

The band played a few songs with nobody dancing. Gradually more were on the dance floor. Smith and Penny were dancing and having a great time. One of the other guys asked her to dance, which she did. Next dance another boy, then the next dance there was another. Finally Smith stepped in and took Penny away from them. Penny said let's get some punch I am really thirsty. Penny filled her cup almost full and drank it down pretty fast.

She became very relaxed and was hanging onto Smith as they danced. The band announcer said, "We are going to speed the tempo up, so be ready." Penny and Smith were on the floor when they played an old jig tune. Penny really got into it and backed away from Smith. She started doing a jig dance her grandmother taught her. Everybody on the dance floor backed up and watched Penny. They were all clapping and yelling, "GO PENNY." She kept it up until the band quit. Smith came and got her and held her up until they got to their table. Someone told Smith the punch had been "spiked." Penny is a little high on the punch. Smith chose not to tell her. They danced and talked until the band announcer said this is the last dance of the night, "everyone on the floor." The number started slow and finished fast. It was a big time for Penny. No one made fun of her. Everyone thought Smith is lucky to have her as his girlfriend. Penny is coming into her own. She and Smith are so in love now. It is too bad that Smith's parents think Penny is not good enough for Smith.

On the way home Penny nodded off to sleep. Smith pulled her over and put her head on his shoulder. When they got to Penny's house Smith gently woke her up. Penny asked if she had slept all the way home. She is so embarrassed. Smith said, "Penny you were so tired." He never mentioned the punch.

Time has flown by since the Parks family moved to the Silver Leaf Farm in the early spring. They came as poor sharecroppers with little more than a few ragged clothes, an old truck and a milk cow. Since then James has gotten a big promotion and a big raise in pay. Plus, the Farm owners have built a new house on the farm and the Parks family will move in to it when it is ready. It is almost finished now. Ruth Hackett and Penny are friends. Ruth looks out for Penny.

Penny has been promoted from a field hand to one of the helpers in the farm office. Earlene has been busy working in the garden and canning vegetables. Missy has been helping her mother. She is learning valuable lessons about canning and cooking, cleaning, and other things that will come in handy in the future. They had purchased a used deep freeze in which they froze vegetables. It really came in handy. They also froze meat from the hog they killed. James Jr. also helps, but every chance he gets he goes to the farm shop to help his daddy. He is learning about working on farm machinery. His dad is teaching him how to weld metal and how to use tools used by mechanics. James Jr. is interested in farming and wants to farm someday.

Smith is getting ready to go to off to school. Penny's school starts later in September, right after her birthday on the 18th. Cotton is beginning to open. Hopefully they will be moved into the new house before school starts and before cotton harvest starts. The rain has been good to the crops: enough, but not too much. It looks like a big harvest.

There is talk of a war with North Korea. Sue and McKenzie keep their radios on to keep up with the news. Sue told Martha and Penny that it doesn't look good for the United States. "Looks like our boys will be going over to fight the North Koreans. They are very concerned. One of the boys who grew up on the farm and graduated from high school this year has enlisted in the Army. His name is Tommy Russell, son of Alec and Ethyl Russell. Tommy is well liked and smart."

Penny is concerned about Smith going to a military school with a war going on. She is wondering if Smith might get drafted after he graduates from the military school. She loves Smith but has no control over his life. His parents are in control. She wonders if they are concerned about the war. Penny tells herself everyday that things will work out, but deep down she knows that when Smith leaves she will lose him. She knows Smith loves her with all his heart, but his parents will do anything to keep them apart.

She has to help her family make a living. She is determined to do the best she can to be a good employee. HB Hackett and McKenzie know that James is one of the best mechanics to ever live on the farm. The promotions were given to keep him. The implement companies would like to hire James so they want to keep him satisfied. The new house and Penny's job will keep him on the Silver Leaf, at least for now.

This will be Smith and Penny's last week for driving lessons. Penny is studying for the driver's test with one more day of driving to get ready. Next day is Tuesday. Smith comes in at noon to get Penny. They drive to Lonoke where the test will be given. Penny drives them to town and they eat lunch at Ketchum's café on Main Street. Penny has to park parallel on the street, something she has not even thought of. Luckily there were several empty parking spaces so she had plenty of room. Smith talked her through it. Penny is nervous but got the truck parked on the third try. Smith said they would practice more after lunch.

They drove around town and found places to practice parallel parking. Penny drove them back toward the farm. Neither was too happy. They only had one more week together. Most of the next week would be dedicated to packing and good-bye parties given by friends of Mark and Mary Hackett. Thursday, Penny would go for her driver's test. She felt confident she would pass. After the driving lesson Penny drove them to the horse barn. It is quite there except the sounds of horses nickering. Billy is riding a horse in the arena so he wasn't paying any attention to Smith and Penny. Penny laid her head on Smith's shoulder and snuggled up. Smith put his arm around Penny and they sat silently for about ten minutes then Penny asked Smith about the school and if he might go to war.

Smith said he didn't know what the future holds for him. His parents are telling him what to do. If he ran away they would come after him so he felt there is no hope of getting out of going off to school. Again, for about the hundredth time, Penny tells Smith how much she will miss him. They stayed until almost dark then headed home.

Next morning, Wednesday, Penny arrived at work early. McKenzie let her into the office. She finished up some pay sheets she had been working on. Sue and Martha arrived and they asked how the driving lessons were going. Sue turned on the radio to get the news. She is following the Korean War very close, as she had relatives in the military. Sue reviewed the time sheets Penny had finished and found one minor error, not enough to cause a correction but Sue did point it out as it is an accounting procedural error. Penny would not make that mistake again.

Penny is busy studying for the written part of the driver's test and that helped keep her mind off Smith. She is a little nervous about taking the driver's test, mainly because she didn't know what to expect. Thursday morning she studied for the test until Sue came in and assigned her some work. Penny felt confident she would pass.

Smith came in at noon to take Penny to take the test. On the way to town Smith asked Penny questions that he knew were on the test. Penny got them all correct. They stopped for a quick lunch and drove to City Hall where the test would be given. There were three more to take the test. Finally the test is handed out and instructions given by the officer in charge. Penny is the first one to hand in the test. The officer told her she would be the first one to take the driver's part. Penny would drive Smith's car for the driving test. She stood nervously waiting for the driving test to start. Smith tried to calm her down by talking to her about horses.

After a while, maybe thirty minutes the officer called Penny's name. She came forward toward the officer. "Are you Penny Parks?" "Yes sir," she replied. He asked her to get in the car. She got in and waited for the officer to get in. Before they started, the officer asked her questions about driver's safety. Finally he asked her to start the car. Once she was all set, she waited for the officer to tell her which way to go. She looked in the rearview mirror and out the windows to be sure there is no traffic. She then eased onto the street slowly and gained speed up to the speed limit. The officer told her to make a left turn at the next street. Penny slowed the car down and signaled a left turn with her hand and arm. This went on a bit. She had to parallel park, which she dreaded most. She did it perfectly. The officer told her to drive back to the drivers testing station.

Smith is anxious to know how it went. Penny said, "I think I passed." They waited around to find out her written score, which is a perfect 20 out of 20. In a while they call Penny to the desk and issued her an Arkansas Driver's License.

Penny is glad to have the driver's test behind her; it is a big load off her shoulders. Next day is Friday and payday. She is very happy to have her job and the money she is making. She has money saved for a pair of cowboy boots and maybe a hat. Penny is in for a big surprise today. McKenzie called her into his office. "Penny, we are going to make some changes. We are assigning you to the cotton gin as a weigher and auditor. Don't worry; it is not as scary as it sounds. This move is good for you and the farm. You will be able to more or less set your own hours. What you will be doing is something you can do as you have the time. You won't have to come in every afternoon after school or all day on Saturday. However, during the peak ginning time you may be needed more."

"Let me see if I can sort it all out," he continued. "I will give you the condensed version. Gins separate the lint from the seed and the seed is sold to pay for the ginning. That is how we make money. Sometimes there is a little money left over after the ginning is paid it's called "seed money" but some farmers call it Christmas money. They will wait until Christmas gets close and they will cash them in to buy presents for the family."

"First off, the farmer brings a wagon load of cotton across the scales. It is weighed; the farmer's name and the name of the farm are recorded in a book and on a tag. The weigher needs to determine how many bales are on the wagon or trailer. Most of the time, the farmer will know because they weighed the cotton in the field. To make it simple, after the cotton is ginned the wagon is weighed empty and recorded. When the bale comes out of the press it is weighed and recorded."

"We have an intercom that is used to call the weight of the bale to the office so it can be recorded. So now we have the amount of seed cotton and the weight of the bale. The cotton bales are loaded onto a flatbed truck. When it is loaded it goes to the compress where the bale is further reduced in size and stored in the warehouse. At that time a Warehouse Receipt is issued and a sample is cut from the bale. This is what the farmer takes to the buyer."

"Now that is the short version. You will pick it up a lot quicker than you think. We have a man hired full time until the cotton is out and the gin shuts down. His name is George Quick; however, he is not very quick. He has a disability but nothing is wrong with his mind. He will show you how to do the scales and fill out the gin book. Now, school is starting and you need to keep your grades up. That is the good part of this job. We want you to come in when you can and do an audit of George's work."

"Occasionally you will need to fill in at the scales. The audit is a sampling of the books to make sure there are no errors. If you find any we will do a more in-depth audit. George has a son that is a senior in high school this year and he is going to learn how to weigh cotton in. His name is Larry. I am sure you will get to know him. Do you see how it is going to come together? There is no pressure on you to put in long hours. It will take a while to catch on but you will have it down sooner than you think. "Questions?"

"Mr. McKenzie, I am willing to do whatever is asked. I need to make some money for things I need and help our family, but I do want to learn to ride horses when time allows." "Not a problem" McKenzie replied. "Until the gin starts running, continue in the office until school starts." "Another thing: you will be working around men, most of them older. We want you to speak and be friendly. If anybody gets out of line let me know immediately. There is a button under the desk you will be using. It is wired to my office and to my home. If there is an emergency use the button and I will come in a hurry. Only you and Mr. Quick know about the alarm. I will show you where it is."

"It is ok if you are working after school to do your school work as you can." As far as riding lessons, talk to Billy and set something up. He will be glad to help." Penny asked McKenzie if she could use the jeep to go to and from the horse barn. McKenzie told her "If it is available you are welcome to use it. Check with your dad; he will be in charge."

This is a lot for Penny to think about but she knows McKenzie would not ask her to do something she couldn't do. After a few questions Penny felt more at ease with the situation. She knows if she does good she will continue to have a good job with good pay. McKenzie dismissed Penny from his office and she went back to her desk. Sue brought her check to endorse and then gives Penny the cash. That perks her up a bit. Sue and Martha wanted to know what is going on. However, McKenzie had already talked to Sue about the move. He is mainly interested if Sue thought she could handle the job. Sue assured him she could handle it and do a very good job.

Smith will be leaving next Wednesday for Wentworth Military Academy. It is a co-ed school, so Smith will get to know lots of female students. The school is located in Lexington, Missouri, which is about three hundred miles from home. He will be taking his car. Mark and Mary, his parents, will follow him in their car. Both vehicles will be loaded with Smith's clothes and things he will need for his room. Smith's dad is an alumnus of the school so Smith knows a lot of what he will be going through.

Mark and Mary don't dislike Penny, but they don't think she is "the one" for Smith. However, if she came from a rich family and not a sharecropper family they would welcome Penny with open arms. Penny knows that. She is not sure if she will see Smith before he leaves but in her heart she knows Smith will find a way to say goodbye. It is Friday and she does not have a date with Smith. In fact she has not seen or heard from him since the driver's test. Right before the noon break Sue came to Penny and told her Ms. Ruth asked her to come over for lunch. Penny is hoping Ms. Ruth had some good news.

At noon she walked over to Ruth's and knocked at the back door. Ruth let her in and told her lunch is ready. They sat down to eat, just Ms. Ruth and her. Ruth first asked Penny how work was going she told her about the new job. Ms. Ruth said, "Penny, I am so happy for you if that is something you will like doing." Penny said, "I think I will like the job. I like to be around people and this will give me a chance to meet new folks."

As they ate, Ms. Ruth brought up Smith. She said, "Mark and Mary have him busy getting packed for the trip. Today they went to Little Rock to buy new clothes. It will be late when they get home. I expect Smith to be here in the morning. I expect he will want to see you too." When they finished eating Penny helped with the dishes. She feels comfortable in Ms. Ruth's kitchen. Before she left for work she thanked Ruth for her help in making her feel more at ease about Smith leaving. Penny gave Ruth a hug, "I love you, Ms. Ruth." Ruth could tell Penny's heart was breaking.

Chapter 7

Penny finished the day figuring up time sheets and going over an inventory list. She didn't say much, but at the break Sue and Martha tried to cheer her up. She appreciated that. She told Sue and Martha, "Thank you both for the kindness and understanding about Smith's leaving for school. I know my feelings show." Sue spoke up and said, "Penny that is love for you." You both are young and have a whole life ahead of you. It is hard now but in time it all will work out for the best. My advice is to meet new people, go on dates if you feel like, and have fun. Smith will back. I know it is hard for him too."

After work Penny walked over to the farm shop where her dad is working. She asked him if she could use the jeep to go to the horse barn. He checked to see if the jeep was in use. It is parked under a shed nearby. He walked Penny over and checked the oil and gas. He told Penny, "It has no headlights on it, so be back before dark." "I will," Penny replied."

As she pulled up to the barn she saw Billy unsaddling a horse. Penny walked over and spoke. Billy said, "Good to see you Penny. Want to go for a ride? Ol' Bones has been lonesome." "Billy I really want to learn how to ride and learn about horses." He understood and said he would do all he can to help. He gave Penny a halter and told her, "Bones is in the corral go catch him and lead him to the hall of the barn." He watched Penny as she approached Bones. She was quiet and slow in her approach. Bones saw her and moved toward her. Gently she patted him and rubbed in forehead and eased the halter on him. She led him to the barn, as Billy told her.

"OK Penny, look in the tack room and get a brush and a curry comb, and clean Ol' Bones up a bit." She liked to pet and brush him. "You won't need to tie him. He won't go anywhere." Penny took the brush and started brushing Bones. He liked that. "When you are finished we will saddle him. Wave at me, I will be on a horse in the arena." When she was done she waved at Billy and he came over and showed her which saddle they used on Bones. "I want to show you how to properly bridle and saddle a horse."

"This is the saddle you will use. Come over to the left side." Billy put two saddle blankets on; he showed how they should go. "Now the saddle; fold the off side stirrups and girth strap over the saddle like this. Good, now Penny, take hold of the saddle like this. Now, you do it." "I will try." She took hold of the saddle as Billy said she lifted it up; it is heavier than she expected. "Ease it up and place it on Bones' back. It took some strength but she managed to get it on. "Good job!" Billy told her. Now I will show you how to girt it up; watch." Billy went through it slowly, and then told Penny to do it. "We don't want to get it too tight but not too loose either." Penny didn't get it all right the first time. Billy showed her how to tell if the saddle is tight enough. Billy explained to her, "When most horses are being saddled up they will 'blow up,' that means they will expand their bellies. Sometimes we girt them up and ride them for a while then tighten the girt up. You will get used to it all. Get aboard and I will adjust the stirrups for you."

"Penny I am waiting for you to get your 'riding balance.'" "How will I know when I get it?" Penny asked. "You will know, and I will too. It may take a few ridings but no need to get technical now. From now own Penny you will be on your own to catch your horse. Brush him then bridle and saddle him. One more important thing I need to show you is how to tell if the bridle and bit fits or not. That is an important thing." He went about showing Penny how to properly bridle a horse and adjust the bit if needed. Penny understood all of it but knew she needed practice.

"All right Penny, you are on your own. Come ride Ol' Bones any time you want. Go slow getting him saddled up. You will know when it is right. If you need me wave at me if I am riding a horse. I am riding my horses early in the morning and late in the afternoon because of the heat so likely I will be here if you come after your work. I am anxious for you to get used to riding. I need a good 'turn back rider" Penny asked, "What's a turn back rider?" "When I am working a horse on cattle, the cattle will try to escape and a turn back rider turns the cow back to the herd. Now for that you will have to be a pretty good rider."

Penny got on Bones and rode him down a turn row. "First at a walk, then a trot." When she got back, Billy told her to come in the arena. "Penny, I want you to first walk around the arena. Then kick Ol' Bones into a trot when I tell you." Penny did as Billy instructed her. Once Bones got in a trot, it was very rough and she was bouncing all over his back. Billy told her to ride over to him. He asked her to let him on Ol' Bones. He got on and kicked him into a trot. He was barely bouncing. "See how still I am on him? There is a way not to bounce on a rough riding horse. He went on explaining how to sit and 'post.' "If you put more weight on your feet that will help, too."

He showed her when to post up. As she watched, she knew she wanted to learn that. Billy pulled up and told Penny to get back on. He stood by and coached her until she knew how to do it. Doing it right would take some practice. She rode until the sun was almost down. She took her time unsaddling. She petted and rubbed Bones for a while. He felt like a long lost friend. She left the bridle on as she led Bones back to the coral. Once there she pulled the bridle off. She put the bridle back in its place. She waved good bye to Billy and drove back to the shop and parked the jeep in its place. No one is there; they had quit for the day.

It wasn't dark yet but pretty close. She hoped her mom and dad were not worried about her. Earlene had her supper ready. As she ate she told her mom and dad about the job and the riding lesson. Penny said she is tired and would bathe and go to bed early. James asked Penny if she might be interested in buying a car. Penny had not thought about it but with school starting soon and with her job and riding she could see that it would be good if she had a car. She said, "Dad, it would be good if I had a car but I can't buy one until I get more money saved. James told her a man came by and had a 49 Ford car he wanted to sell. "It has a bad motor so I can get it pretty cheap." If it is in good shape besides the engine I will make him an offer. If he sells I can overhaul the engine and make it run like a brand new car." You might have to ask McKenzie if they would loan you some money. They loan to the labor if they need money and if they can pay it back. They hold a payment out of their pay so they are sure they will get their money.

Don't mention it until we agree on a price. I think I can get it for $400. Of course we will need to buy a few parts." "Dad I have almost $200 already saved plus I got paid today." I will see the man next week. I will look the car over and make an offer."

Penny asked her mother if she had heard anything about the new house. Earlene said, "Matter of fact, McKenzie came by today and told me it is almost finished and I need to meet with the builder and pick out the colors we want. I told him we all would come over and decide." He said it may be a few days but would be back.

Friday night and Penny is at home; no date with Smith. She is really missing him but knows he loves her and will find a way to say goodbye before he leaves. This is a good time for Penny and Missy to visit. Penny tells her about her dates with Smith, her work, and learning to ride horses. Missy tells Penny what she has been doing this summer. Overall it has been a good summer. Missy had a birthday and Earlene drove Missy and James Jr. to the swimming pool in Lonoke and let them swim. They enjoyed snow cones and ice cream. Missy had a boy trying to flirt with her, something new for Missy. Missy didn't say, but she liked that. Penny gave her some advice about boys. Missy had tons of questions. The farm is getting much needed rain. It was a good night.

In the morning Penny woke up early and began to get help her mother with the housework then got ready for Smith if he came. She was ready and sitting on the front porch when Smith drove up. She ran out to greet him. Smith gave her a big hug and a kiss. He spoke to Earlene and Missy; James is with his dad at the shop. Smith asked Penny to come with him. He is going to see Ruth and HB. HB was coming out the door when they drove up. "Hello Penny. Smith, are you going to be around here today? I have to go to town on business but I will be back by lunch and I would like to see you before you leave for school." Smith said, "Yes, we will be around. Granny Ruth invited us to eat lunch with you and her." HB said, "Good will see you then. Penny I hope you are eating with us too" Smith answered for her. "Yes she will be here."

Penny and Smith drove around mainly just to talk. He told Penny what he knew about the school. Penny didn't really want to hear it but knew it is important to Smith's future. Penny told Smith "I know it is a co-ed school and I know you will meet lots of girls. I want you to go on dates and have fun. I hope you keep me in your mind and in your heart. I pray for the right outcome."

"OK, I guess we better head back to Granny Ruth's." Penny agreed. They drove up and parked under a shade tree. The sun is very hot. They went in and immediately Penny started helping Ruth with lunch. She set the table and asked if there would be others coming. Ruth said "no one else that I know of. We will wait for HB, he should be back anytime. "Is there anything else I can do?" Ruth said, "No, go on into the living room and keep Smith company." She and Smith both sat in a big lounge chair. Penny laid her head on Smith's shoulder and he had her hugged up to her when HB drove up.

They waited until he could get washed up then the all sat down. She sat by Smith on one side of the table and HB and Ruth on the other side.

Ruth had fixed fresh veggies from the garden with a large roast she had been cooking all morning. HB said the blessing and prayed for Smith as he went off to school and for all those that are affected by the war and all those that are sick. He delivered a passionate blessing. When he was finished Ruth started passing the food around. As they ate they talked about the school. HB said, 'Penny I know you two are going to miss each other, but that's part of life. We all have to go through it. You will be just fine. We are going to keep you busy this fall, maybe that will help." She appreciated his comment. After they ate, Penny helped Ruth clean up the kitchen. Smith sat in the living room with his granddad, and they had a nice visit. Ruth and Penny sat at the kitchen table and talked. Smith asked to be excused. He went in the next room and came back with three packages wrapped in bright gift paper.

He said, "Penny, I won't be here for your birthday so I want to give you my gift before I go. Hope you don't mind." Penny looked stunned, she never expected this. Smith sat the gifts down at her feet and handed her an envelope with a birthday card. Smith said you can wait until later to open the envelope. She didn't know what to say. Smith said, "Go on Penny and open your gifts, the big one first." Penny is not used to getting gifts. She teared up but proceeded carefully to open the gift.

She is so surprised when she found a new pair of women's cowboy boots. They were beautiful. Smith knew what style to get. "Try them on Penny." Good thing she wore socks that day. She slipped out of her shoes and slipped her foot into the boots and pulled them on. They were a little tight but she expected that. "I don't know what to say, they are beautiful and a perfect fit." Smith said, "Penny go ahead and open the next one." She did and found a beautiful western belt that had her name stamped on the back and a silver buckle. Penny is shocked. Now Penny opened the last one. It is a small package.

She opened it and found the most beautiful necklace with a silver heart. Smith told her, "That is to remember me by." Penny sobbed and said, "I will never take it off." Ruth and HB looked at each other and grinned.

Smith said they were leaving for school early the next day, Saturday, and his mother and dad had set up a going away party for Smith at their house. Smith invited Penny. She was a little surprised, thinking they were trying to keep them apart. This is a special event. They knew Smith wanted Penny there. Smith asked her if she could be ready by six o'clock. She assured him she would be ready. "Come on I will drive you home." As they drove off Penny asked, "When can I open the envelope you gave me?" "Well I guess you can open it now." Penny carefully unsealed the blue envelope and carefully took out the card. "It is a beautiful card, Smith. She read what was printed on the front then opened it. Smith had written a long note to Penny. She read it slowly then tears began to well in her eyes. Then she put her head down and sobbed. "Oh Smith, this means the whole world to me! Thank you for the gifts but this means a lot more to me. I love you too, Smith Hackett, and I always will no matter what."

When they arrived at Penny's house Smith helped her take the presents into the house. Earlene and Missy were wondering what the presents were for, but said nothing. Penny told them, "Smith bought me birthday presents and gave them to me today because he wouldn't be here on my birthday. Look at the necklace he gave me; isn't it beautiful?"

"My goodness it is beautiful." Earlene said.

"Penny, how long do you need to get ready for the party?" Smith asked. "Probably a little more than an hour, is that ok?" "Sure, I will be back in an hour."

Smith had brought clothes to wear for the party. He showered and got dressed. He put on some of his best cologne. He sat in the living room with Ruth and HB. They talked about the school and gave him lots of encouragement. Ruth was concerned for Penny, even though there is nothing she could do.

The time came for Smith to go get Penny. He is thinking this may be the last time he would ever pick Penny up at her house. He is very sad for that. He drove up to Penny's, and Missy is sitting on the porch swing. She let Smith in the house and loudly announced his presence. Penny came from the next room and told smith she is ready. Smith said, "You look so very pretty." Penny said, "Thanks." Penny is in a talkative mood mainly because of the gifts Smith had given her. Sad too, because it is her last night with Smith until he comes home from school on a visit. Smith is glad Penny is in a good mood. Hopefully both would have a good time at the party. When they arrived, Smith drove his car around back to there would be another parking place for the guests.

Smith and Penny came in from the kitchen entrance. His mother, Mary, is in the kitchen cooking. She spoke to Smith and said, "Penny you look nice." "Thank you," Penny replied. Then she said, "What can I do to help, Ms. Mary?" "Penny you don't have to help." Penny said, "I want to help." Mary told her she could take some of the plates and stack them on the table set up in the dining room. She had a very nice table cloth with decorations placed in the center of the table. Penny is not sure how to go about setting them up but she did the best she could do. She asked Mary to see if it is okay. Mary made one quick change and told her it looked good.

Penny went in the kitchen to help with the cooking and cleaning. "Ms. Mary, do you have an apron I could put on? I don't want to splash water on my clothes." "I am sorry Penny I didn't think about that. I will get you one." Penny washed the pots and pans as Mary got through with them. Penny kept up with the dirty dishes so when Mary got through cooking there would be no dishes to wash. As they worked, Mary did her best to carry on a conversation with Penny. Penny did enjoy being with Mary and working with her. Penny asked her if she knew that Smith had gotten her presents. Mary said, "I did know about them. Smith showed them to me. In fact I did the wrapping."

"Did you like them?" Mary asked. "Oh yes! I like them, especially the necklace. It is so pretty, and I like the heart pendant." "Good," Mary said. She went on to say that she hope Penny wasn't mad at them for sending Smith off to school. Penny said, "No, I know Mr. Mark went to school there his senior year and I know it had been planned long before I knew Smith. Still, I hate to see him go." "I understand, Penny. I hope you two will meet other people and move on with your life. Smith will be coming home on holidays and for some special occasions. You two will see each other then."

In a few minutes the guests started to arrive. Smith came for Penny to stand with him and great the guests. Penny knew most of them, and they were friends. Penny forgot to take the apron off and when one of the guests said, "Boy, Smith you already have her trained to do housework." Penny and Smith looked a little puzzled until Penny noticed she still had the apron on. They all got a good laugh. The party went well; all had a good time and the food was great. They spent a lot of time reminiscing and telling stories about them and Smith. Penny listened mostly, and laughed at the stories. Smith gave a going away speech. It was upbeat and not at all sad. At the end of that some of the guests started leaving. Smith and Penny said goodbye to them. Smith assured them that he would be back holidays and on spring break.

Soon all the guests were gone and Penny and Smith helped clean up and move the tables and dishes back into their place. Mark came by and said to Penny, "Even though Smith will be gone we hope to see you. You are always welcome here." Penny thanked them and said she would be busy with school and at the gin and the office, but she hoped to see them too. At last, Smith and Penny were on their way back to Penny's home. She and Smith tried to put on a happy face but both knew that wasn't the case. Smith stopped at their regular parking place and they did lots of hugging and kissing. Penny knew what Smith is thinking. His hands began to move toward her breasts. She tolerated it for a while, and finally said, "Smith, I know you want to go all the way with me but I can't and

I won't. I want to be a virgin for the man that I marry. I love you. As much as I want to, I have to be strong and stop it before we go too far." Smith seemed disappointed but said, 'I understand." Penny replied, "If we get married I want to be your first and only love." "I respect you for that." Smith said.

They sat and talked a while and finally Smith said he should go, "It is going to be a long day tomorrow. Promise me Penny, you will write me every week and tell me what you are doing. I will do the same to you. I am not sure of my mailing address so I will send it to you as soon as I can." With that, Penny tried to hold back the tears but broke into a hard sob. Smith held her and tried to reassure her things will work out. At Penny's doorstep Smith hugged her tight and gave her a goodbye kiss. He said, "Penny I love you so much. I hope that one day we can be married and have a family. I plan to raise them here on the Silver Leaf." Penny said she wanted that too. Then she said, "Goodbye Smith. Know that I love you so very much and it will never die. Good night and I will pray for a safe trip."

Penny sat in the porch swing until Smith is out of site. Slowly, she made her way into the house and started getting ready for bed. Missy is awake and asked Penny about Smith. Penny just said he would be leaving in the morning for School. Penny put herself to bed but didn't immediately fall asleep. She woke up early and got up to start breakfast. Earlene came in and they sat at the table and talked. Penny realized all conversation in the past few months had been about her and Smith. "Mother, I am sorry. I have been so wrapped up with my dates with Smith I have neglected the ones I love most, my family."

Earlene said, "You haven't neglected us. It has been a pleasure to see you so happy. You deserve that." "I promise to be more attentive. I have hardly seen dad, he is up so early and works so late." Earlene assured her she had kept him up to date on what is going on.

After breakfast Penny told her mother to sit down and rest. "I will do the cleaning." Earlene appreciated that. She finished before noon and it is time to prepare for lunch. They had plenty of fresh food from the garden that needed to be eaten before it spoiled. She and Earlene teamed up and cooked a big meal, enough for supper too. When her dad came in for lunch she asked if she could use the jeep to go to the horse barn. He said it would be okay, just be careful. She knew Billy would not be riding until later in the day but she wanted to catch Ol' Bones and give him a good brushing. She got a halter and went to find him. He is standing in the shade out in the pasture. Penny walked up to him and put the halter on. Ol' Bones acted like he is glad to see her. She led him into the hall of the barn in the shade and got the brushes and curry combs to clean him up. There is a breeze blowing through the hall and if felt good to Penny and Bones.

As she brushed and combed his mane she took her bare hands and just rubbed him. A peaceful feeling came over Penny. She knew horses would be her next love until Smith came home.

Chapter 8

In a little while Billy drove up in his truck and stopped to say hello to Penny.

They talked a few minutes and Billy told Penny to saddle up and ride in the shady part of the arena. He asked if she needed any help. Penny said, "No, I want to do this by myself." Billy said, "Suit yourself. If you need me give me a holler I will be behind the other barn tending to a sick horse." She got the saddle blankets and saddle and took them around to the left side of the horse. She slowly put the blankets on being careful to get them on proper. Then she slowly took the saddle and folded the right stirrup and girt back over the saddle seat.

Then she picked it up and placed it on Bones back. She pushed the stirrup and girt back over. Bones just barely moved as she reached under his belly to get the girt. She noticed she had forgotten the bridle. She found the one that fit and removes the halter and gently put the bridle on. When she put the bit into bones' mouth he readily accepted it and she pulled the bridle head stall over his ears. Then she fastened the throat latch. She was actually proud of herself.

She is careful not to get anything twisted. After she had him saddled and the bridle on she looked everything over to make sure it all was correct. Then she remembered what Billy had told her about horses swelling up when they were saddled. She took the girt and pulled it more to be sure it is tight. Now she understood what Billy was saying. She knew she had lots to learn, but she had plenty of time.

She led Bones into the arena and climbed aboard. She sat still a few minutes looking around to make sure nothing is in the arena that she needed to be aware of, like a cow or some equipment. In a few minutes she was riding around the shady part. In a while Billy drove up. He told Penny to kick Bones up into a trot. She had no trouble getting him to trot. Then Billy said, "Now kick him up into a canter or lope." She had not done that before so she is a little reluctant.

Billy said, "go ahead, Penny, make him lope." She kicked him in the sides harder, then he started the lope. Penny grabbed the saddle horn to hold on Billy told her to turn it loose and relax. It took a minute but she let go and is riding without holding. Billy told her to relax and keep him kicked up in a lope. Penny rode this way for another five minutes. Billy said, Okay Penny, make him stop." Penny eased back on the reins and told Bones to stop. He stopped quicker than Penny is ready for, and she almost fell off.

She said, "Billy I almost fell off, I see I have a lot more learning to do." "OK Penny," Billy told her. "It is time for you to move up to a better horse. I have one that will suit you to a T." She is one of our turn back horses. I need some turn back help. Go unsaddle Bones and I will bring the horse to you." Penny did as Billy said. She unsaddled bones and petted him and turned him out in the pasture. Soon Billy came up leading the horse he told her about. She is not as pretty as Bones. She is a solid color with black stockings. She is not as gentle as Bones, and she seemed a little nervous. Billy said, "Penny meet Molly. She is about 14 years old and is a good cow horse. I want to alert you that she is a lot quicker than Bones. She will help you get your riding balance." "Ok Billy, I will try." Billy said, "Penny try to relax and pay attention to what she is doing. She is quick and if you relax too much she might jump out from under you. If you fall off don't get too excited or scared. Everyone falls off some time or another." Penny said, "I understand; just promise me you won't laugh when I do." Billy said, "No way! I will have a big laugh."

Billy helped Penny saddle Molly up to make sure the saddle is tight enough. He told Penny to lead her to the arena and walk her around until he got there. Billy saddled one of the horses he is training. He went to the back pen and ran in five head of cattle. This is for training. Billy told her to hold on the saddle horn and told her where to put the horse. "Be ready Penny. When a cow turns and starts to run to your end of the arena, it is your job to turn her back." Penny is a little anxious but tried not to show it. Billy eased his horse up to the cattle and pushed one out in front to cut. The cow didn't move much but that is okay; Billy is teaching the horse to wait.

In a minute the cow came running toward Penny. She reined her horse toward the cow. Molly knew what she was doing. The cow moved to the right and suddenly turned back to the left. Molly kind of squatted down and ducked back toward the cow. Penny flew off the horse and landed square on her butt. "Ohhhh!" she yelled. Billy said, "Penny, are you hurt?" She said, "I don't know. Wait till I get my breath and I will check to see." She got up and dusted herself off and said, "I'm okay." "Ok, get back on and try again. This was a good lesson. This will help get your riding balance quicker than anything." Penny knew this was a good lesson. She did not want that to happen again. She began to catch on to what Billy wanted her to do. It was fun.

Before they quit though, Penny fell off three more times. Each time she got up and got back on. They both got a good laugh. "That is what you have to do. When you get throwed, get back on and keep on going. You are getting the knack of turning back cows. We will do this often. You will be good at it." When she got back home Missy said, "Penny, how did you get so dirty?" Penny looked in the mirror and said, "oh my gosh! I didn't know I was this nasty." She said she would tell them all about it after she got cleaned up. Penny went to the bath room and peeled of her dirty clothes. She soaked in the hot water to get some of the soreness out. Finally she got out and got dressed. She wasn't planning to go anywhere else that day. She had checked herself over for any bruises and scratches. She did find a few bruises. She is glad she got a chance to ride a good horse. She is determined to keep on riding.

Penny told Missy and her mother about her getting thrown four times. As she is telling how it happened they all had a good laugh. James came in and said, "Tomorrow we go look at the new house and start getting ready to move. McKenzie said the house is very close to being finished. We need you girls to pick out the colors of the walls and pick out the flooring. The contractor won't be there tomorrow, but will be there Monday. You need to be thinking about what you want. Ms. Ruth said they are waiting for them to move the furniture they are buying from her and HB." They were excited.

The next morning Penny told Missy to help her out of bed. She is so sore from being thrown from the horse and could hardly move. Finally Missy pulled her up and told her to lean on the dresser. It took Penny about fifteen minutes before she could walk into the kitchen where her mother and dad were sitting at the kitchen table. They laughed at Penny. Penny said, "Hey, it's not funny. I am hurting. I have never been this sore before." Earlene told her, "Sit down and have some coffee. You will feel better once you start moving around."

James told Penny he is meeting the man with the car that he wants to sell Monday after work. He said, "Penny you really need a car. With your job at the gin you really need to come home from school and not wait on the bus. James Jr. and Missy can ride with you some of the time. Plus you will want to go to town some. I think it would be to your advantage not to depend on someone else." Penny agreed and said, "In another week I will have $400 saved up." James said there would be a few parts to buy but maybe not too many. He said he might be able to find them on a wrecked car somewhere. "Anyway, we can work it out."

After breakfast they loaded up in their car and drove over to the new house. It is beautiful and smelled so good. It is that new house smell. They never talked much about it before because they didn't want to be disappointed if they didn't get the house. They walked through the rooms. The living room is large by their standards, and the kitchen is a dream come true for Earlene. It had large cabinets and sink and a work area. The house had two bathrooms one for Penny and Missy and James Jr.; the other for James and Earlene. Theirs is larger than the kids' bathroom. The master bedroom for James and Earlene is big. Penny got the next largest one, and Missy and James Jr. got the smaller ones. Actually there were only three bedrooms but there is a utility room large enough for James Jr. Everyone would have their own space, which is so nice for them. McKenzie told them there would be a washer and dryer in the utility room and, sure enough, there is a brand new washer and dryer. It is hard for them to imagine them living in a new house. Sunday, Penny stayed home from church and nursed her bruises. She is anxious to get back on Molly. She thought a lot about what Billy told her about riding a good cow horse and how to turn back cattle.

Next morning, Penny is up and at the door of the office when McKenzie drove up. They spoke and McKenzie told Penny the gin is going to open in a few days. "The cotton is opening real fast and those that did not have a mechanical cotton picker are hiring cotton pickers out of the surrounding towns to hand pick the cotton. Some cotton has already been picked and others will start the following week. I am asking Mr. Quick, the head weigher, to come and start work. He can get things cleaned up and the office in order to start the ginning season. Penny, this afternoon right after lunch I want you to walk over to the gin office and meet Mr. Quick and his son Larry. Larry is a senior in high school but will work part time like you are doing. I will be there to get you started."

After lunch Penny walked over to the gin office and went inside. The office is pretty big. There is an area partitioned off where the scales were located and another area partitioned off where the gin secretary is located. Penny and Larry had desks in the back of the office for their reviewing of the gin records. There were stairs to a second floor where the gin samples were stored by the name of the farmer who owns the cotton. It would be Penny's and Larry's job to keep the samples organized so that a farmer could come and get his samples anytime.

McKenzie came in and spoke to Penny, Mr. Quick and Larry, his son. Penny found out Larry goes to the same school Penny goes to. She doesn't remember him from last school year. He is a nice looking young man and has good manners. After things settled down and while they were waiting for Mr. Quick to start the training Penny and Larry talked. They had a good conversation. Mr. Quick told Penny and Larry to come to the gin scales. He showed them how the scales worked. He told Larry to drive his truck onto the scales. "This is to show you how to weigh. In a minute Larry drove the truck on to the scales and stopped. Mr. Quick said, "Now look at the scales and tell me how much the truck weighs. Look at it and write the weight down."

Penny went first and wrote down the weight she saw. Then it was Larry's turn. Mr. Quick said, "Ok Penny, let's see your weight." She had written down 3,350 pounds. Larry had also written down 3,350. Mr. Quick said, "Very good, you both are correct. Now, understand if that was a trailer load of cotton, after it is ginned they will pull the trailer back onto the scales and weigh it empty. We say that weight is, "empty weight." This weight is recorded in the gin book. The man at the gin press will call in on the intercom and give a bale number and the weight of the bale. Some trailers will have more than one bale on it. Some might hold up to four bales. You will learn how to judge about how many bales are on the trailer when it comes in loaded."

"You two are expected to speak to every farmer that comes in the door. Sometimes farmers have a lot on their minds but you speak to them anyway. Be friendly. If they say crude things to you be sure you let me know. That will not be tolerated here. If they don't like it they can take their cotton elsewhere. Learn their names and something about them. They like that. Any questions?"

Neither Penny nor Larry had a question. Mr. Quick said when the cotton starts coming in we expect you both to be here. McKenzie will let us know. Penny hung around the office doing some cleaning that was missed by the cleaning crew. She spent time looking at the gin book and talking to Mr. Quick. He had lots of stories to tell about things that have gone on in the gin office. Some were really funny. By now, she learned farmers like to tell funny stories. At quitting time Penny walked over to where her dad is working and asked him for the jeep.

Penny drove home and changed into her blue jeans and short sleeved shirt. She also put on her new cowboy boots and the belt she bought in Stuttgart. She bought a new ball cap at Stuttgart she wore that too. She drove up to the arena and Billy had Molly saddled and tied to the fence. She waved at Billy and went over and climbed aboard Molly. She rode her to get her loosened up and herself too. After a while Billy rode up on one of the horses he is training and asked Penny if she is ready. Penny said, "I am ready. I am going to try not to fall off, but if I do don't laugh." Billy chuckled and said, "Penny you already know I am going to laugh so you better stick like glue to Molly."

Billy already had the cattle in the arena all huddled in a group. He told Penny a little about the horse he is working. It belonged to one of the cattleman in the area. He wanted it trained for competition. Billy said it is a really good horse. "Ready Penny? Move over to your left a bit." Penny did as Billy said and got ready. Billy eased into the herd and cut a cow out. The cow made a move toward the herd and the horse stayed in front keeping it out. After a few tries the cow ran toward Penny. She kicked her horse in the side and pulled on the rein which didn't take much. The cow moved back to the herd just like it was supposed to. Billy quit that cow and went after another.

Penny's eyes were glued on the cow. Billy pushed it out and it tried very hard to get back to the herd. The horse really got down and kept it out of the herd. The cow moved toward Penny and she kicked Molly and ran toward the cow pushing it back. This went on for a while. Billy said, "That is enough. Penny, you are going to make a real good hand with horses. You did real good." He led the horse up to Penny and asked her to take the reins and lead him around so he can cool off. This is new but she caught on real quick.

By the time Penny had the horse cooled out; Billy came in the arena leading another horse. He told Penny to tie the horse in the back of the arena. Billy said, "I guess I better show you how to tie a horse up properly." He led the horse over and showed her how to tie a horse up. He let her practice a few times and they were ready to go again. Penny is ready. Billy eased the horse into the cattle and pushed one away from the herd. The cow stood there and looked around and ran away from the herd. Penny and Molly were ready. The cow came to them pretty fast and Molly headed the cow and made her turn.

Penny thought the cow is going back to the herd but suddenly stopped and turned. Molly stopped very hard and turned to the cow. When she did, Penny came sailing off the horse and landed on her feet. Billy and Penny had a good laugh. Penny climbed back on Molly and this time Penny is ready. Another lesson learned. They worked another horse and by then it is getting dark.

Penny help Billy unsaddle the horses and rub them down. These horses had individual stalls. Billy told Penny which stall to put the horses in. Billy said the stall is their home while they are in training so Penny needs to be sure to put each horse in the right stall. Penny told Billy she had to go before it got too dark. She said she would be back every afternoon she could. Billy thanked her for her help.

Penny drove back to her house. It is dark by the time she got there. She would return the jeep in the morning. James told Penny the man came to see him about the car and they looked at it. It is not in running condition because of the motor. James thought it could be fixed. James offered the man $350 for it. The man hesitated, but then said, "Ok, it's a deal. When can you get me the money?" James told him to come by in the morning and he would have it. This is good news for Penny. She said, "I have $350 saved. I will go get it." She had it hid, same as her mother hid her money. She brought it back to James and gave him a big hug and said, "Thanks Dad!"

Next morning Penny met McKenzie at the door of the farm office. She asked him if she was to go to the gin. McKenzie said, "Not right now. Stay here until Sue gets here and check with her if she has anything you need to do or need to know." In a few minutes Sue and Martha arrived. They spoke and visited for a few minutes. Penny told Sue what McKenzie had said. Sue told Penny, "Everything is under control for the moment, but remember when the ginning get underway and lots of cotton starts to come in we all will be behind and working long hours to catch up." Penny understood this, but is disappointed she could not help Billy with the horses.

The gin is just a few hundred yards from the office so Penny walked over. On her way, she had to pass the shop where her Dad worked. She spoke, and asked if he had the car yet. James said, "Not yet but I will get it this afternoon. I will have to tow it in. Mr. Johns is going with me to help pull it back." "Good, I will be by to see it when I get off work." She went into the office and spoke to Mr. Quick. Larry was not there. Mr. Quick gave Penny another lesson in weighing cotton. About that time a farmer pulled a trailer onto the scale. "Good," Mr. Quick said. "OK Penny, here is lesson number two. Come over here and pull a chair up next to me." She did as she was told and Mr. Quick went through the weighing of the cotton, recording the information in a book that had carbon paper in it so there would be three copies of the ticket. Penny thought that is not too hard to do, but she knew she would need more training.

The farmer introduced himself to Penny. He said, "Hello, young lady. My name is Luis Jones." Penny said, "Hello Mr. Jones, I'm Penny Parks. I will be working here time to time." He said, "Good. Glad we finally got a pretty girl working here. I am tired of seeing a bunch of old ugly men." Penny and Mr. Quick laughed at that.

Mr. Quick showed Penny how to take the gin tags and record who brought the cotton in. Mr. Quick told Penny to ask which farm the cotton came off of. He said, "That is very, very important. We don't want to get the cotton on the wrong farm."

After a while another load came in and they went through the procedure again. By lunch time there had been five trailer loads to come in. The gin wasn't running; they were waiting to get enough cotton to make it run all day. Mr. Quick said they would start the gin up in the morning. Later in the day another load came in and Mr. Quick asked Penny if she was ready to weigh and fill out the book work. She said, "I will try." Mr. Quick said, "Take your time, Penny." She introduced herself to the farmer and told him she would be working there part time. She asked for his name and the farm the cotton came off. She also made sure he was the owner of the cotton and not just a hired hand that brought the load in. Penny recorded the information and filled out the tags, went out and tied them onto the trailer.

Mr. Quick told the farmer, "Pull it down to the gin and get it in line." He did as he was asked. Most farmers have ginned there for years and they know the drill. Mr. Quick checked over Penny's work and said Penny, "You did it just right. I will be here to see that you understand how it all works. Tomorrow you will get to weigh the trailers after they are ginned, and the bale weight." Penny understands it is a big responsibility to do the weighing and recordkeeping. That is why they have extra help.

Mr. Quick told Penny to go on home. Penny walked to the shop where her dad is working. They spoke and James asked Penny how her day went. They talked about that for a while. James said they were going after the car as soon as he finished the job he was working on. He said the man brought the title and a receipt for the money Penny paid on the car. She asked if she could use the jeep to go home and change clothes and go to the horse barn. James said, "Its okay, but this week may be the last day you can use it because it will be needed at the gin."

Penny drove home and changed into her blue jeans and a short sleeved shirt. She also put on her new cowboy boots and the belt she bought in Stuttgart. She had bought a new ball cap at Stuttgart and she wore that too. She drove up to the arena, where Billy had Molly saddled and tied to the fence. She waved at Billy and went over and climbed aboard Molly. She rode her to get her loosened up, and herself too. After a while Billy rode up on one of the horses he is training and asked Penny if she is ready. Penny said, "I am ready. I am going to try not to fall off but if I do, don't laugh." Billy chuckled and said, "Penny, you already know I am going to laugh so you better stick like glue to Molly."

Billy already had the cattle in the arena all huddled in a group. He told Penny a little about the horse he is working. It belonged to one of the cattleman in the area. He wanted it trained for competition. Billy said, "It is a really good horse. Ready, Penny? Move over to your left a bit." Penny did as Billy said and got ready. Billy eased into the herd and cut a cow out. The cow made a move toward the herd and the horse stayed in front, keeping it out. After a few tries the cow ran toward Penny. She kicked her horse in the side and pulled on the rein which didn't take much. The cow moved back to the herd just like it was supposed to. Billy quit that cow and went after another.

Penny's eyes were glued on the cow. Billy pushed it out, and it tried very hard to get back to the herd. The horse really got down and kept it out of the herd. The cow moved toward Penny and she kicked Molly and ran toward the cow pushing it back. This went on for a while. Billy said, "That is enough. Penny, you are going to make a real good hand with horses. You did real good." He led the horse up to Penny and asked her to take the reins and lead him around so he can cool off. This is new but she caught on real quick.

Chapter 9

Billy is in the arena working a horse. Penny waved at him. He rode up and asked her to saddle Molly and they would work cattle. Soon Penny had Molly saddled and rode up to the arena gate. It is open so she rode inside. She got Molly in a lope and rode her in a circle for a while; first to the left, then to the right. After a bit Molly was settled and ready to go. "Are you ready, Penny?" Penny said, "Yep, I'm ready to go." Penny rode back to the gate and closed it so the cows wouldn't get out. Billy brought out the good horse he rode the other day. He is a beautiful animal. Billy ran some cows into the arena. Penny took her place and is ready. Billy ran the horse across the arena a few times and spun the horse around to the left and right. The horse is really fast. Billy said, "OK, Penny hang on." "Me and Molly are ready," Penny said.

Billy eased a cow out and waited until it moved. It didn't do what it was supposed to; it ran toward Penny and Molly. Penny kicked Molly and she ran toward the cow. Penny slapped her leg and said, "Go back cow." The cow went straight toward the herd and the horse is ready; he headed her off. The cow tried about three more times and each time the horse headed the cow, and did not let her get back to the herd. Billy stopped the horse and patted him on the neck saying, "Good job, Pete."

Penny and Molly were cooling Pete out. Directly Billy came back with another horse. Billy said this is Roany, another one of Mr. Hackett's cutting horses. He is a good one too. In a few minutes HB drove up and got out of his pickup. "Hey Billy are you fixing to work Ol' Roany?" Billy said. "I sure am. You came just at the right time."

HB is surprised to see Penny on a horse helping Billy. HB spoke to Penny and said, "Penny I didn't know you liked horses and sure didn't know you could ride a cow horse." Penny said, "Mr. HB, I love horses, especially cow horses. I have been helping Billy. He is teaching me. In fact I've been thrown off about eight times." HB laughed and said, "That is the way you learn."

Billy eased Roany into the herd and he quietly pushed one of the cows from the herd. It immediately tried to get back. Roany jumped in front of the cow and the cow headed the other way. Roany then headed her off and she tried again. This time the cow gave up and headed toward Penny. She kicked Molly and ran her toward the cow. Penny slapped her leg and said, "Hey, hey! Get back cow." The cow went back to the herd. Billy pushed another one out and it tried really hard to get back to the herd. Roany lowered his front end and went head to head with the cow. Billy quickly stopped the horse and said, "What do you think HB?" "Hey Roany is really getting good! Think we can show him next month at the cutting show in Little Rock?" Billy said, "I think he will be ready." HB turned to Penny and said, "Penny you surprised me! You are making a good hand."

Billy said, "Yeah HB. Before too long I am going to start her cutting cattle. She is really coming along. She needs a pair of spurs though." HB told her to come by the office in the morning. He had a pair that would just fit her.

Next morning Penny met McKenzie at the office door and told him what HB said about coming to see him. McKenzie said, sure Penny I think he is in the office. Come on, I will go with you." McKenzie knocked on the door and opened it. He said, "Penny is here to see you." "Thanks, tell her to come in." Penny walked in and said she was on her way to the gin office but wanted to stop by on the way.

HB said, "Sure Penny, here are the spurs I promised you. I bought them for Ruth but she never had much interest in horses. They are really good cutting horse spurs. Let me show you how to put them on."

Penny propped her foot on the edge of a chair and HB put the spurs on her boots and showed her how they should go. "Remember the buckle goes to the outside." He adjusted the spur straps and told Penny to put the other one on. She took her time but got it just right. She said, "Thank you so much for letting me borrow the spurs." HB said, "You are welcome. Good cowboys and cowgirls never take their spurs off their boots. When I see you wearing boots, I want to see the spurs on them." "Yes sir." Penny thought that is kind of strange, but accepted it. She took HB at his word.

Penny said, "Mr. HB, do you mind if I help Billy and ride your horses?" HB said, "Of course not, Penny. I am tickled you are interested in horses. When you are ready you will be riding and showing cutting horses for the Silver Leaf." That really got Penny's attention. She thanked him and walked proudly to the gin.

Penny never knew it, but HB called McKenzie into the office. HB said, "I want you to arrange the work schedule so Penny can help Billy with the horses. Make sure when she is helping Billy she gets paid for it. Right now Billy is working the horses early in the morning and late afternoon. You can tell her about the arrangement. When she is not helping Billy she can work at the gin." McKenzie said, "I will take care of it."

As Penny approached the gin she could hear it running. It is loud. She went into the gin office and closed the door. She could still hear the gin, but it is not so loud in the office. She could also smell the smoke from the burning of the gin trash. She spoke to Mr. Quick. His son Larry is there. Mr. Quick said, "Ok you two, we are going to the gin and show you how it works. You need to know it is very loud in there—and dangerous—so keep your hands to yourself. The gin likes fingers and arms. It will get you. Most workers put cotton in their ears."

The gin is only about a 30 steps from the scales. First they watched as the cotton was being sucked into the gin by a big telescoping suck pipe operated by one of the workers. He is skilled at the job and made it look easy. Mr. Quick motioned for them to follow him. Once inside the gin, he pointed to where the cotton is going. He pointed to the gin stands where the cotton is being separated from the lint. The seed went into a suck pipe that took it to the seed house. The lint went to the gin press, where it is packed down until there is enough for a bale. The workers had a bagging made of jute read to wrap the bale when it is ready. They watched as the press is packing the cotton.

When there is enough for a bale, a horn blew and the workers turned the press so another bale could be started while they unloaded the one with the bale. The workers quickly put metal straps around the bale and fastened them. Then the press door opened and the two workers pushed the bale onto scales. The weight is recorded in a ledger and called in to the scale person, who took the weight and recorded it to the name of the farmer who owned the cotton. This helped Penny and Larry to get a clear picture of the ginning process.

Mr. Quick went on to say that the last step is when the seed is separated from the lint. It goes into a pipe that blows the seed to the seed house. The seed is then transported to a Cotton Oil Mill in Rose City, AR, where they press it into oil. What is left is fed to cattle.

Penny and Larry were silent, trying to absorb all that in their mind. Mr. Quick said, "Now do you understand the cotton gin business a little more?" Penny said, "I know it is a big responsibility to run a cotton gin." Larry agreed.

School is starting in two weeks. They put the start date back a week so the kids could pick cotton and help their families out with money. Penny is glad. That meant more time with the horses. Penny and Larry both helped with the scales. More cotton is coming in. It is good practice for them both. At the end of the day Penny walked to the farm shop where her dad is working.

He said, "Want to see your new car?" "YES! I do, Dad!" He walked Penny over to the shed outside. "There it is." Penny said, "Oh Dad! It is so pretty!" She opened the door to look inside. "It looks like brand new!" James said, "It only has a few hundred miles on it. We sure got it for a bargain. That is, if it doesn't cost too much to fix it up." Penny asked, "When do you think you think you will have it running?" James said, "I will tear into it this Saturday and get the parts maybe next week, so it may be a couple of weeks."

Penny said, "Oh Dad! I really need it now! Is there any way we could work on it sooner?" James said, "Well, we could work on it some at night after work." Penny said, "I will help you. Right now, I need to go home and change clothes and go to the horse barn. Can I use the jeep?" "If it is in its parking place, you can use it." James said.

"Dad, I just thought if the jeep had lights on it I wouldn't need the car so soon. I have to leave the horses before we finish because the jeep doesn't have lights." Her dad replied, "Tomorrow I will rig up something. You will have lights by tomorrow afternoon." "Dad, thank you so much," Penny said.

Penny changed and headed to the horse barn. Billy is saddling Molly for Penny. He had a horse saddled that Penny had not seen before. "This is a new horse HB bought from an outfit in Texas. He is supposed to be a good one. We will find out soon enough. Ok Penny, you are ready to go. Hold up, I forgot, there is something I need to tell you. McKenzie came by and said HB wants your work schedule arranged so you can help me with the horses. When you are helping, you will be paid same as if you were at the gin or anywhere else on the farm. He will work out the time sheets. I am glad you are helping. We do have an old fellow that does the feeding and mucking out the stalls so you won't have to worry about that."

Penny told Billy, "Oh that makes me so happy I want to holler!" Billy said, "Go ahead Penny." Penny took her cap off threw it in the air and yelled "YIPPEEE!"

"Good for you! Ok let's get going. Penny be careful when you use your spurs. They really wake a horse up. If you are not careful, Molly will get out from under you." Penny climbed on Molly, and rode around the arena to warm her up. Billy watched Penny ride and thought to himself how good she looked sitting on a horse. He is determined to get Penny on a good cutting horse and get her good enough to show.

Billy mounted the new horse. As he did, Penny asked, "What's his name Billy?" Billy said "You know, I don't know. We will have to come up with a good name. Got any ideas?" Penny said, "Well, he has a pretty blaze on his face. Why don't we call him Blaze?" "Good as any; that's what we will call him." Penny asked if he is a gelding. Billy said, "He is a three year old, so he is what we call "green broke." That means he is a little more than just starting. He has just started working cattle." Penny understood what Billy is saying. Billy rode the horse around to warm him up. The horse caught Billy by surprised and bucked him off. Penny ran over to Billy and said, "Billy, are you hurt?" Billy got up and dusted himself off and said, "Alright, go ahead and laugh. I sure laughed at you." Penny couldn't hold it any longer. She let out a big laugh. "OK Billy, now we are even."

Billy got back on the horse and was more careful with him. He rode him around for a good while until he could get all of the buck out of him. "OK, I think he is ready; I am going to ride in and get a cow out. For right now, don't turn the cow back. I want Blaze to just follow it. When the cow breaks back to the herd, I want him to head it off." Penny watched as Billy cut a cow out and made Blaze just follow the cow. They took it slow and, about halfway down the arena, the cow broke back to the herd. Billy spurred Blaze really hard and made him jump in front of the cow. The horse is sure looking at the cow. It is easy to tell he is a cow horse, but he needs training on the cutting part. Billy is a good trainer and will get him going. In no time he will be showing him.

They worked Blaze, then put him up and saddled Pete. He needed some work. Billy got him warmed up and went into the cattle that were bunched up. He rode in and eased a cow out of the bunch. He is really quiet; none of the cattle were spooked. Billy eased Pete out front and, when the cow broke to go back to the herd, Pete headed it off. It tried again and Pete held it back. In a few minutes the cow broke toward Penny's end of the arena.

Penny spurred Molly hard on the right side to make her go left and head off the cow. Molly jumped so fast Penny almost fell off. But she didn't. She knew she is gaining her riding balance that Billy talked about.

They worked until it was very near dark. Billy knew the jeep didn't have lights so he told Penny to go on home. Penny said, "I hate to go, but it is close to dark." Penny asked Billy if he needed help in the mornings when he rides. Billy said, "I sure could use the help. I start riding at six o'clock. Is that too early?" Penny said she will be there at 6:00.

When Penny got home Missy ran out and said, "Penny, you got a letter from Smith." "Oh, good!" Penny exclaimed. Missy handed the letter to Penny and she ran in her room to read it. It is a long letter. The first words were "I love you and miss you very much." Smith spoke of his room and roommate, who is also from Arkansas; from Stuttgart, in fact, which is only about 25 miles from England. Smith said his name is Andrew, but he wanted to be called Andy. They could ride home together. He wrote that his classes were going to be hard and he would really have to study.

Smith gave Penny his mailing address and said, "Please write me and tell me what you are doing. Do you miss me?"

Penny could tell Smith is homesick. She is so happy to hear from him. Smith gave Penny asked her mother if she had writing paper and an envelope. Earlene told her to look in the middle drawer of the Penny couldn't wait; she had to write him tonight. She went to her mother and asked if dresser. Penny found paper and an envelope, but no stamp. She sat down by the lamp in the kitchen and wrote Smith a beautiful letter. She told Smith how much she missed him and could hardly wait to see him. She told him about helping with the horses and about getting thrown about eight times. She knew he would get a laugh about that. She told him about working at the gin and then told him about her new car.

Penny wrote almost five full pages. She has a pretty handwriting and writes really well. She put the letter in an envelope and sealed it up. She would get a stamp from the office in the morning after she finished with the horses. At supper Penny told the family that she will get paid for helping Billy with the horses. She said, "I am so excited! I enjoy the horses so much!" James said, "We are glad you are going to be paid for something you love to do. I know you will be good at it." She told them about what HB had told her about riding cutting horses for the Silver Leaf Farm. Then she showed them the spurs she had on her boots. Penny told them that Mr. HB wanted her to never take the spurs off her boots. They liked that. Penny liked the way they jingled when she walked.

After supper Penny bathed and put on her pajamas and laid out her clothes for the next day. She needed a few more pair of jeans. She asked Earlene if they could go to town Saturday if she wasn't working and get them, maybe a shirt or two. Penny said, "I get paid Friday and I will have the money. Oh, I have to be at the barn before six in the morning. Will you please wake me up if I am not already up?" "Yes, one of us will get you up."

With that Penny went to bed. It is early for her, but she was tired. In the morning Penny was awake when her mother came and told her it is 5:00. Penny got up and dressed, and helped her mother fix breakfast. Missy and James Jr. were still asleep. After breakfast, Penny got in the jeep and drove to the horse barn. Billy wasn't there yet, so Penny caught Molly and saddled her up. She was riding in the arena when Billy drove up. He waved at Penny and went and saddled one of the other horses he is being paid to ride.

He rode into the arena and wave for Penny to ride over. Billy said, "Penny, this is Lady. She is in training. I want you to tie Molly to the fence and get on this horse." Penny wasn't sure what to expect. Billy went on to say, "As a part of your training you need to ride different horses. It is the best training you can get." Penny tied Molly up just like Billy had showed her a few days ago. She then walked over to Lady and gave her a rub on the nose. She said, "Lady, you are not going to throw me off so you just better behave yourself."

Penny got on and sat there just a few seconds. She gathered up the reins and kicked the horse forward.

Penny could tell this horse had a lot more fire in her than Molly. Penny showed no fear; she rode Lady around the arena, then pulled her to a stop and reversed her circle. Billy rode up on Blaze and told Penny to watch. "I am going to show you how to spin a horse around." As he went through the drill, he talked to Penny. "Now watch close; you will be doing this next." Billy started turning the horse slow, and then got the horse spinning on his hind feet. Not fast; he didn't want to scare Penny off. Then he spun the horse in the reverse direction. "Now Penny, I want you to watch and do what I do." Penny watched closely as Billy picked up the reins and pulled the horse's head to the right, then kind of leaned back. The horse got on its hind feet and turned the horse around. Penny did that and almost got it right.

Billy said, "Take your time; let's do it again." This time it worked out just right. "Ok, now to the left. She gathered the horse up and reined it to the left. The horse gathered its hind feet underneath her so she could turn on them. Billy said, "Penny that is good for the first time. I want you ride Lady around the arena and, about every time around, stop and make her turn over her hocks; first one way, and then the other." Penny is determined. It took her a good bit of trying before she got it good enough to suit Billy.

There were lots of things Penny will need to learn before she can ride like a pro. One thing is the basic 'leads.' Billy chose not to tell Penny anything about leads until she got a little more experience. He really needed Penny to ride more than she is now. With the new work schedule Billy felt he could ask more of her. They rode in the arena awhile, and then Billy asked Penny to take the horse down the turn row. He told her ride her around the field by the barn. "That will be about a mile. Ease her along. If she wants to stop and look, that's okay. Be careful not to spook her. Watch out; you may think everything is going good and she will jump out from underneath. You she's quicker than lightning."

Chapter 10

She eased Lady down the turn row and Billy was right; Lady is a little spooky. Of course she is still very green. Penny took her time with the horse and, about halfway around the field, Penny could feel Lady loosening up. She kind of dropped her head and got into a steady walk. Penny knew she had made progress with the horse. When she got back she dismounted and walked her into the arena where Billy was riding another young horse. Billy waved to Penny to come over. Billy told Penny to change horses with him. "Take this horse on the same trail as this one." Penny asked, "Do you want to change saddles?" Billy said, "I think it would be better if we did." Penny unsaddled her horse and then saddled the other one.

Billy said, "This is another young one, so be careful." Penny spoke to the horse and gave him a rub on his face. She took a few minutes to get on the horse. They slowly started down the turn row. Penny liked this horse; he seemed like he enjoyed what he was doing. It was a good riding session. Billy called Penny over and told her he needed her to put in more time helping him. "Don't worry; HB and McKenzie know I am going to ask you for more hours. They assured me there would be no problem for you at the gin. You can still work there when we are not riding. We will skip some days and let the horses rest."

"Now, can you be back about 4:00 this afternoon?" "Yes sir, I can. My dad is supposed to put lights on the jeep today and if he does I can stay longer." "Good," Billy said. Penny drove straight to the farm office and asked Sue if she had a stamp she could buy. "Sure, Penny. How are you getting along at the gin and with the horses?" Penny said, "Okay. Did you hear about me falling off a horse eight times?" "No, I didn't did you get hurt?" "No, but I was so sore the next morning Missy had to help me out of bed. Billy got a good laugh. He got bucked off yesterday so I got to laugh at him." Sue said, "If you want, just drop the letter in the out basket and we will get it in the mail."

"Do you think I could get a book of stamps from the mailman?" she asked Sue. "Yes, you can but I have some extra stamps here. They are three dollars a book." Penny had some dollar bills in her hip pocket. She got them out and counted out three dollars. She thanked Sue and asked her how work is going. Sue said, "Good so far. We will be on overtime starting next week." Penny told her she would be putting in more hours helping Billy. She said, "I will still work at the gin as much as I can. I need the money. My dad found me a car. I bought it but it needs some work."

Penny Spoke to Martha and they visited briefly. She said, "I will see you two later. I have to take the jeep back to the shop, then go to the gin." Sue and Martha noticed the spurs on Penny's boots. They could hear them jingle. Penny drove to the shop and parked the jeep in its regular parking place, then went to see her dad. He is busy helping one of the workers pull an engine out of a tractor. She went by and spoke to him and asked if he is going to have time to put lights on the jeep. He told her that he planned to but it might be rigged a little rough. "I will fix it better when I can find the time, but for now at least you will have lights. When you come to get it this afternoon find me, and I will show you how they work." She is glad of that.

She walked on over to the gin. Mr. Quick and Larry were at the scales weighing in a load of cotton. They spoke and Penny watched as they weighed the load and put tags on the trailer for the gin. Mr. Quick told Penny and Larry that they need to know how many bales are on a trainer or wagon. He told them, "Most of the time the farmer will know because he has the weights that came from the field records."

"If they don't know, ask them about how much the trailer weighs and you have the gross weight. You can subtract the estimated weight of the trailer and divide it by 1300 pounds. That is approximately how much seed cotton it takes to gin out a 500 pound bale."

Penny and Larry thought they could do that with no problem. After the trailer is pulled of the scales and to the gin, Mr. Quick said to Penny, "We need to talk." She said, "Yes sir." Mr. Quick said, "McKenzie came by and told me about you helping at the horse barn. That is okay with me; it will let Larry get in more hours. He needs the work too." Penny said, "That is fine with me. School will be starting soon and we won't get as many hours in. Since I will be working with Billy Rosewell, it will help us both."

Penny is glad Larry is available to work at the gin. That freed her up to help Billy. Penny stayed at the gin until noon. Mr. Quick told her to go home and rest. "You will be working late today." Penny said, "that's fine, but if you need me I can stay." Mr. Quick told her to go. "You can't work all the time. You need some time off." Penny was walking back to the shop to look at the car again. As she approached the shop she saw a military car easing down the road toward the Russell's house. She knew something is wrong. She ran to the farm office and told Sue about the car. Sue ran into McKenzie's office and told him. He then alerted HB.

HB came out and asked Penny about the car. She told him it had two soldiers in it. HB figured something was bad wrong. He told Penny to go get Ruth. She ran over and told her. Ruth dressed hurriedly and drove to the office. She told HB she thought they should go to the Russell house. HB told McKenzie to go find Alec and bring him to the house. He asked Sue to follow them to the

Russell's. When they got there the Chaplain had told Mrs. Russell that Tommy had been killed in action in Korea.

This is terrible news. Ruth is holding on to Mrs. Russell; she is about to faint. In a minute McKenzie came up with Alec. He knew what the news was. He talked to the Chaplain; he had some information about how Tommy died. He died trying to save another soldier. Sue came up and helped Mr. Russell and Mrs. Russell. She led them to the porch and asked them to sit down. They did and held onto each other as they grieved.

McKenzie went and told all the other workers the bad news. Some wanted to go immediately to the Russell house. McKenzie told them to wait about 30 minutes as the Russells were both in shock. They needed some time to grieve. Before long the word spread to the surrounding towns. Tommy had many friends, including Smith Hackett.

It took a few hours for things to settle down. HB left and went home but promised the Russell's if they needed anything let him know. Penny walked to the shop and told her dad. He went home to tell Earlene. They decided to wait until late in the day to go see the Russells. Earlene had baked a cake earlier and she would take that over. She would cook more the next day. Penny drove the jeep to the horse barn. Her dad did get some lights on the jeep. She told Billy about Tommy getting killed in action in Korea. Billy is saddened by the news. He asked her how he got killed; Penny said she hadn't heard.

Penny and Billy went about riding the horses. Billy told Penny to get Blaze out and saddle him. She got him out of his stall and tied him to one of the tie rings mounted in a heavy post. She brushed him hurriedly then saddled him. She put the bridle on and checked to make sure it fit correctly. She led him in the arena and mounted him there. He is a little frisky at first but soon calmed down. Billy ran six cows into the arena. Penny is busy warming Blaze up. Billy got on one of the other new horses and rode him in a circle, making him spin left, then right.

He told Penny, "Ok, be ready! No telling what might happen." He eased his horse in the herd and pushed one out. First thing, the cow ran toward Penny's end of the arena. She kicked Blaze in the side and he jumped at the cow and ran it back. Billy and Penny rode horses until after dark. The arena had good lights and they kept working. Finally Billy said that is enough. They unsaddled the horses and Penny led them to their stalls. She made sure they had water. They did. They had plenty of feed, too.

Billy and Penny talked for a few minutes. He told Penny she was coming along really good. "I am proud of you Penny." Penny said, "Thanks Billy." Penny drove back to her house. Her dad and mother were at the Russell's. Missy and James Jr. were home. Earlene had food out for her. Penny ate, then bathed and put on her pajamas. Afterwards, she sat down and wrote Smith a letter. She wondered if Smith would come home for the funeral. She is sure his mother and dad called him and told him the bad news.

Penny didn't get a lot of sleep. She thought about Tommy Russell. She knew him, although not well. She knew he was a nice looking and gentle person. Smith and Tommy were real good friends; they had been hunting and fishing buddies. She would ask Ms. Ruth if Smith is coming home for the funeral. Next morning, Penny is up by five and drove to the horse barn. She and Billy rode horses until about 10:00. They talked about the horses. Billy said he is going to the Russell home this morning.

She drove to Ms. Ruth's house and knocked on the back door. Ruth told her to come on in. Ruth asked her if she knew Tommy. Penny said, "Yes, I knew him. I know that he and Smith were good friends and hunted and fished together."

"Ms. Ruth, "I hate to ask but do you know if Smith is coming for the funeral?" Ruth said she had not heard. "I am sure I will know if he is coming or not, and when I know I will make sure you get the word. It might take several days for the body to arrive. HB called the Senator and he has promised that his office and Red Cross would do all they can to bring him home soon."

Penny said, "It is awfully selfish of me to even ask." She and Penny talked for a while. Penny told her about the car she bought. Ruth asked Penny if she knew when they would be moving into their new house. Penny said, "It should be pretty soon. We have been over and picked out the colors for the rooms." Ruth said she is glad they were getting a new house. Penny replied, "We have not said too much about it because, if something happened, we wouldn't be so disappointed. But now all of us are getting really excited."

Penny went to the gin and helped Mr. Quick and Larry. Mr. Quick wanted to go to the Russell's' home. He left Penny and Larry in charge. Two loads of cotton came in and Penny and Larry teamed up on weighing and recording the loads. They spoke to the farmers and asked them if they had heard about Tommy Russell getting killed in Korea. One of them had not heard. He is also a friend of the Russell family. He asked about funeral arrangements and they said they had not heard anything about that.

The funeral director came to visit the Russell's and asked about the arrangements. He told them he could arrange for the body to be escorted to the funeral home if they wanted that. The Russell's asked if he could arrange that. The military is supposed to have a person to help coordinate the military funeral if that is what they wanted. They agreed on a military funeral but they wanted the family's preacher to deliver the last rites. The funeral director asked if they wanted Tommy to be buried in a Military Cemetery or a cemetery of their choice. They wanted him buried in the family plot next to them.

The community is busy preparing food and places for relatives to stay overnight. It is a terrible time, but work had to go on. Penny is busy helping Billy. James had some time to work on Penny's car. He got the car to start. It had a 'knock' in the motor that did not sound good. He is afraid he would have to overhaul the whole motor. Since the engine is practically new, it should not have to be overhauled. He was about to take the motor out when he noticed something on the side of the motor that looked out of place. He looked at the fuel pump and noticed the whole pump is loose. In fact, it is so loose it is almost off. James looked it over and decided to tighten it back on the motor.

When he did, he turned on the ignition and pushed in the starter. It cranked right off and ran as smooth as silk. He let it sit and run to make sure there were no oil or gas leaks. After he was satisfied he got in it and drove it to the gin where Penny is. She saw her dad drive up and walked out to meet him. He told her the good news and she said, "Thank you Dad! You have made my day!" James said, "I will leave it here for you and I'll drive the jeep back to the shop."

Mr. Quick told Penny she did not need to stay if she wanted to go. Penny said, "I think I need to stay a couple more hours to see what is going on. If you don't mind, I will leave a little before 4:00." Mr. Quick knew not to send Penny home, so he said that will be fine. "While you are here, look at the gin book and check some of the figures. Larry will be here to help." Penny and Larry talked about Tommy Russell. Larry said he knew him, but not all that well. Larry knew Penny and Smith were dating. He asked if Smith would be coming home and Penny told him she didn't know. She said they don't know when the body will arrive.

Earlene had fixed food for the Russell's. Penny had forgotten she is supposed to come home and go with her mother to take the food. She told Larry she should go. She got in her new car and drove it home. She is so excited to be driving her own car. She drove up to the house and went in to help her mother gather up the food. Penny said, "Come see my new car. Let's put the food in it and I will drive it to the Russell home." That is the first time Earlene had seen the car. She liked it. Penny drove up to the Russells and helped with the food. Penny hugged Mrs. Russell, then Mr. Russell. She told them how sorry she is for their loss.

They stayed and visited for a while. They knew Mrs. Russell pretty well. She is a good seamstress. She made clothes for Penny and Missy. Mrs. Russell couldn't work out in the sun so she bought her a sewing machine and started sewing. They stayed and helped clean the house and the kitchen. Mr. and Mrs. Russell tried to lie down and rest. They had relatives coming in. They needed a place for them to stay. The church had places for them; they also provided food. They did not know when the body would arrive. The Senator's office and Red Cross told them the body would arrive this Monday. Since today is Thursday, most of the relatives went back home and would come back Monday or Tuesday. It would be a long weekend for the Russells.

Penny drove her mother home then drove to the horse barn. Billy had a horse in the round pen giving him a workout. "Penny, come watch." Billy stood in the middle of the round pen with a rope and had the horse running around the pen. Billy took a few steps toward the horse and shook the rope. The horse stopped on its hind feet, reversed himself and went the opposite way. That was the first time Penny had seen that. In fact, they had just finished the round pen that day. Billy later told her he had been trying to get one built for a long time. Billy told Penny to come into the pen. She walked up to Billy. He stopped the horse and told Penny he wanted her to learn how to work horses in the pen. He told her where to stand and gave her the rope, which is only about eight feet long. Billy showed her how to get the horse doing what she wanted him to do. It took a while, but Penny caught on real quick. Billy told her not to get the horse too hot; he wanted him warmed up, and stopping and going the opposite way.

Now is a good time for Billy to teach Penny more about leads. He spent about an hour with Penny and the horse to make sure Penny understood how a horse is supposed to be on the correct lead; clockwise then counterclockwise. Penny is a quick learner but training horses takes time and patience. After they had finished with that horse Billy told her to bring Pete out. She got the halter and went in the stall and slipped the halter on Pete. She led him into the round pen and handed the lead rope to Billy. "This is the first time for Pete too. Let's see if we can get him to go. Billy took the lead rope off the halter and pushed Pete toward the boards in the pen. Billy shook the rope and got Pete going around the pen, first in a trot then in a lope. Pete wanted to stop or slow down but Billy kept him going.

After a few minutes Billy took quick steps toward the horse and shook the rope. This caused him to stop and reverse his direction. Billy said to Penny, Okay, watch and tell me which lead he is on." "Left lead." "Good," Billy said. After a while Billy said, "Whoa." The horse came to a quick stop, sliding on his hind feet. After that, they saddled up two horses. One is one of the green broke horses. Billy got Blaze and rode him to the cattle.

He eased one out. Penny's horse was alert; he is looking at the cow. In a few seconds Penny had to head the cow and push it back to the herd. She knew better than to really spur the horse hard. He would probably buck her off. She kept the cows turned back without any trouble from the horse. After a while the horse settled down and started to get into the turn back roll. Penny spurred him a little more and asked more from the horse. When they stopped, Billy told Penny, "That is a good job turning back."

They unsaddled their horses and caught two more to ride. They took turns working them in the round pen. Penny could see that is a good way to work horses and get them ready to ride. She took her horse in first and started him trotting around the pen then in a slow lope. After a bit, she motioned for the horse to reverse and go around. Billy then told Penny, "That is enough; go ahead and get on him, and ride him in the arena." She did this while Billy worked his horse. It wasn't long before they were both in the pen with the cattle. Penny's horse is acting lazy. The cow came at them and Penny really got after him with her right spur. This woke the horse up and she had no problem after that.

"Good job!" Billy said.

It started to get dark as they unsaddled their horses. Billy told Penny he is going to take two of HB's horses to a Jackpot Cutting on Saturday, and asked if she wanted to come and watch. He said, "It will be a good time so see how a cutting horse contest is put on. It is not far; about 20 miles from here. My wife is going and we will have room for you if you want to go." Penny said she would go and asked what time to meet them. Billy said, "Be here around 9:00. We will get there and be unloaded by ten." Penny had never met Billy's wife; in fact he had never mentioned her.

Penny drove home in her car with the lights on. They were bright, and the car rode like a cloud. She went in and ate supper. She told her family she is going with Billy and his wife to a cutting horse show this Saturday. They were glad Penny had something to do to take her mind off Smith. She bathed, put on her pj's, and got her pen and writing paper. She wrote Smith a long letter. After that, she got a book out to read. Billy had loaned her a book on horses. He had told her it had lots of good information on horses— how to train them, and how to groom and take care of them. She settled down on the couch by the electric lamp to read.

James came in and told her the new house is 99 percent finished and they might move in next week, but might wait until after Tommy's funeral. Penny read for a while then went to bed. Tomorrow is Friday and payday. She should have a full 40 hours' pay. Next morning at 6:00 she is at the horse barn. Billy is already there and told her which horse to saddle. He is going to work the two horses he is taking to the cutting show. Penny is riding one of the younger horses. First he rode Pete. He got a fresh cow out of the herd and she really tried to get back to the other cows. Pete got down low on his front end and kept the cow back. Finally the cow ran toward Penny. She kicked the horse with her spurs and made him turn the cow back. "Good job Penny!" Billy said.

Billy worked both horses, and he was a little rough on both of them. This would get them ready for the cutting competition. After they worked those two, Billy said, "Penny we need to clean them up and get them looking good for the cutting. Billy told Penny to hold Pete so he could clip around his feet and fetlocks. The horse didn't want to stand still so Penny had to really hold him. She talked to him and he settled down. Billy showed Penny how to pick up a horse's feet and dig the "crud" out. He said the horseshoer would be there this afternoon to put new shoes on them. He also showed Penny how to tend to a horse's mane. He said, "I like a good long mane on my horses. When the mane is swinging and swaying it makes the horse look like it has more motion." He told her that you have to break the ends off the hair and not use clippers. Penny got the curry comb and combed the mane out. She broke ends off the mane, and made it look better. She liked doing that.

Billy led the horse to the wash rack and Penny held him while Billy hosed him down. He applied some soap made for horses and he and Penny scrubbed him down all over, even his "private" parts. Billy really knew what he was doing and Penny is glad to have him as a teacher. When they finished they scraped the excess water off and took a towel to help him dry off more. Billy didn't want the horse to lie down and wallow, like horses do. He didn't want him to get dirty. He tied him up, and Penny had Blaze ready to work on.

Blaze got the same treatment. Neither horse wanted to stand still while they washed them but Billy didn't make a fuss about it; he said that is something they will get used to. After they were finished with the horses Billy pulled the truck and trailer up to the wash rack and they gave both a good washing, inside and out. Billy then pulled the saddles, bridles and halters and grooming stuff out of the tack room and they gave all the equipment a good cleaning. Billy said, "Ok Penny, we are ready. In the morning we will load all the tack in the trailer. Help me make sure we haven't forgotten anything. We could put the stuff in the trailer tonight but it might get stole. The tack room has a good strong lock on it. Penny, we are done until in the morning. I hope you enjoy the cutting."

Next morning Penny is so anxious. She drove to the farm office and went in to get her check. Sue handed it to her and asked her to look over it and sign on the back and she would cash it. Sue said, "Penny you had quite a bit of overtime." Penny said she had put in hours helping Billy and at the gin. "Mr. HB knows about what I am doing." Sue said, "Oh no, Penny. I wasn't questioning your hours. McKenzie told me what you are doing. I am glad you are getting them." Penny said, "School will be starting and I won't be getting any overtime then so I hoped to get some in now. I appreciate HB giving me a chance to make some more money."

Penny left the letter to Smith for the mailman to pick up. She drove to her house to eat lunch. She told Missy and Earlene what she had been doing and told them about the cutting horse show tomorrow. Penny is so happy. It is the first time in her life she had something to do that she loved. The Parks family had spent all their time trying just to put food on the table. HB Hackett knew that. So did Ruth. Both were determined to help Penny enjoy some things in her life.

Chapter 11

Penny drove to the gin and parked away from all the gin traffic. Mr. Quick is glad to see her. He asked her if she minded working the scales. He said, "I have to take my wife to the doctor. I may be gone all afternoon but I will back to close the office when the gin shuts down. Larry won't be here either. If you run into some difficulty, contact McKenzie; he will take care of it." "I think I can handle it; don't worry," Penny replied. Mr. Quick left in a hurry. She sat at the scales and looked at the gin book. She knew the next empty trailer coming across the scales belonged to Luid Jones. She had to weigh it and record the weight in the book with his name.

Soon Mr. Jones pulled the trailer across and Penny weighed it and recorded the weight. Mr. Jones came in and spoke to Penny. He said, "I am waiting for the gin to call in the weight of the bale." It took about five minutes. Mr. Jones got a cold drink out of the vending machine and sat down to visit with Penny. The bale weight came in at 475 pounds. She told Mr. Jones what it weighed. He wrote it down in his day book. He said, "The cotton is turning out pretty good."

He stayed a while and mainly talked about his family. He had four kids: two boys and two girls; all teenagers. All were in the field picking cotton. Mr. Jones told Penny he would see her next trip if she is there. Penny figured up the gin ticket. She checked it over three times to make sure she had it correct. In a few minutes a load of cotton came in on a pickup truck. The driver got out so the truck would be weighed empty.

The driver came in and told Penny the cotton belonged to the Joe Saddler farm. "There is one bale on it. In fact, I have the weights here in my book." Penny said she only needed to be sure there is enough for one bale. It is, if the weights were correct. She filled out the ticket and tag and went out and tied the tag on the opposite side of the truck so when the truck pulled under the suck pipe the ginner could easily reach the tag.

Mr. Saddler came back in and sat in one of the soft chairs where some farmers waited until they got their trailer or truck ginned off. It would be over an hour before they could gin it off. They ginned the cotton in the order that they came in so Mr. Saddler had to wait his turn. He is a friendly man and liked to talk. He also talked about his family and asked Penny all kind of questions about hers. He noticed the spurs on her boots and asked her about them. Penny liked to talk about horses. Soon another trailer came from the gin and pulled on the scales. Penny took the weight and recorded it in the gin book. Soon after the bale weight is called in. Penny put all the information in the book.

She is getting into a rhythm doing the work at the scales. She knew anything could happen to cause errors. She did not want that. She is glad when the Saddler truck was ready to weigh empty. One of the gin hands drove it across the scales and got out so it could be weighed empty. Penny told Mr. Saddler his truck is empty. He thanked Penny and said he had to hurry back to the field. Before long the bale weight came in 465 pounds.

In a few minutes Penny heard the gin shutting down. She went to the door to look. The gin hands were all gathered in a group. The main ginner is James "Pepper" Cates. He was trying to figure out what is wrong. In a few minutes one of the gin hands came in and said a belt had run off a pulley and they were waiting for James Parks to come have a look. James went in the gin to inspect the pulley. He found a bearing had worn out and caused the belt drive to freeze up. He got his tool box out of the truck and took the bolts holding the pulley on the shaft. He asked Mr. Cates to get a new bearing. He came back in a few minutes with the bearing. It took almost an hour to get the old bearing off and the new one put in. James told Mr. Cates the old bearing had not been greased. James made sure it is greased properly and warned the gin hands if it happened again he would have to report it to McKenzie.

Once James is out of the gin they restarted it and continued ginning. When Mr. Quick came in, it is getting dark. Penny told him about the gin breaking down. Penny asked about his wife. Mr. Quick said, "She got a good report. She had an infection but the doctor said it is something medicine would take care of." He told Penny she is free to leave. Penny said, "I will stay if you need me. If you don't, I will go on home and get ready for tomorrow. I am going with Billy and his wife to a cutting horse show and we're taking two horses." Mr. Quick said he would be there all day.

Penny hurried home to get ready. Missy came out with a letter from Smith.

He had heard about Tommy Russell getting killed and said how sorry he was. "I hope I can arrange it with the school officers to take a couple of days off. I think they will let me since this is a military school and one of our own was killed in action." Penny hoped he could come. Not for her sake but because he and Tommy grew up together.

Next morning Penny was up early and dressed for the horse show. She wore her new hat Smith had bought for her and a new western shirt she had bought. She wore her best pair of blue jeans and her new belt. She looked in the mirror and thought she looked okay. Missy came in and said she looked like a cowgirl. "Thanks" Penny said. Earlene also thought she looked very good. She ate a big breakfast because she didn't know if she would have lunch or not.

When it was time she drove to the horse barn. Billy and his wife were driving up. They got out and Penny walked over to meet Billy's wife. "Penny, meet my wife Shirley." Penny walked over and shook her hand and said she is glad to meet her. Shirley is a lot younger than Billy, with dark hair and a slender build. Shirley said, "I am glad I finally got to meet you, Billy has told me so much about you. He said you are catching on real quick." Penny said, "I never dreamed I would love horses the way I do and now I have a chance to ride them and take care of them."

Penny asked her if she rode horses. Shirley said, "I do sometimes to help Billy, but to tell the truth I am scared of them." Billy came up leading Pete and told Penny to get Blaze out. She got a halter and put on Blaze and led him out. Billy said, "Just tie him to the trailer. There are rings welded to it to tie them to." Penny tied Blaze just like Billy had taught her. He said, "Okay, get a brush and give him a good brushing. They brushed the horses good and they looked great. They had their manes trimmed and all the hair on their fetlocks and off their chin. Billy took the electric clippers and trimmed a place where the bridle fits on their head. Billy came up with some leg wraps which Penny had not seen. "Here Penny, let me show you how to wrap their legs so they won't hurt them in the trailer."

"Watch me, start just above the hoof and wrap from the inside out, like this. Pull it tight enough so they won't come loose. Go up to the knee and tie it off. Okay, your turn." Penny took the wrap and started where Billy said to. Billy said, "Pull it tight. Good job Penny. Now tie it off."

She did the hind legs; she wasn't scared of getting kicked. She is gentle with the horse and finished the job and asked Billy to check it to make sure it is right; it was. By then Billy had Pete's legs wrapped. Billy asked Penny to help him get the saddles and bridles out of the tack room and all the grooming stuff as well as water buckets and feed buckets. It was a lot to do to get ready for a horse show. A lot more than Penny expected. Finally they were ready to go. Billy loaded the horses and opened the windows for air. It is going to be a very hot day. Shirley sat in the middle, with Penny by the window. She rolled the window down to get cooled off.

This was the dawning of a new day for Penny. She is trying to take the whole experience in and enjoy it. Before long Billy is heading the trailer close to the arena. Thank goodness it had a roof and they could hear the big fans blowing on the spectators seats. Billy did manage to park under a big shade tree. They got the horses out and tied them to the trailer. Billy told Penny not to worry about them they would stand still and not panic. Shirley and Penny walked to the seating area. There were a few riders working their horses. Penny's eyes were glued to them. She wanted to see how real professionals rode their horses.

Some had leather chaps on they looked good in them. There is one girl about Penny's age riding one of the horses. Shirley told her they knew her; her dad is a trainer. "Her name is Suzy Pugh. She will show a horse here today." She looked so at ease on the horse. Shirley asked Penny if she wanted a cold drink. "Yes I do," Penny replied. "I will walk with you." The concession stand is inside the covered part away from the dust. Penny and Shirley got their drinks and when Penny pulled out her money to pay, Shirley said, "Penny, these are on me." Penny wanted to pay Shirley insisted. "Thanks a lot. I will pay for the next one." Shirley showed her where the restroom is located. Penny thanked her.

By then a tractor with a rake behind it pull into the arena. The announcer said, "Clear the arena. We are getting it ready for the cutting horses." Billy saddled both horses and left them tied to the trailer. In a few minutes he came over to Penny and asked her to ride Pete around in a walk to start getting him loose. Penny took the halter off and put Pete's bridle on. She checked the girt strap to make sure it is tight enough. She mounted Pete and started easing him around. There is a group riding in a big shaded area and Penny took Pete over to join them and get him out of the heat. She fell in line with the others and is very careful to stay out of their way. About thirty minutes later Billy waved for Penny to ride over to him.

He said, "Thanks Penny. I will take him now. I think I go in the first group. Take a seat and enjoy the cutting." She sat with Shirley and she pointed out some of the technical things to look for in a good cutting horse. It took a while to get the cattle settled, but finally the announcer called for the first horse. It is a good looking horse; the rider is a trainer for one of the owners. Shirley said he owned quite a few horses and they show all over the country. The rider eased a cow out to cut. Penny noticed there were four turn-back men and she watched to see how it is done. The horse did a good job but the cow didn't move all that much. The rider stopped him and rode in for another cow. This cow was a little wild and didn't do much.

Time is running out and the rider cut one of the cows that is standing by its self. It did try to get back and the horse did a good job keeping it back. The horn blew to signal time is up. The horse got a pretty good score according to Shirley. Billy is working Pete, getting him ready. Billy had on his chaps. Penny thought he looked good on the horse. At last it is Billy's time to ride. About that time HB and Ruth came walking up. They asked if Billy had ridden yet and they said, "He is next." HB and Ruth spoke to Shirley and Penny, and asked Penny how she liked the cutting horse business. Penny said, "It makes me more determined. I love it." They sat down to watch Billy and Pete. Billy eased a cow out of the herd and let it settle a few seconds. He cow started toward the herd and Pete cut it off. It tried again and Pete held. Then it tried a lot harder to get back and Pete held it out front.

Billy quit that cow and got another good cow. Pete worked it to a standstill. Billy then just "peeled" one off the front and Pete held that one. The horn blew and they all clapped for Billy and Pete. HB said, "That should get a good score." It did. Billy is leading the class. Ruth came up and sat by Penny and Shirley; HB walked off to find Billy. Penny walked over to see if she could cool Pete off. Billy said, "Yes, thanks." Penny got on Pete and rode him over to the shade and walked him around; he was really blowing. The cutting really got him tired.

As Penny continued walking Pete, Suzy Pugh came up and introduced herself to Penny. Suzy rode her horse alongside of Pete and they talked. Penny told Suzy this is all new for her but she said, "I like cutting horses." Suzy said, "So do I." They talked and rode around the shady area. They talked about school. Suzy went to Stuttgart high school. She and Penny are in the same grade. Penny asked her if she knew Smith Hackett, she said "Yes I do. He is a good looking man." Penny told her she and Smith were going together. She told her about him going off to military school and about Tommy Russell getting killed in Korea.

Suzy said, "I am so sorry to hear about Tommy." By then it was getting close to Suzy's turn to ride. She said, "I will be back here after I show my horse." With that she rode off and Penny continued to cool Pete out. She would ride him until Billy said to stop. After a while Penny heard the announcer call Suzy's name. Penny hoped she did well but not beat Pete. She listened for the score after Suzy's ride. It was three points less than Pete got. Pete is still leading. After a time Suzy rode back to cool her horse out. Penny asked her how it went. Suzy said "I am very pleased with "Rider," which is her horse's name. Before long Bill rode up on Blaze and asked Penny to ride him and get him warmed up. He said, "Ride him at a walk and at a trot."

Penny said, "I have to go." She and Suzy said they would visit more later. She rode Blaze around and let him get used to the sounds and the other horses. He is a little spooky at first but soon settled down. She rode for about twenty minutes then Billy came and got Blaze. They had another cattle change and they also ran the rake over the part where the cattle and the horses had dug up. Soon it is time for the next cutter. Shirley pointed out that this is a different class than the one Pete showed in. She said this is for the younger horses that are just starting out.

Two horses worked before Billy. He eased Blaze into the herd and let them move around the horse. Billy pushed one out front and held Blaze until the cow started to move. The first cow was a good one; the second was a little slow. Billy got the third one out and it really tried to get back to the herd. Blaze got a little behind. Billy had to spur him really hard to catch up with the cow. Shirley told Penny, "That will count against the horse but it was still a good job." Blaze's score came in it was a pretty good score. Billy rode over to where HB is standing. They talked a few minutes. Ruth had spotted one of her friends and she went over to visit with her. HB went over to Ruth and told her he is ready to go. She came to tell Shirley and Penny bye. "Penny, I am so glad you are riding horses! From what I hear, you really like it." Penny said, "Ms. Ruth, I love riding them! I have lots to learn before Billy will let me cut ride one working a cow. Ruth said, "Take your time it will come soon enough."

Billy came over as HB and Ruth were leaving. The announcer gave the results of the first class. Pete came in first. They called out his registered name and Penny didn't recognize it. Shirley told what it was. She said, "It is easier to have a short name like Pete or Blaze. I guess you could call it a nickname." The next rider is Suzy Pugh. She rode in the herd and got a good cow out. The horse really got down on his front end and held the cow. The crowd hooted and clapped. She only cut one more and did a good job. Shirley thought she would probably win the class. There were four more to show, but none of them were as good as Suzy's horse.

Billy led Blaze over for Penny to cool out. That gave her a chance to talk to Suzy. Penny told her she enjoyed watching her ride. Suzy thanked her she said, "This is a good horse." Penny asked questions about riding a cutting horse. Suzy told her how it is for her. Penny said, "I can't wait until I ride my first one." She said she had to learn how to stay on first. She told Suzy about falling off eight times the first time she rode a turn-back horse. Penny said, "I was so sore the next morning my sister had to help me out of bed!" Suzy laughed at that. She said, "Penny, just keep on riding. That is the only way you will learn. I busted my butt many times trying to ride." She said, "I still get throwd sometimes. I guess that will make you tough." Penny liked Suzy and she could tell Suzy liked her.

After the horses had cooled down they tied them to the trailer. Billy said he still had one class to show in; it is what we call the "Open" class. That class will pay the most money. It is the toughest class too. Billy sat and talked to Penny and Shirley for a while. He gave Shirley money their lunches and asked Shirley to bring him a sandwich and a cold drink. Penny said she had money to buy her lunch. Billy said, "No, you don't" Our lunch is on the Silver Leaf farm. "Eat whatever you want, it's paid for." Penny and Shirley went to the concession stand and got their lunch and a sandwich and drink for Billy. They went back to the bleachers and found a place near the big electric fan and ate their lunch.

Billy came up and sat with them. He asked Penny what she thought of the cutting so far. "Thanks to Shirley for pointing out some of the technical things. I know a lot more than I did. I want to learn more." She told Billy about meeting and getting to know Suzy Pugh. She said she thought she was nice. Billy said she comes from a good family her dad is a horse trainer and she helps out. Penny said, "I can't wait until I get on a cutting horse." Billy said it might be sooner than you think. "HB just bought a cutting horse that is a real good one. I think he bought it just for you. It is a mare maybe ten years old."

Penny said, "Oh, I can't wait." "Billy said; see that horse tied to the fence straight across the arena?" Penny said yes I see it, it's pretty." Billy said that is the one HB bought. From now on you will be the one to ride it on cattle and show it at the next horse show. Penny could not believe her ears. "Oh my goodness Billy do you think I can really do it?" Billy said, "Sure you can, I will help you every step of the way." Penny is so excited. Billy said, "They are going to show it in the next class so you can see her work. We will take it home with us. We take ownership of it after the show."

Penny asked Billy if she could walk around to the fence and look at the horse. He said, "Sure go ahead." She walked over not taking her eyes off the horse. She is so nervous she approached the horse cautiously. The horse looked at Penny like she knew her. She has a pretty head and a partial blaze down the front. She is a sorrel in color and has two white sox on back and the front legs had stockings on both legs. That meant they were white almost to the knee. Penny had never seen a prettier horse. She wanted to reach through the fence and pet her but didn't she is afraid she might scare her.

She stayed with the horse until the owner came and lead her away. Penny went back where Billy and Shirley were setting. "Well, what do you think?" "Oh she is so pretty. I can't wait until we get her home. Did Mr. HB really buy her for me to ride?" Billy said well sort of, you will ride her until you are ready for a better horse. She stayed with the horse until the owner came and lead her away. Penny went back horse then he will breed her to his stud." That satisfied Penny. Do you know what her name is? Billy said I know about her bloodlines but I don't know what they call her but I will ask."

"Ok it's time to start warming Pete up. Go get him and start riding him out by the shady area." Penny got on Pete and was warming him up when Suzy rode by. Penny didn't say anything about Mr. HB buying a horse. Suzy and Penny talked as they rode around under the shade. They had become good friends. Suzy said "Mr. HB has a cutting every year like this one. He usually has it right before the state livestock show in Little Rock." Penny said, "Oh good will you be there?" "Yes I will, I usually show a couple of horses there." Penny said I hope I can have one to show too." The conversation drifted toward school and what they would be taking. Suzy told Penny she would be a cheerleader for this year. She is looking forward to that. Penny continued to ride Pete until Billy called for him. "Ok it's time to start warming Pete up. Go get him and start riding him out by the shady area."

Penny didn't want to miss her horse working. She went and sat by Shirley. A rider was on Penny's horse getting her ready to show. Penny thought she looked so pretty. Soon the called the horses name the called, Ms Peppy McCue, Penny saw that is her horse. Penny said "Peppy." That is what I will call her." The rider rode her in the cattle and got one out front. Peppy's eyes were fixed on the cow. The cow tried to get back to the herd but Peppy headed the cow and kept it out front. The cow tried again and Peppy had to hurry but she headed the cow. The rider quit that one and got another one. This cow tried a couple of times and Peppy held her. She ran toward the other end of the arena and the turn back rider pushed her back.

The rider quit that one and got another this cow really tried to get passed Peppy but she held. As Peppy is locked up head to head with the cow the horn blew ending the ride. The score came in and Peppy is now leading the class. Penny just couldn't wait. She let out a loud "yippee" and stood up and clapped. Billy said, "Come on Penny and I will introduce you to your horse. Penny walked with Billy up to the rider. Billy said, "Jimmy meet the new owner of your horse. Her name is Penny and she will be showing her." Jimmy said, "Nice to meet you Penny you are getting a very good cutting horse." Penny said I hope I can do a good job of showing her. I might fall off a few times but I will keep trying until I get it right." Jimmy said, "That's what you have to do. Get up, brush yourself off and get back on."

Jimmy said, "If you want to ride her and cool her out you are welcomed to." Penny looked at Billy he said climb on Penny and be careful the stirrups are too long for you but you can go ahead and ride. She got on and petted Peppy before she started off. She rode over to the cooling off area and rode her around at a walk. She looked for Suzy but she is not riding. Penny heard the announcer call Suzy's name. She is going to be the next rider. Penny listened for her score and it is lower than Peppy's. Penny thought Peppy might win the class.

Soon Suzy rode over to the shady area. Penny asked her how she did. Suzy said, "I thought it was ok. We might get in the money. Suzy recognized Peppy. Suzy asked. "Are you riding her for Jimmy?" Penny said, "No, Mr. HB just bought her and told me I would be showing her. I am so happy about that." Suzy said, "She is a really good cutting horse good luck with her. They rode around together and talked mostly about nothing. Penny asked her if she had a steady boyfriend. Suzy said, "No I don't have much time for a steady. I do date but these horses keep me so busy I can't commit to any kind of relationship. They kept riding and talking until it is time for the next class. Penny asked if she is showing in that class. Suzy said, "No this is the open class, it is the one that pays the most. The entry fee is a hundred dollars so they only have the best horses. They come from all over to ride in this class." By then Peppy is cooled down Penny rode her over to Jimmy and asked him what to do with her. Jimmy said go get a halter and I will take my tack off her and she will be all yours. Good luck with her she is a good one. Penny went to Billy and told him what Jimmy had said. Billy said, "That is ok get a halter and tie her to the trailer." 'Penny said, Billy do you mind if I wipe her down." Billy said sure Penny go ahead. I want you here to watch the open class and when I am done come get on Pete and cool him off. Pete had a good run in that class and finished fourth which is good he beat a lot of good horses.

It was getting late when they loaded up and started for home. On the way Billy said to Penny. "I know you are anxious to ride your horse but let me make it clear HB's horses and those in training come first. Remember that. I will make time for you to ride and help you learn how to work a cutting horse. Trust me on that." Penny said, "I understand that and I will put the other horses first but I want my turn on Peppy. She belongs to Mr. HB too." Billy said, "You have a good point but I don't want you to get your feelings hurt. I would never do that intentionally."

Once they got home they unloaded the horses. Billy walked down the hallway of the barn and looked for a good clean stall for Peppy. He found one and told Penny to bring the horse and put her in the stall. Billy said there is a water bucket in there get it and wash it out and give Peppy a good drink of Silver Leaf water. She did that and asked about feed. Billy said for tonight put some hay in the hay rack. Sam will feed her in the morning. She hated to walk off and leave Peppy but she had other duties to attend to. The stalled Pete and Blaze and gave them water and hay.

They unloaded the tack and put it in the tack room. Billy said Penny I hope you understand what I told you I didn't mean to hurt your feelings but that is part of the cutting horse business. Penny assured him her feelings were not hurt. "I want you to tell me if I am doing something wrong. I am just starting out and I need direction." "Penny you did good today you were a lot of help. Mr. HB appreciated your help too. I will make sure you get paid for helping." That's good I appreciate that but you know I didn't do it for the money." Billy said, "I know Penny but you worked and you should get paid. HB would tell you that too."

Chapter 12

It was almost midnight when Penny got to bed. She lay awake for a while and thought over the day's activities. She woke up about seven the next morning but stayed in bed for another 30 minutes. She got up and went in the kitchen to start cooking breakfast. In a few minutes Earlene came in and helped. Penny told her about the new horse and what she did at the horse show. Earlene told Penny, again, "I am so glad you have something to do that you like." "Me too." Penny replied.

At the breakfast table James told Penny about them going to see the new house. Earlene said, "Tomorrow we will go over and start cleaning it up. Ms Ruth said she had an extra vacuum cleaner we can use." Penny said she would help after she helped with the horses and if they didn't need her at the gin. "Penny don't work yourself so hard it makes you sick." Earlene told her. "Mama I won't, school starts next week and I need to make as much money as I can. I have to have gas for the car and I still need a few clothes."

After breakfast Penny got ready for church. She asked if anyone wanted to go with her. Missy said, "I do, can I go mama?" "Yes you can get in the bath tub first. "Mama I took a bath last night." "Ok get your clothes out," her mother said. Penny asked her mother if she would like to come along. She said, "I have too much getting ready to do for the move." Penny and Missy left for Sunday school and church. Missy enjoyed being out with her big sister. She asked Penny lots of questions about horses and boys. Mostly boys. They found a place to park and went inside. Missy went to her class and Penny to hers.

Penny's Sunday school teacher is a teacher from her school. Her name is Ms Peters she taught Penny math. Penny liked her. The class had 12 high school age kids. It is a good class Ms Peters made the lesson interesting. All the students listened very attentively. After Sunday school there were a few minutes until the main service started. Penny walked out with one of her friends and they sat together for the worship service. Missy sat with one of her friends.

The pastor announced that Tommy Russell's Funeral will be Wednesday at Caney Creek Baptist Church at two o'clock. There will be a Wake at the church Tuesday night. After church Penny told Missy she needed to get gas at a service station if there is one open. She found one and told the attendant to fill it up. The attendant checked the oil and washed the windshield and cleaned the headlights; they had lots of bugs.

The bill for the gas came to $8.00. Penny asked Missy if she would like a cold drink. "Sure if you have one." "Yes I am would you mind going and get them?" Penny paid for the drinks plus deposit on the bottles. She would have to return them to get her deposit back. The ride back home was mostly more boy talk. Penny told Missy Smith might come home for Tommy's funeral. "I sure hope he does. Mostly for his sake."

When they arrived home they told their Mother and Daddy about the funeral. Then they both got out of their "Sunday" clothes and put on shorts and an old shirt. They were clean but ragged. Penny asked her mother if she could go over and see the new house. "Yes, you can, I need to go and do some measuring for curtains." They went in Penny's car.

The house is so nice and smelled so good. Penny went to see her room. Missy would have her own room as well as James Jr. Their lives have changed so much since the moved on the Silver Leaf farm. They are all thankful. The floor in Penny's room has a nice thick carpet. She sat down on it then laid down. It felt so good. She fell asleep and slept until her mother came and woke her up. Penny said, "I'm so sorry I went to sleep." Her mother assured her that was perfectly ok. "Now", Penny said, I am anxious to move in.

Earlene told her they had lots of decisions to make. She wanted to bring some of the furniture and give the rest to a needy family. She said, "Most of the furniture we have belonged to my mother and she got it from her mother. It may not look so good but all of it is antique and you kids will get it after we are gone. Ms Ruth is waiting for us to move so she can move the furniture she is selling us out and in to our house. That is a blessing to get that furniture it still looks like new. No dings or scratches on the pieces that I looked at. Maybe we could do some refinishing on the antique pieces. That would make them look better in a new house. Earlene thought that was a good idea but said she didn't know when she would get around to doing it. Most of it is bedroom stuff and that won't show up when we have company.

Penny wanted to keep her bed it is one of the antique pieces. Earlene will put some furniture pieces in hers and James's bedroom. So for now problem solved. They stayed at the new house doing some cleaning and taking trash left over by the builders. It would take a day to get it ready to live in. They drove home and Penny got her clothes ready for the week. She would wear jeans mostly she might change to pedal pushers for the gin. She also went through some of her older clothes and piled them in the floor. She would never wear them again. They were too ragged to give away so she would trash them.

She sat down and wrote Smith another long letter and told him about the new horse, among other things. Next morning, Monday, Penny was at the horse barn petting Peppy when Billy drove up. They spoke then Billy said they were going to have a busy day. All the horses needed attention and riding. He would tell which horse to saddle then and go to the round pen for about seven or eight minutes. Once the horse had all the "buck" out of them and the rough edge worked off Billy would take the horse to the arena for work. A good way to train horses. Before he was finished with that horse Penny would have another one ready. This went on for a good two hours. Penny rode two horses around the field while Billy was working in the arena.

It was getting close to noon when Billy said, "Ok Penny go get your horse out and saddle her then go to the round pen for a few minutes. By the way what do you call the horse?" "Peppy," Penny said proudly. "Ok this is going to be your first lesson in riding a cutting horse," Billy told her. Once Peppy was warmed up Penny climbed on and rode up to Billy. Billy said, "I will be telling you what to do sometimes things happen very fast. Don't be offended when I talk loud to you. It is just my way. I want you to be relaxed don't get tense the horse knows when you are nervous. Riding here is not the same as riding in a contest. You will soon find that out. First off I want you to ride in the herd and cut a cow out just like in competition. This will give you a reference point. Ride to the edge of the herd easy, move through them all the way to the back gate and cut that black steer with the white face." Penny eased in and moved toward the steer. Three cows came out with the steer. Billy said, "Keep your reins up and move your horse toward your steer. Penny eased up and the other two cows went back to the herd." Billy said, "Ok put your reins down, this lets the horse know to keep the steer away from the herd. Hold your reins in your left hand, low on the horse's neck with your right one on the saddle horn.

As the steer moved Peppy did too heading the steer off. The steer tried to get to the herd and Peppy headed her and went the other way. Peppy had to hurry to catch up. The cow suddenly stopped and changed directions Peppy had to turn really hard to keep up with the cow. Penny, however, didn't make the hard move. Off she went into a pile of cow manure. She looked at Billy as if to say now what do I do? Billy was not laughing but said, "Penny you will get thrown a lot more times before you learn to sit a cutting horse." Peppy walked over to Penny before she got up and gave her a nudge in the back. She said, "Billy did you see that?"

Penny got up and went over to the fence and got a sack and wiped the manure off her the best she could. Billy asked if she wanted to stop. Penny did not answer; Billy knew what her answer was. She got back on Peppy and started over. Billy said, "Easy, easy, don't spook the herd. Stop and let them settle them go cut the solid black steer." She guided Peppy toward the black steer and it moved out front just right. Billy said, "Ok let your hand down and cut the cow. The steer moved to Peppy's left and Peppy cut him off then the other way and Peppy held. Penny's eyes were glued to the steer. It turned and went the other way. Billy said, "Quit that one. Put your right hand on her neck just in front of the saddle. This lets her know you are finished with that cow." Penny did and Billy said now you cut the one you want.

Penny eased Peppy in the herd and one peeled out in front just in front of Peppy. She guided her toward the cow then dropped her reins down on the neck. Peppy took over. The cow tried hard to get back to the herd and Peppy held. The cow turned and ran off. Billy said, "That is enough" He rode up to Penny and asked if she is hurt. Penny said "only my pride." Billy told her she did very good. "You looked like you have been riding cutting horses all your life. Remember though sometimes things won't go your way. That is why we practice and work these horses hard. We don't want mistakes in a cutting contest."

Penny found some clean feed sacks to sit on; she didn't want to get cow shit on her new car seats. Once she got home she peeled the soiled clothes off and got in the bath tub and scrubbed herself clean. It is lunch time and Earlene fixed Penny lunch. Penny told her about getting thrown into a pile of manure. Earlene laughed and asked her if she was hurt. Penny assured her she was not. After she ate she finished dressing for the gin. She put on pedal pushers and slip on shoes. She looked real nice; she drove to the gin and parked in her regular place. She went in and spoke to Mr. Quick and Larry. More cotton was coming in and it is getting really busy. She asked if she could help. Mr. Quick said, "You can help Larry audit the gin books and let me know if you find an error."

Penny got one of the completed books then sat down by Larry in case she had a question. Mostly they were quite and checked the books. No errors were found but Penny had a question about one load that came in. She wondered if Mr. Quick had written the right name on the tags. She showed it to Mr. Quick and he admitted he had misspelled the name. No other errors were found. This continued until 3:30. Penny told Mr. Quick she had to go to the horse barn. Mr. Quick said "Ok." Penny hurried home and put on a clean pair of jeans and her boots and headed to the horse barn.

It is dark when they finished riding. The arena and barn had lights so there was no problem. There was a problem with mosquitoes. Billy had Sam to spray out the barn and turn on the big fan. This would keep some of them blown off the horses it wasn't a perfect system but the best they had. She and Billy talked about how they were coming along with the training. Billy said, "He is well pleased. We will have some good horses to show at our cutting here and the state show in Little Rock. I want you to be ready to show Peppy. Keep thinking about that."

"By the way, HB wants you to go to the Silver Spur Western Store and get measured for chaps. Shirley and I have to go there this Saturday. I need some supplies. If you want you can go with us and let them measure you." That is a surprise she wondered if she would get a pair. She thought they looked neat on people riding cutting horses. Billy told Penny they would not ride Wednesday in respect to Tommy Russell. We will ride tomorrow morning, Tuesday and we will quit early in the afternoon. I will go to the church and sit at the Wake.

Penny is back at the arena at six the next morning. All the horses were scheduled to be ridden. When they finished with the horses, Billy told Penny to saddle Peppy and she would get some work cutting the cows. Penny hurriedly saddled Peppy and warmed her up. She told Billy, "We are ready." Billy said, "Ok ease into the herd and cut that black one with the white face. She eased Peppy toward the steer. "Easy, easy, slow, now wait until the other cows peel back to the gate." Penny did exactly as Billy told her. That left the black steer with the white face standing alone in front of the herd.

Penny dropped her reins and Peppy went to work. The steer never got passed Peppy. She quit that one and asked Billy, "Which one?" "You decide Penny," Billy said. Penny looked over the herd and decided to get the black one with spots. She eased Peppy through the herd and eased the spotted one out front. Penny dropped her reins and the cow ran to the fence and got passed Peppy and got back to the herd. Billy said, "Stop. I was waiting for that. That is a no, no in cutting. You let Peppy get behind and the steer beat you to the fence. Don't let that happen. If she gets behind, eat her up with your outside spur. She got careless and maybe lazy. You have to keep the cattle "shaped up" in cutting contest. Now, do you understand Penny?" "I think I do, I know I wasn't watching close enough. Maybe I got a little lazy."

"Penny that is the way you learn. Work one more and we will quit for the day." She worked a brown cow and never let Peppy get behind. Billy never said but he saw that Penny had a natural instinct about cattle and what they might do. She cooled Peppy out and rode her to the barn. She unsaddled her and got a cloth and rubbed her down then put her in her stall. She checked to make sure Peppy had plenty of water and hay. She did. Penny finished helping Billy check on the horses for feed and water. Billy is very careful to tend to the horses and make sure they are not neglected by the persons responsible for feeding and watering.

Penny drove to the gin to see if she was needed. If not she would go to the new house and help her mother get ready to move. Mr. Quick said he could handle it. She drove to the new house. Her mother was there. Earlene said, "Penny go talk to Ms. Ruth." Penny wondered what it might be about. She drove over and knocked on the back door. Was she ever surprised! Smith opened the door. "SMITH! Oh, my goodness!" She hugged him and kissed him right in front of Ms. Ruth. "Smith, I am so glad to see you." Smith said, "They let me off, but only enough time to attend the funeral. I have to go back after the funeral tomorrow." Penny said, "I am sorry for the Russell family and you too. I know you were good friends."

Smith asked if she would go with him to visit the Russells. Penny said, "Yes, I will, but I need to clean up and put on some clean clothes." Smith said, "Fine. I will wait here with Granny Ruth." Penny hurried home and bathed and put on clean clothes then drove back to pick up Smith. Penny asked Smith to ride with her in her new car. Smith told her what school was like and that he liked it ok but he would rather be home. Penny told Smith, "I am helping Billy with the horses." Smith said, "I had heard that you were, and that you are really good at it." Penny said, "I love doing it. I hope Mr. HB continues to let me." "He will, I guarantee it." Smith said.

Once they got to the Russell home, Smith and Penny walked up to the front door. Alec is standing at the door and shook Smith's and Penny's hands. Ms. Russell came to the door. Smith told them how sorry he is. He and Tommy were good friends. "We hunted and fished together ever since we were in the first grade." They talked about Tommy. Smith and Penny felt so sorry for them. They told Smith they had his name down for a Pall Bearer. Maybe it is honorary because the Army is providing a military funeral and they would carry the casket. Smith said, "I will be honored to do it." They stayed another half hour then told the Russells he would attend the Wake.

Penny drove them back to Ms. Ruth's. Smith asked Penny to come in while he visited with his grandmother. HB was not home; he had to go to Little Rock on business. After they visited for about an hour, Smith asked Penny to eat supper with him at his house. "Mother and Dad asked me to bring you." Penny said, "Sure I'll go." They stayed about an hour more. Smith talked about school and some of the people he had met. They enjoyed listening to him.

Then he said to Penny, "I am ready to go if you are." "I am ready but I need to let my folks know." Ruth said, "They already know. I saw your mother earlier and she knew Smith was here." "Good," Penny said. On the way to town Penny couldn't keep her hands off Smith. She said, "Smith, I have missed you so very much. I don't know how I can wait until you are out of school." Smith told her, "Penny I feel the same way but I can't do anything about it for now."

They arrived at Mary and Mark's and went inside. Both gave Penny a hug and said they were glad to see her. They visited a while and Mary started putting supper on the table. Penny went in to help. Penny felt more at ease this time than before, when she was at their house. Penny helped with the food and the table setting. When they were ready, Mary told Smith and his dad to come to the table. Mark, Smith's dad, gave a real nice prayer for the Russells and his own family. He did not leave Penny out.

It was a good meal and they had a good conversation. Penny thought Mary and Mark had finally accepted her. When the meal was over Penny helped Mary clear the table and started to wash the dishes. Mary said, "No Penny, You go be with Smith. I will take care of these." Penny said, "Thank you but I will help if you need me." Smith told Penny he would take her home, then he was going to attend the Wake at the Church. On the way home they were not in a very talkative mood. Penny said, "Smith I know I am selfish when it comes to spending time with you and I can't help it. I know you are here because you lost a dear friend in a bad war."

Smith said he would see her at the funeral, and after the burial he would come to her house. Penny would settle for that. She told Smith that they were moving into the new house in a couple of days. She said, "I am looking forward to that. Our lives have changed so much since we moved on the Silver Leaf. It has been a God send."

After they talked and held each other it was time for Smith to go to the Wake. He said he couldn't stay all night then drive back to school. Penny didn't see Smith before the funeral. The church is packed, and people were standing outside. The church did have a speaker so they could hear the service. The army had an escort for the body. The casket was draped with the United States flag. The soldiers were very precise in unloading the casket and bringing it into the church. The pastor delivered a passionate speech. One of Tommy's cousins made a talk about Tommy. It was a beautiful service.

The burial would be at the Weeden cemetery just up the road from the church. Penny and her family followed the hearse to the graveside. The military detail unloaded the body and placed it by the grave. The pastor spoke and offered a prayer for the Russell family. Then the military did a twenty-one gun salute. Two of the soldiers took the flag and very carefully folded it up military style and presented to Mr. and Mrs. Russell. It is all so very sad.

The Parks family drove back home all were silent. When they got home, they all got out of their church clothes and got into something more comfortable. Penny did change, but she put on clothes to meet Smith. In about an hour Smith came driving up. He said he had talked with his mother and dad and decided it is too late for Smith to start out for Missouri. He would have more time with Penny. Smith still had on his suit and tie. He asked Penny to ride home with him so he could change clothes. Penny is happy too.

On the way Penny asked if he had any concerns of being drafted and having to go to Korea. Smith said, "I hope not, and as long as I am in school I don't think they will draft me but when I finish I might get drafted. Since I am in a military school I would say there is a real good chance they will draft me. If there wasn't the Korean conflict, I don't think they would get me. But if they do call me up I will have to go. I want to serve my country."

Penny thought about that. She said, "Oh Smith, I hate for you to go. You could end up like Tommy. I can't even stand to think about that." Smith said, "Let's not talk about that. Lots of things can happen before I finish school." They were at Smith's home by then. Penny went inside to wait for Smith to change clothes. Mary is there and they talked about the funeral and Tommy and his family. Soon

Smith is finished dressing. He told his mother he and Penny would eat out somewhere but he planned on being home early to rest up for his trip back to school.

They drove to Stuttgart and ate at the Seafood Restaurant. It was a fantastic meal. Penny said, "Oh I am 'stuffed' that was so good." Smith said he was too. Smith talked more about school and asked Penny how things were going with her. He wanted to know every detail. He asked her about Larry. Penny said, "I hardly know him. But I am not going out with anyone and I won't. Not as long as you and I are together." Smith said, "I will be jealous if you did go on dates." Penny said, "I am in love with the horses. I am so busy with them I don't have time anyway."

"By the way," she said. " I met Suzy Pugh and we have become friends." Smith said, "I know her. I see her at all the cutting shows. She is a nice girl."

Smith took another way home which would come out at the farm headquarters. Smith stopped at their parking place and they held on to one another. Smith didn't try to get fresh with Penny; by now he knew she wouldn't let him. Penny didn't say much, she just held on to Smith. Soon Smith started the car and said, "Penny as much as I hate to, I have to go home and get ready to travel tomorrow. Penny said, "I know Smith, but I hate to see you go."

Smith drove up to Penny's house and gave her a long kiss goodbye. Penny told Smith again, "I loved you so very much." Smith told Penny, "I love you with all my heart." Penny went to the front porch and stood until Smith was out of sight.

Chapter 13

Penny is sad when she went to bed. She prayed for a safe trip back to school for Smith. In the morning she would be at the barn at six o'clock. She finally dozed off to sleep. Next morning she is up and ate a jelly sandwich for breakfast. She is at the barn on time. Billy came driving up and they talked about the horses they were going to work and which ones they would work on cattle. Billy said they would work Peppy but she would be the last to work. He said, "That way I can give her more time to work." Penny was busy saddling horses and working them in the round pen. Billy would ride them and work with them on stopping and turning and spinning, all the moves it would take to cut a cow.

It was a busy morning and Billy didn't feel he had to watch over Penny as much as he had been doing. Penny knew that and is careful to do the things Billy taught her. She is fast becoming a real cowboy—or cowgirl. After all the horses had worked and cooled out and stalled up, Billy told Penny to bring Peppy out. She did, and she brushed her real good, talking to her while she cleaned her up. She saddled Peppy and took her to the round pen to get warmed up.

When she was ready she put the bridle on her and mounted up and rode her to the arena. Billy is waiting; he is riding one of the horses he is getting paid to ride. Billy said, "Ok, you know what to do. Before you ride to the cattle make her turn around both left and right." Penny took the reins and kind of pulled Peppy back on her hind legs and asked her to spin around. She did left then right. "Very good," Billy said. "The purpose of that is to wake her up and let her know she is going to cut a cow and be ready."

Penny eased Peppy in and cut a brown steer and set it up in the middle of the arena. The steer tried to get back. Peppy held, it ran toward the fence and Penny is ready. She kicked Peppy in the left side with her spur and Peppy headed the steer. It stopped and ran off. She quit that one. Billy said. "That is the way to do it. Remember that." She got a heifer this time that had ears like a Brahma. Billy said, "Get ready; this is a wild one." It was. Penny had to really get on Peppy to head the cow. Soon as she could, she quit that one and got a better one. Peppy was right on the money with that one. Peppy held it center of the arena and really made some hard moves. Penny was relaxed in the saddle. When she quit that one Billy said, "That is enough. Penny you looked like a pro on that horse. HB is going to be proud of you." "Thanks Billy, I am trying." Billy said, "I know you are."

After the horses were taken care of and stalled, Billy said, "That is all for this morning, we will work again at four this afternoon." Penny said, "I will be here." She went home and ate lunch then drove over to the gin office. She went in and spoke to Mr. Quick. More cotton was coming in. Silver Leaf had started picking. They had some field hands hand picking and two mechanical pickers picking, and they were bringing in lots of cotton. Mr. Quick told Penny when Silver Leaf cotton comes, ask which field it came from. Each field has a name. They were named for the family that used to sharecrop the field. There were names like Smith, Jones, Dixon, Parks, and so on. McKenzie wants to keep a record of what each field makes. That was not too hard to do. Mr. Quick said Larry would be here in about an hour. "If you don't mind take a turn at the scales and let me take a break."

Cotton was coming in and then an empty trailer would weigh out. It was busy but Penny kept it straight and got it all right. There would be a farmer drift in. There were the usual loafers that like to hang around a gin, especially now that Penny was working there. They always asked when she would be working again. When Penny wasn't so busy she would talk to them and joke with them and tease them. They loved Penny Parks.

Finally Larry came in and told Penny he could handle it. Penny went over to the older men and sat down right in the middle of them. Jokingly she would tease them about flirting with the widow women at the rest home. That would get them to talking and laughing. Then they would try to tease Penny. One asked why she had spurs on her boots. Penny said, "Now just why do you think I have them on?" They laughed so loud you could hear them over the noise of the cotton gin.

After a bit Penny said goodbye to the men and said she would be back tomorrow afternoon. She stopped by at the farm office and checked in with Sue and Martha. They were really busy. Penny said, "I have a couple of hours I can help if you need me." Sue said, "Yes, if you don't mind we are checking gin receipts against the weigh book and we are figuring seed tickets." Penny knew how to do that so she sat down at her old desk and checked the receipts as Sue asked. Penny figured seed tickets too. Time passed fast; soon it is time to report back to the horse barn. Penny told Sue she had to go but if they didn't need her at the gin she could help after lunch until she had to go back to the barn.

Sue said, "Penny if you have the time, come on back." Penny said, "I sure will." She is back at the barn waiting for Billy. She walked down to Peppy's stall and is brushing her when Billy rode up. Penny went out to meet him. Billy told her which horses they were riding. He told Penny to saddle one of the new horses and ride him down the turn row around the field. She put the horse in the round pen first to get the edge off so maybe she wouldn't get bucked off.

She put the bridle on and adjusted and mounted up and started down the turn row. She is paying attention to the horse and is letting him look around and explore the new surroundings. She looked up and saw a man walking toward her. He is walking with a limp. She thought it might be someone in trouble. She kicked the horse up into a gallop. Pretty soon she saw it is Mr. HB. She rode up, jumped down off the horse real fast and took hold of him. "Mr. HB what is the matter? Are you hurt? Let's go over here to the shade." She helped him over to the shade and there is a broken tree there. She asked him to sit down. She is still holding him. HB said, "I drove my truck off into a mud hole where irrigation water had run and I got stuck. No one knew where I was so I figured I had better start walking."

Penny said, "Oh my goodness! I am so thankful I was riding this way. "Mr. HB, can you get on the horse? If you can, I will lead him back to the barn." HB said, "No, I don't want you to have to walk. Why don't you ride back and get some help." Penny said, "Mr. HB I don't want to leave you by yourself and that is not too far for me to walk. I am going to lead this horse into the ditch and you won't have to climb on, you can just step over his back. I will lead him because he is a green horse and no telling when he might get spooked." HB said, "Ok, Penny but if you get tired just stop." Penny said, "Don't worry I can make it." With that she led the horse in the ditch and HB walked over and climbed on. HB said, "I am ready." Penny led the horse out of the ditch and started back to the barn. As they went she did she had HB had a good conversation. She told him how much she appreciated letting her help with the horses.

She talked about how good all the crops looked and asked him how he is doing. He said, "Fine now Penny, since you came riding up to rescue me." Penny talked about Ms. Ruth and how much she loved her. Mainly she is talking to keep HB calm. "See Mr. HB, we are already back. I will lead us over to get Billy." Billy saw them coming and he had his horse tied to the fence and is waiting.

Billy said, "Dang HB! Are you trying to steal my help?" HB laughed, "I tell you, I think she saved my life." Penny asked him to get in her car and she would take him home. Penny and Billy helped him off the horse and got him in Penny's car. She drove him home trying to keep things calm.

In a minute they were at HB's back door. Ruth saw them coming and hurried out to see what happened. HB said, "Now Ruth, don't get excited. I got in the back of the big field and got stuck. I started walking and Penny rode up and helped me. I will be all right. Penny do you mind stopping by McKenzie's office and ask him to get someone to take a tractor and chain to pull my truck out of the mud hole." Penny said, "I will, don't worry. I hope Ms. Ruth makes you get some rest. That was a strenuous situation." "Thanks Penny." She stopped by the office and told McKenzie about the truck being stuck.

McKenzie said, "I will get one of the men to get a tractor, and I will get another one of the men and we will go pull the truck out and drive it back to HB's house." Before too long they came driving by the horse barn in HB's truck. It sure was muddy. She knew McKenzie would have the truck cleaned up before they took it home.

Penny still had horses to ride, she caught another green one and they rode around the big field. She rode by where Mr. HB got stuck; it was a big mud hole there. She knew McKenzie would get it drained so it would dry. The horse was a little spooky of the water but Penny coaxed him into wading through it. It is good for the horses to learn not to be scared.

Soon she was back at the barn. Billy asked her to ride the horse in the arena. Billy said, "Make him stop occasionally and start him learning to spin over his hocks." Penny nodded ok. She did as she is asked. The horse is a quick learner. All she had to do is be patient with him.

Next morning Penny is back at the barn at six. This is the last week of summer vacation before school started. She had that on her mind when Billy drove up. She told him she had to start to school the next week but would be in as soon as she could get there after school. Billy said, "I knew you had school. If you could come help me after school, that will be good. We have to get Peppy, Pete and Blaze and two more ready for the cutting that HB will have here the weekend before the State Livestock show in Little Rock."

"Penny, I want you to saddle Blaze and warm him up. I want you to ride him on the cattle." That is a surprise. Penny got him ready and Billy gave her instructions. He said, "I want you to take a rein in each hand keeping them low and kind of 'mule rein him,' one hand on each side of his neck. We won't worry too much if he misses a cow but we want him to get use to turning and stopping. Make sure he knows what 'Whoa' is."

Penny got on Blaze and took a rein in each hand; she had done this before. Billy talked her through cutting a cow out of the herd and setting it up. As the cow moved, Penny would coax Blaze to move. When the cow stopped she made Blaze stop. As the cow turned she would make Blaze turn over his hocks. They didn't do much more than that. Finally Billy said, "That is enough. We will do this again tomorrow. Good job Penny."

She cooled Blaze out and put him in his stall. Billy told her to bring Peppy out. Penny warmed her up and gave her a real hard work out. Penny couldn't let Peppy get lazy. This pleased Billy. They worked until noon. Penny went home to the new house and ate lunch. Then she drove to the gin to help if she is needed. Mr. Quick is glad to see her. He needed to go to town and tend to some business. Penny sat at the scales and weighed in cotton and weighed out the empties. She had confidence that she could do this job.

Mr. Quick was gone over two hours. Penny is glad he is back; she didn't want to be late for the horses. Larry came in with Mr. Quick so he could help if needed. Penny stopped by the farm office and told Sue she had to help Mr. Quick at the gin. "No problem," Sue told her. Penny spoke to Martha and they talked about horses. Penny told her what she was doing.

Penny is at the barn before four o'clock and as usual had Peppy out giving her a good brushing. She put the bridle on Peppy but no saddle. She led her into the arena and pulled herself up on Peppy bareback and is riding her around the arena when Billy drove up. She wasn't holding on. Billy said, "Penny that is good. Can you kick her up into a lope?" Penny did, and rode like she had been doing it all her life. She made Peppy change leads and come to a sliding stop. "That's amazing Penny! I would say you have reached your riding balance." Penny took Peppy back, got Blaze out and saddled him. She took him to the round pen and got all the buck out of him then she saddled him up.

Billy wanted her to work a cow on him the way she did this morning. Penny took the reins like Billy told her to do. She eased in and cut a cow out. The cow was going from side to side of the arena. Billy said, "that is what I want her to do. Make Blaze head the cow and pull him around when he turns." Penny caught on to that. Pretty soon Blaze is working the cow on his own. "That's enough, good job."

It is well after dark when they finished riding. Penny helped cool out the horses and stall them. Billy said he would see her in the morning. Penny drove home. The new house is now the Parks' official residence. Penny went straight to the shower and put on her pj's and ate supper. Then she sat down and wrote Smith a nice long letter. She told him about Mr. HB getting stuck in a mud hole. She stayed up and visited with her family. She hadn't seen much of James Jr. the whole summer. He had been off helping his dad or fishing in the bayou. She had a good visit with him and Missy.

Next morning she is back at the barn. She and Billy worked horses until noon, same as always. Penny went by the gin and helped Mr. Quick with some gin samples making sure they got the right sample with the right bale. They had bins upstairs with the farmers' names on them. She made sure they got the samples in the right bin. The farmers could come and get them any time they wanted to. They had to have them when they sold their cotton. Another lesson learned for Penny. She worked there until it is time to go back to the horse barn.

This time she was riding Peppy bareback with a halter on. She kicked Peppy into a lope, first one way then the other. She stopped when Billy drove up.

Penny worked Blaze first, turning back cows then cutting a cow out of the herd. Blaze is doing good. He is learning fast. Billy told Penny she might get to show him at the cutting show on the Silver Leaf. That is okay with Penny. They worked Pete and Roany and the brown horse but not too hard. Billy asked Penny to ride Brown around the field. Billy said he is still a little spooky and it takes his mind off what he is doing. Penny put her saddle on Brown and rode him around the field. He is still a little jumpy when she got back so she told Billy he needed more riding. That is okay with Billy. It is dark when they finished, same as always.

Penny is learning fast. She had no fear of getting thrown or falling off. She is learning the nature of horses. She could get in their head and know what they were thinking. This is something that can't be taught. Horses liked her, mainly because she liked them. Billy is pleased with the whole horse operation. The owners of the horses Billy is riding were very pleased at the progress their horses were making. Penny could be a little more at ease.

Penny drove home and did her same routine: a shower, supper, writing Smith, and visiting with her parents. Penny is giving her mother a big portion of her paycheck to help support the family.

Penny told her mother she would start getting her school clothes out and ready for school. She would start the next day. She told her mother she wanted to go to town Saturday and get a couple more outfits. Earlene said, "I will go with you. We need groceries, and I will pick out a few outfits for Missy and James Jr." They wouldn't need much.

James asked Penny if James Jr. and Missy could ride to school with her. Penny said, "I would be glad to have them, but tell them they need to be up and ready. I will leave here at 7:30. I can bring them back home too. I will still be riding horses after school." James said, "Most likely you will be having some flats, these old roads are rough and are hard on tires. Your car has good tires. I have two spare tires and a good jack and wrench to change a tire. I will put them in the trunk of the car. James Jr. knows how to change a tire so you won't have to do it all." Penny thanked him for that.

She wrote Smith another letter, then went to bed. The horse riding had become a routine. Penny could do anything Billy asked her to do. Penny also spent time at the gin and the farm office. Billy told Penny they would ride Saturday morning and then would not ride any more until Monday. Billy said, "I can handle it in the mornings, but I would like you to be here as much as you can after school." Penny assured him that she would leave school as soon as possible, change clothes and come straight to the barn. Billy said, "The cutting show we put on here is in two weeks, so we have lots of getting ready to do."

Penny and Billy rode horses Saturday morning and quit to go home by 11:00. Penny went home and cleaned up, then drove her mother and Missy and James Jr. to town. Penny picked out some clothes and bought her another pair of western jeans. Earlene picked out some things for Missy and James Jr. She bought them a new pair of shoes. After that they went to a café where Penny treated them all to burgers, fries and drinks. They liked that. She asked if they wanted to stay in town a while or go home. They wanted to stay a while. Earlene gave them each a dollar and told them to meet them back here in an hour.

Missy and James Jr. liked walking up and down the street and going in stores to see if they had something they could buy. When they got back to the car James Jr. had bought some fishing tackle and Missy bought a bracelet. It is pretty and she could wear it to school. By then they were all ready to go home.

Sunday morning Penny and Missy got ready for church. Penny drove them and they were there a little early. Penny saw Ruth and went over to speak to her. Ruth said, "Penny, I was looking for you; one day this week I would like for you to drive me to Little Rock to do some shopping." "Oh, Ms. Ruth I would love to. Do you think

I can drive in Little Rock?" "Sure you can," Ruth replied, "I will show you where to go. Which day is the best for you, Penny?" "Any day is okay. I'll need to let Billy know where I am so he won't get worried." Ruth said, "How about Tuesday morning, about seven o'clock?" "That sounds good to me. I will come to your house." "Fine," Ruth said.

Penny and Missy sat together at the Sunday Worship Service. It was a good sermon. Penny thought the church had a good preacher. After church, Penny went by and filled up with gas, and had the oil checked and the windshield washed. They got two cold drinks and used the two empty bottles they had bought there last Sunday for deposit. They drank the drinks as Penny drove home. They changed from their Sunday clothes to their loafing clothes. They did not plan to go anywhere that afternoon.

Chapter 14

Monday morning Penny is riding Peppy bareback when Billy drove up. He walked over to Peppy and took the halter off. "Whoa!" Penny said. "Show me how you can control Peppy now," Billy said. Penny kicked her off in a walk and moved her body over some to give Peppy a cue she wanted her to turn. Then Penny kicked her up into a canter. She rode Peppy in a circle then made her turn and go the other way on the correct lead. Then she leaned back to let Peppy know to stop. Peppy slid on her hind feet. Then Penny spun Peppy around to the left then to the right. Billy could absolutely not believe it even though he saw it. What Penny could do that no other trainer could do is to make a horse work without switching its tail, which is a sign the horse is irritated. Billy is flabbergasted. "Penny, you have been holding out on me."

When she stopped she asked Peppy to ride over to Billy and put her head on his chest. Billy is so surprised he couldn't speak. Penny told Billy that Ms. Ruth wanted her to drive her to Little Rock the next morning. "She said we might be back in time for me to help in the afternoon." Billy said, "That's okay, you sure can't say no to Ms. Ruth."

They did their usual thing with the horses. They rode until noon. The horses were getting better but they still had a way to go to be top cutting horses. After they got the horses put away, Penny did her usual thing. She went home for lunch, then drove to the gin and talked to Mr. Quick. He said he didn't need any help, although cotton harvest is in full swing, with lots of cotton coming in. Penny visited with the usual loafers sitting around. They teased each other. Penny said she had to go.

She drove to the farm office where Sue and Martha were very busy. Penny asked what she could do to help. Sue asked her to audit the money against the gin weights for the hand picked cotton. The office had lots of money in the form of rolls of pennies, nickels, dimes, and quarters. Along with rolls of one dollar bills. The weigh boss comes in each morning and tells Sue how many hands are picking. Then she hands him a money sack with so much money in it. The coins are all in rolls and the one dollar bills are separated in to one hundred dollar rolls. The money is counted and the weigh man signs a voucher saying he has a certain amount of money.

Each afternoon he brings Sue the weight figures and the money he has left over. All the money has to be accounted for. Penny's job is to add up the wagon weights and multiply that time the amount they were paying for picking, in this case two cents a pound. At the end of the day, if the weights come to 6,500 pounds times two cents a pound equals $130.00 that should have been paid out. It gets checked every day. If there is a big difference the weigh boss has to account for it. The Silver Leaf wants every picker to get all that is due.

Penny worked there until it is time to go to the horse barn. She and Billy worked until dark. Penny drove home and got her clothes out for the next day. She told her mother she is going to drive Ms. Ruth to Little Rock to do some shopping. Penny ate supper, bathed and wrote Smith a letter. She is tired so she went to bed early. She is up by six the next morning and helped cook breakfast. She is ready to go by 6:45 and decided to drive on over to Ms. Ruth's house. When she pulled up into Ms. Ruth's driveway, Ruth is waiting for her. Penny got out and spoke Ruth, asking if she is ready. Penny got in Ms. Ruth's car and adjusted the seat and the mirror. Ruth said, "Penny, just take your time; no big hurry. I will tell you how to get where we are going. We are not going to go the same way we went last time you and I drove up there."

Penny said, "I am little nervous about driving such an expensive car." Ruth said, "You will get used to it." The car had an air conditioner which would make the ride more comfortable. Ruth told Penny, "Turn left out of the driveway; we will take the blacktop road. It may be a little longer but a whole lot better ride." In a few minutes Penny had gotten into driving the Cadillac. She drove the speed limit, and maybe a little more. She and Ms. Ruth had a good talk on the way. Soon they were in Rose City. Ruth told her, "Watch for the traffic lights and stay in the right lane." Penny is a little nervous but did not show it. When they came to the Main Street bridge, Ruth told her to get in the left lane. Penny checked the rear view mirror and moved over into the left lane. Ruth told Penny, "The lever on the left of the steering wheel is the signal light. Push down if you are turning left and up for a right turn."

As they drove down Main, Ruth told her the next street is a one way, going east. She said, "You will need to turn on the signal light and, when the light is green and no cars are coming toward you, then turn left and get in the right lane." Penny figured that out pretty quick. Ruth said, "Okay, put on your right signal and turn in at the parking lot. Drive up to the little building." She did. Ruth got out and spoke to the attendant. The attendant said, "Hello Ms. Ruth, good to see you." Ruth told him to take good care of her car. He said, "You know I will." Penny got out, leaving the keys in the car. The attendant would park it and takes the keys out.

Penny and Ms. Ruth walked around the corner to one of the department stores. Ruth is buying clothes for her and HB. They went to a men's store and bought HB some pants and shirts, along with other accessories he needed. They then went to Blass department store. She bought clothes for herself; she tried on several pair and asked Penny for her ideas. Penny told her which outfits she liked.

Ms. Ruth said she liked them too. Ruth asked Penny if she needed anything. She said, "I do need some underwear." Ruth said, "Let's go over the women's department." Penny bought her some much needed underclothing. She also got some for her mother and Missy.

They walked down the street to Pfeiffer's and shopped some more. Ruth offered to buy Penny an outfit, but Penny told her she had all she needed for now. They went to one more store and Ruth bought her a new pair of shoes. Finally Ruth said she is through with her shopping. Penny is carrying most of the sacks. They walked back to the parking lot and Ruth handed the attendant her parking ticket. He got the car and drove it up to Penny and Ruth. Ruth paid him and gave him a generous tip. Penny eased the car back onto the street. Ruth showed Penny which way to go.

Ruth said, "Penny we will stop at Fishers restaurant and have lunch." Penny had seen the restaurant as they drove by. Soon Ruth said, "Penny turn left in the parking lot. I see a good parking spot near the front door." Penny eased the Cadillac into the parking spot and they went in and had a very good lunch. Soon they were back on the road home. The talked about lots of thing going home and Penny enjoyed the trip with Ms. Ruth. When they got home, Penny parked the Cadillac in its parking place and helped Ruth with the packages. Ruth told Penny, "You did a good job of driving. I enjoyed the day." Penny said, "I enjoyed it too. I will make myself available anytime you need me to drive for you." Ruth's said, "I will call you Penny, and thank you again."

Penny got her packages and drove back to her house and took them inside. She showed her mother and Missy what she had bought them. They were pleased. Penny changed clothes and drove to the horse barn. She is on time to ride.

Billy is glad to see her. He told her to get Brown out and saddle him. Penny did as she was told. She took him to the round pen and warmed him up. He bucked all the way around the pen and settled down. Billy said, "Horses buck in the round pen because they feel good and they know they are going to get to work." Penny rode

Brown in the arena a few minutes. Billy wanted her to turn back on him. Brown is a little lazy and slow. Penny kicked him hard with her spurs. That woke him up. He didn't get behind anymore. When Billy was done with the horse he was riding, he told Penny to swap horses. "Saddles too?" Penny asked. Billy said, "No I can ride in your saddle." The stirrups were as long as Billy's.

They worked for about thirty minutes and then Billy quit. He gave the horse for Penny to cool out. She rode Brown and actually cooled both of them out. Billy told Penny it is her turn on Blaze and Peppy. She caught them both and tied Peppy to the fence. She would ride Blaze first. Soon he is warmed up and ready. Billy said, "Go cut a cow." Penny eased in and pushed a steer out that she had seen work before. She is still "mule" reining Blaze. She moved the steer to her left and stopped him, then moved him to the right. Blaze was right on the money. He stopped and waited for the steer to move. When it moved Penny kicked Blaze and made him move. She mule reined him and made him head the cow. Billy is giving instructions as they went.

Billy told her to get Peppy and saddle her up. Penny took the saddle off Blaze and put it on Peppy. She warmed Peppy up and rode her into the arena. Penny made her stop and turn hard then made her spin to the left and to the right. Finally she is ready. Billy didn't give her any instructions. Penny knew how to make a deep cut into the herd and get a cow out. She cut the one she was looking at. She had it out front and dropped the reins. Billy ran up and made the cow move. Penny stopped it just right. It went the other way and Peppy got behind. Penny dug her left spur into Peppy and she headed the cow. She quit that one and made another cut but didn't take much time getting one out.

Peppy is right on the money. Peppy knows Penny will spur her hard if she doesn't hustle. Penny cut one more and Peppy held. Billy said, "Very good Penny. I think Peppy will be ready."

It is well after dark when they finished riding. Penny helped Billy unsaddle and wipe the horses down. Billy said, "We got a lot done today. Thank you Penny, for coming to help." "Billy, I know I have told you a hundred times but I like riding and helping you get them ready for competition. I hope I get a chance to show Peppy." Billy said, "Penny you are going to show Blaze too. They have a class for beginning horses and beginning riders. It is called the Novice class. I expect you to win it." "Wow, Billy! You don't expect too much."

Penny finished up and drove home. She went in and took a shower and put her PJ's on before she ate supper. She told the family about driving Ms. Ruth's Cadillac in Little Rock. Penny told them it has an air conditioner and it is very comfortable inside the car. The Cadillac rode so smooth you never knew when you hit a bump.

Penny had a letter from Smith and she went into her room to read it and write him back. Smith said he made the trip okay. He is sorry for the Russells. He said he would never forget Tommy Russell. Smith said he is looking forward to the next trip home.

The next day, another round of riding horses. They rode until noon, same as always. Penny rode two horses around the big field, and worked some of the horses in the arena. After they finished, Penny ate lunch and went to the gin. Mr. Quick asked her to stay for a while and do the weighing. He had some paper work he had to finish. Penny sat at the scales and was very busy, cotton coming across the scales and empties coming across from the other direction. She took her time to make sure she got it right. Mr. Quick had his eye on Penny as he did his work. About 3:30, Mr. Quick finished up and told Penny she could go. Penny had some words for the loafers. They all laughed.

The evening riding went well; they didn't work any horses on cattle. Billy said they don't want the horses to get soured. They actually quit about an hour early and Penny got to be home before dark. That is a big change. Penny walked around the yard and picked up some sticks and limbs that had fallen out of the trees. Penny wanted the yard to look as good as the house. She asked James Jr. if he could get a water hose and water some of the bare spots in the yard. Earlene assured her that he would get it done.

Penny showered and put on her pj's before supper. After that, she went to her room and wrote Smith a letter. Next day is Wednesday and Penny followed the same routine. All went well. Next day is more of the same. Friday came and after working the horses she went by to pick up her pay check. It is a few dollars over a hundred dollars. "Wow!" Penny thought to herself. "That is a lot of money but when school starts the paychecks won't be so big." She is glad to get the money. She helped Sue and Martha until time to ride. They all talked and enjoyed the afternoon. Penny left and went to the horse barn. It is time for her to ride Blaze and Peppy. She gave them a hard workout and they both responded. Billy said they were really doing good. Billy rode Pete and Roany and gave them a heavy work too. Penny cooled them out then unsaddled them and put them in their stalls. Billy said, "See you in the morning Penny." Penny said, "I will be here." He said we will quit early and won't ride anymore until Monday.

Saturday morning was busy riding. Penny rode two more around the big field. They were a little spooky but they seemed to get over it. She rode Peppy without a saddle. Actually, she turned back on her with only a halter. Billy thought as long as she got the job done it would help Penny set a horse better. Pretty soon Penny is riding without holding on the horse's mane. Billy could not believe what he is seeing.

It is about eleven o'clock when they quit. Penny drove home and ate then drove to the gin. Larry is there to help his dad, so Penny was not needed. She went by the farm office and it is closed. Penny went back home to help with the house work and tend to the yard. She told her mother she wanted to plant flowers in front of the house. Earlene said, "I know where some are that I can get a cutting off of." Penny said, "It makes the house look better with pretty flowers." Penny said she would talk to Ms. Ruth and see if she might know which flowers would be the right ones to plant. Penny just had a thought, "School is starting Monday." She had forgotten all about that. She was ready; she had all her clothes bought and sorted out.

She reminded Missy and James Jr. She would leave for school every morning at 7:30. The bus runs before that. Missy wouldn't be late but James Jr. might.

Penny stayed around the house for most of the afternoon. She asked her mother if she needed anything from the grocery store. Earlene said, "Yes, I do need a few things." Penny said, "If you would like I will drive you to the store, or Missy and I can pick it up for you." Earlene said, "I haven't been anywhere this week. If you don't mind I will go with you."

Penny drove them to England and they shopped at Cleek's Meat Market and Grocery. Earlene said, "You know I don't have anything for your lunches." She bought sandwich meat and bread and snacks. She wanted them to have a good lunch. They all had lunch boxes which would come in handy and keep the lunches from spoiling. They shopped and then drove by the drug store, where they all had an ice cream sundae. It was very good.

Penny drove them home and they all helped with the groceries. Penny gave her mother fifty dollars to help with groceries and whatever else she needed. The extra money will come in handy. Life now is good for the Parks family.

On Sunday Penny and Missy went to church. She saw Ruth and HB. Penny asked him how he is doing; he said he is fine and thanked her again for helping. He also thanked her for driving Ms. Ruth to Little Rock. Penny said, "It is my pleasure. I enjoy being with Ms. Ruth anytime I can. I really enjoyed driving her car."

After church Penny got her car filled up with gas, and she and Missy got a cold drink to drink on the way home. At home they changed into shorts and t-shirts. After lunch Penny took a nap. Later she went out and did some work in the yard. She picked tree limbs up and placed them in a pile in the back of the lot. Her dad had cut the tops out of two 55 gallon barrels to burn household trash. When they were full of cans and things the Silver Leaf had a crew to pick them up and take them to a dump.

The rest of the day Penny just rested and wrote Smith a letter. She is getting a letter from Smith almost every day. Finally it is bed time; school tomorrow. She is looking forward to it but hated that it took time away from the horses.

Next morning they were all up and ready for school. At 7:30 Penny said, "Okay, let's go." Penny drove to school and found a good parking place. She went to her to the 11th grade room and took a seat. Eventually someone came in and had a list of names and which courses they would take and which teacher, as well as which room. There were lockers, so they had a place to store their books and lunch.

Penny would take algebra, English, history and social studies; not too bad a schedule. They ran a short schedule and were out of school by two o'clock. Missy and James Jr. were out too. Penny put her books in the locker, as there were no assignments for the next day. She ran into Larry; he is looking for her.

He said, "Penny I hate to ask but could you give me a ride to the gin? I will help dad and ride home with him." Penny said, "Sure Larry anytime you need a ride you are welcome." Larry rode in the front and Missy and James Jr. rode in the back. They all talked on the way home. Penny drove Larry to the gin first. Larry said, "I can't thank you enough Penny. Can I pay you or buy you some gas?" Penny said, "No, I was coming this way anyway." She drove home and changed into her riding clothes then drove to the horse barn. It is too early for Billy. She got Peppy out and brushed her and got on her bareback and rode to the arena.

Penny didn't see Billy drive up. She is riding Peppy without a halter or a saddle. Billy stopped and didn't let Penny see him. Penny is putting Peppy through her paces. She had her at a lope in a circle then changed direction, then in a figure eight. She asked Peppy to stop then back up. Billy is stunned; he had never seen anybody with that kind of control over a horse.

He walked over and waved at Penny. She put the halter on Peppy and led her over to the tack room. She and Billy visited for a while.

Billy told Penny to saddle Blaze. "We have to get him ready for the cutting contest." Penny saddled him and took him to the round pen and warmed him up. Billy told her, "Go and cut a cow out. This time don't mule-rein him. Put the reins in your left hand and keep them low like you do Peppy."

Penny did her usual thing. She eased in the herd and cut a cow out without scattering the herd. She held the reins up until she had Blaze positioned. Then she dropped her hand and let Blaze cut the cow. The cow moved and Penny had to kick him up. Finally Blaze caught on to what he is supposed to do. After that he did a good job. Penny cut two more cows then Billy told her that is enough. Penny stopped Blaze and petted him, saying, "Good job Blaze." Billy is pleased.

This time Billy told her to go get Pete. "It is time you rode a real cutting horse." She caught him and put her saddle on him. Pete is a stud horse and Penny has to be careful around him, but he is a good mannered horse. She warmed him up in the round pen and climbed on. "Okay, ride him like you are in a cutting contest," Billy said. Penny eased him into the herd and stopped him while the cattle filtered by. She set a good cow up and dropped the reins. Pete is a big strong horse. When he stopped and turned, he almost lost Penny but she stuck to the horse and appeared not to be tense. She rode Pete just like she had been riding all her life. Billy is impressed. Now he knew Penny could set a cutting horse.

She cooled Pete out after she finished. Penny asked, "What was my score Billy?" He said, "Good enough to win most any cutting horse contest. Penny said, "That was a good ride." "I can't wait until we have our cutting. I expect you to win," Billy replied. Penny said, "I will give it a good try." "It is coming up in three weeks. We have lots of getting ready to do. I mean cleaning up around the arena and getting the bleachers cleaned up the fans put in place. Plus the trailer parking area needs mowing. We want it all to look nice for the visitors," Billy told her.

Billy went on to ask, "Would your brother and sister like to help clean up around here and earn and earn some extra money? They sure would just tell me when to have them here. I need to get the bleachers swept off they are so dusty then hose them off the day before the cutting." Penny said, "I will tell them."

They rode until dark as usual. Penny is getting really good at sitting a horse. After they had the horses stalled. Penny went and looked at the bleachers. She said, "Billy some need new boards some are broken." Billy said, "I will ask McKenzie to get us some help with that."

Penny went home and cleaned up and dressed for bed. She ate supper and told Missy and James Jr. what Billy had said about sweeping off the bleachers and picking up trash. They were glad to get to make some money. Missy and James Jr. were going to try and pick cotton after school to earn extra money too. Neither had ever picked cotton before.

Penny got on Peppy and was riding her around and she saw Suzy. They rode around together and they had a nice visit. Pretty soon it is time for the next class. She asked Suzy if she is showing in this class, she said she was. Penny said she is showing Peppy. Suzy said she is showing first and didn't want to go first. Penny said, "Good luck Suzy. If I don't win I hope you do. Suzy went inside the arena and is waiting for her turn to go. Finally they called her name. Her horse worked well, but the cow didn't really try to get back to the herd. There were other good rides and finally they called Penny. Billy had the turn-back riders in place.

Penny took Peppy deep into the herd and cut the cow Billy told her to cut. She set the cow up just right. She tried Peppy really hard and Peppy is almost down on her belly holding the cow. The crowd is screaming.

She quit that one and it didn't do much, so she peeled one off the top and that cow is a good one. It tried hard and Peppy got down and is holding it out front when the horn blew. The Hackett family gave Penny and Peppy a standing ovation. They were glad Penny had done so well. They thought she would win the class. She did. She rode Peppy back where Suzy was and they visited some more. They liked each other. Penny said, "When Smith comes home do you think we could go on a double date?" Suzy said, "I would like that." When Peppy was through cooling out Penny gave her some water and put her back in her stall. One of the horse owners approached Billy and asked if he thought HB would sell Peppy. Billy said, "I really doubt it but he won't mind you asking." The man went over where HB and Ruth were sitting and he asked if he would sell Peppy to him. Ruth butted in and said, "That horse is not for sale." HB laughed and said, "Tom I guess you heard that." He said, "I did and I don't blame you for keeping her."

Penny went over to sit with her family. They were all so proud of Penny. Penny and Missy went over and got cold drinks for them. They sat together as long as Penny could. She had to help Billy with the horses. Penny gave her family a hug and said, "Thanks for coming. Now you know what I do."

Penny and her brother and sister fell right in to the school routine. All liked their teachers. Larry is riding to the gin with Penny. Each day Penny got a little better with the horses. Every chance she got she worked Peppy without any equipment. Penny felt it would help her riding balance.

Next week on September the 18th Penny would have her 18th birthday. Everybody that knew Penny knew she is older than her years. One day Billy asked Penny if she wasn't scared she would fall off Peppy while she was riding with out a saddle or bridle. She told Billy, "The only thing she is scared of is not having anything to eat." She had been there before. Billy thought that is a good answer.

Things went on as planned. Sunday is her birthday. On Saturday Ruth asked Penny to drive them to Stuttgart and have lunch. Penny is happy to. She drove to Ms. Ruth's and they got in the Cadillac and took off for Stuttgart. They had a good time talking on the way over. They ate at the Circle J Steak House. Ruth told Penny to order anything she wanted. Penny said, "Ms. Ruth, "I have never eaten a steak in my life do you think I could order one?' Ruth is not surprised. She said, "Yes you can Penny their steaks are delicious. I recommend the porterhouse, it is tender. There will be more than you can eat but you can take the rest home with you. "Oh good," Penny said. Ruth ordered a seafood plate. When they brought their meal Penny had to ask Ms. Ruth how to cut it up. Ruth showed her and told her about the steak sauce that most people put on their steak. Penny caught on fast. It came with a baked potato with butter and sour cream.

All this is new to Penny. A green salad also came with it. She put blue cheese dressing on it. It was all very good. The steak was tender, the salad fresh and the potato tasted so good. Penny ate all the salad and almost all the baked potato and almost all the steak. She ate until she was stuffed. "Oh, Ms. Ruth I am so full I have never had a meal this good. Thank you for bringing me here." Ruth asked Penny if she had any room for desert. She said, "They make the best Pies. Penny said, "Do you mind if I get one to take home to mother?" "That is very thoughtful of you.' Ruth said.

Ruth is pleased; she loves Penny and will do anything to help her. Penny asked Ms. Ruth if she needed anything before they started back home. Ruth said Penny if you don't mind I do need a few groceries and they have one of the best Safeway stores her in the country. She told Penny how to get there. "Oh, I almost forgot, Penny we are supposed to go by the Silver Spur and try on your chaps, they are ready, if they fit. "Good," Penny said. She knew how to get to the Silver Spur. They went in and told the sales lady they were there to try on the chaps for Penny Parks.

The sales person is the one who measured Penny for the chaps. She said, "They are beautiful I think you will like them." She took them out of the box and helped Penny try them on. "They are so pretty." Penny said. She got them on and Penny asked Ms. Ruth what she thought. Ruth looked and checked them out and said, "Penny are they comfortable?" Penny said, "Yes they are. Are they too long?" Ruth said, "They are supposed to be a little long so the judge can't see you spur your horse. Penny I think they are beautiful. I like the Silver leafs with the green leather coming out of the Conchos's." Ruth told the sales lady to send a bill for them to the Silver Leaf farm."

They were about to leave when Ruth asked Penny if she had a hat good enough to be a show hat. "No, I don't Ms. Ruth but let me buy it." "No, Penny as long as you are showing horses for the Silver Leaf Farm you won't have to buy anything. This is a business and all this is deductible on our taxes." Ruth and Penny picked out a white women's straw hat and had the sales girl to shape it just right for Penny. Penny tried it on and looked in the mirror until she had it just right. Ruth had the sales lady to put it in a hat box. Ruth said, "Penny, the chaps and hat are to be worn only when you are showing." Penny understood. Ruth said, "Penny you need a shirt to go with the chaps and hat. Ruth asked the sales lady they needed a blouse, something that will be used as a show shirt. Something with sequins would be good." The girl said, "I have the perfect one if it fits. She found it and it is a perfect match to her chaps and hat. Penny loved it. She asked, "Can I try it on?" The sales lady replied, "Sure go right in that changing room." In a few minutes Penny came out wearing it and asked, "What do you think?" Ruth said, "It looks like a good fit to me." Penny said, "It feels good." "Ok, we will take it," Ruth told the sales lady.

"Now," Ruth said, "Let's go down to the Safeway grocery and get some groceries. They did. Penny went in and got a shopping cart. Penny followed Ms. Ruth with the cart and she put what she needed in the cart. When they were finished they went to the checkout counter and they added up her bill and sacked up the groceries. They loaded them in the car and Penny drove them home to Ms. Ruth's.

On the way home Penny said, "That was the best meal I have ever eaten." On the way, they talked about girl things and the chaps, shirt and hat. Penny loved Ms. Ruth. When the got home Penny helped unload the groceries and helped Ruth put them away. As Penny started to leave Ms. Ruth handed her an envelope with a card inside. "Oh thank you Ms. Ruth is it ok to open it now?" "Yes you can," Ms. Ruth said. Penny carefully opened the envelope and found the most beautiful birthday card she had ever seen. Inside Ms. Ruth had written Penny a note thanking her for being so good to her. Penny read it and she started to cry a hard sob. She said, "Ms. Ruth you are the best person I have ever known. I love you so much."

Ruth told Penny she loved her too and is glad she lived on the Silver Leaf. Penny drove home and her mother is in the house by herself. Penny said, "Mother, I brought you a piece of pie from the place where we ate. Earlene sat down and when she tasted the pie she said, "Penny this is the best pie I have ever had."

Next day is Sunday Penny didn't go to church she had lots of things to do. James and Earlene had a special supper for Penny and a pretty birthday cake and homemade ice cream. Penny appreciated them doing that. Earlene gave Penny a package and asked her to open it. It is a nice pair of blue jeans and a western shirt. Penny hugged them thanked them. Penny had never been this happy in her life.

This was the last week before the cutting horse contest put on by the Silver Leaf. Billy had some helpers cutting the grass and picking up any trash and limbs or anything that needed picking up. Penny brought Missy and James Jr. with her after school to sweep off the bleachers. They swept them off then Billy told then to get a water hose and washed them down. They took turns doing that. Missy watched Penny work her horses. She had never seen anything like that. Once the bleachers were washed down and all the trash picked up Missy and James Jr. sit down and watched Penny and Billy work the horses. It was fun. When Penny was finished with the horses she drove them home. They all showered and ate supper. They all had some homework to do.

The week went fast Billy and Penny worked the horses hard then Billy said they would only get a light workout the day before the show.

Chapter 15

Show day is finally here. Horses started coming in early there were lots of them. Folks like to come to the Silver Leaf cutting. It is scheduled a week before the State Cutting Show and HB and Ruth are good hosts. There were wind fans set up in the bleacher area. The announcer is a good one. He knew all about cutting horses. Billy and Penny had a surprise for all the spectators and competitors. Most surprised would be HB and Ruth Hackett and Mark and Mary Smith's parents as well as Earlene and James. One of the hired hands ran a tractor with a rake to smooth down the arena. In a few minutes after that the arena was ready, the announcer told them to close the gate and keep all horses out. He announced, "There will be a special exhibition sponsored by the Silver Leaf farm." Penny had Peppy bright and shiny Billy had helped her.

Once they were ready the announcer said, "Ladies and gentleman I want to direct your attention to the north gate. This exhibition features Penny Parks and her horse Peppy." Billy opened the gate and Penny came riding Peppy in the arena in a run with no bridle or saddle or any equipment. She had on her new chaps, shirt and new hat, she looked absolutely stunning. Penny rode the horse around the arena in a run with her hands out to her side. Once she went around she dropped her arms and asked Peppy come to a sliding stop. Peppy backed peppy up then spun to the left then to the right. Penny rode around a few more times asking Peppy to spin and stop. Once she had finished Penny had Peppy to bow to the crowed. The crowd all stood up and clapped.

The announcer said, "Would you like to see Penny cut a cow on Peppy? Of course the crowd yelled, "Yes!" The cattle were ready at the south end of the arena. Penny eased Peppy into the herd and turned her and let the cattle filter back to the herd. All but one this one Peppy cut. The cow tried to get back but Peppy stopped her. She went the other way and Peppy did a swinging gate turn and stopped the cow. By now they were locked up head to head and Peppy is almost touching the ground holding the cow. By now the crowd is on its feet and screaming.

Penny quit the cow and rode Peppy around the arena waving to the crowd. Before they rode out of the arena Peppy rode Peppy to the center of the arena and turned her toward the audience on one side of the arena and bowed to the crowd. Then she turned her toward the other side and Peppy bowed to them. No one ever expected to see anything like that. HB and Ruth were stunned. They couldn't believe what they saw.

The announcer called for the first class which is the Novice, Novice class for beginning riders and horses. There were five in the class Penny is due to go last. She is riding Blaze. The first horse lost a cow; the second did a pretty good job. So did the third one. The fourth rider fell off his horse and now it is Blaze and Penny's turn. She had Blaze warmed up and ready. She eased Blaze into the herd same as always and cut a good cow. Penny dropped her hands and let Blaze have at the cow. The cow tried to get to the fence but Blaze headed the cow. It went the other way and Blaze lock up on her head to head. When Penny got a chance she quit that cow and peeled another out of the herd. Blaze held the cow in the center of the arena. Penny got one more out and was locked up head to head when the horn blew. The crowd went wild again. The announcer told the crowd, "This is the first cutting horse Penny has ever shown." Penny won the class.

She is out riding Blaze cooling him out and Suzy Pugh rode up. She said, "Penny that was so good of you riding the horse without a bridle or saddle. Penny said, "Thanks, I am proud that my horse won the class."

After a while Billy waved Penny over and told her to put Blaze in his stall; he was through for the day. He said, "Go see Ruth and HB, they want to see you." Penny walked over where they were sitting with Mark and Mary. They all stood up and gave Penny a hug. HB said, "Penny, I have been around cutting horses for thirty years and I have never seen anybody do what you did on Peppy." Penny thanked them and said, "I want to thank you for letting me ride your horses. I love them and I want to learn all I can. Ruth said, "Penny, I want to get a picture of you and Peppy to send to Smith. Penny said, "I will have Peppy out before long, I am showing her in a class."

Penny sat with the Hacketts until it is time to get Peppy out and start warming her up. Billy is showing three of HB's horses today so he would be busy. Penny told Ruth she was getting Peppy out and would bring her around to get a picture. Penny got Peppy and brushed her good and had her shiny. She lead her around to where Ruth was and she got a picture of Penny on Peppy without a bridle or saddle. She told Ruth she is going to saddle her up and would bring her back for another picture.

She saddled Peppy and rode her over to get another picture. HB is so proud of Penny. He asked Penny if she is scared? Penny said, "I will tell you what I told Billy. The only thing that scares me is being hungry." HB said, "Penny as long as you are on the Silver Leaf you won't have to worry about being hungry."

Penny got on Peppy and was riding her around and she saw Suzy they rode around together and they had a nice visit. Pretty soon it was time for the next class. She asked Suzy if she is showing in this class, she said she is. Penny said she was showing Peppy. Suzy said she is showing first and didn't want to go first. Penny said, "good luck Suzy. If I don't win I hope you do. Suzy went inside the arena and is waiting for her turn to go. Finally they called her name. Her horse worked good but the cow didn't really try to get back to the herd. There were other good rides and finally they called Penny. Billy had the turn back riders in place.

Penny took Peppy deep into the herd and cut the cow Billy told her to cut. She set the cow up just right. She tried Peppy really hard and Peppy was almost down on her belly holding the cow. The crowd is screaming.

She quit that one it didn't do much so she peeled one off the top and that cow was a good one, It tried hard and Peppy got down and was holding it out front when the horn blew. The Hackett family gave Penny and Peppy a standing ovation. They were glad Penny had done so well. They thought she would win the class. She did. She rode Peppy back where Suzy was and they visited some more. They liked each other. Penny said, "When Smith comes home do you think we could go on a double date?" Suzy said, "I would like that." When Peppy was through cooling out Penny she gave her some water and put her back in her stall. One of the horse owners approached Billy and asked, "If he thought HB would sell Peppy." Billy said, "I really doubt it but he won't mind you asking." The man went over where HB and Ruth were setting and he asked if he would sell Peppy to him. Ruth butted in and said, "That horse is not for sale." HB laughed and said, "Tom I guess you heard that." He said, "I did and I don't blame you for keeping her."

Penny went over to sit with her family. They were all so proud of Penny. Penny and Missy went over and got cold drinks for them. They sat together as long as Penny could. She had to help Billy with the horses. Penny gave her family a hug and said, "Thanks for coming. Now you know what I do.

The bigger classes were coming up and Billy had three horses to show: Roany, Pete and Brown. It is a good day and a good cutting. HB and Ruth were good hosts and all had a good time. HB had free watermelons, as much as you could eat. They were all excited and proud of Penny. She said, "Missy come go with me and we will bring us back a cold drink." They got the drinks and visited until Penny had to go help Billy. The main classes were coming up. Billy would show Pete and Roany in the open cutting and Brown in the Novice horse class. They had a good number of entries. This is serious business for the trainers and owners.

Roany was first to go. He did a real good job. Pete would go much later. After Roany finished Penny got on him to cool him out. She went to find Suzy; she was just getting on a horse to warm up for her dad. They had a few minutes to talk. They talked about seeing each other when Smith came home for Thanksgiving. They made plans. After Roany was cooled out Penny gave him some water and put him in his stall. She went back to sit with her family. Soon it was Pete's turn. Billy had him really warmed up and ready to go.

He eased Pete into the herd and cut a good cow and held. The cow really tried to get back to the herd. Billy got another and same thing. The third was locked head to head with Pete until the horn blew. Billy thought he would win the class. He did. Roany finished third and Brown did not place. It was a good day for the Silver Leaf horse operation. HB and Ruth again told Penny and Billy they were really proud of them. Billy said, "Give Penny some of the credit. She works very hard to make the horses do what they are supposed to do." Billy asked HB if he was surprised to see Penny work Peppy without a bridle or saddle. HB said, "If I hadn't seen it I would not have believed it." Ruth said, "Me either."

After the spectators left, Billy made one last pass to make sure all the horses were tended to. Penny was waiting until Billy told her she could leave. He waved her over and handed her a roll of money. He told her she could count it later. HB said to give you all the money you won today. Billy again bragged on Penny's performance and her winning two cutting classes. He said, "The State Cutting horse show is next week. Can you take a few days off from school?" She said she would not ask the school for days off; she would just tell them it is part of her job to be off. "I will be ready." Billy said, "We will talk Monday."

Penny went home and cleaned up and dressed in her new jeans. She asked her family if she could take them to town for supper. James Jr. and Missy were all for it. Finally James and Earlene gave in. On the way to town Penny handed the roll of money to Missy and asked her to count it. She counted it three times. She said, "Penny, do you know how much money you have?" Penny said, "I have no idea." Missy said, "It is almost two hundred dollars." Penny said, "What? Two hundred dollars?" Missy said, "That is right." "Oh my goodness," Penny said. "I tell you what, we will eat good tonight." Penny said, "Billy told me HB wanted me to have all the money I won today." I had no idea it was that much."

The Parks family ate a big meal. She asked her mother if she needed anything from the store. Earlene said, "We could use a few things for your lunches next week but if you don't feel like shopping I will come back Monday." Penny said, "Mother, I don't mind. I guess you can tell I am a little wound up over the horse show today." She asked her dad if it was okay with him. He said, "Sure Penny, I am a little wound up too." They went in and filled up a shopping basket. They bought more than they usually do. When they checked out, Penny asked Missy and James Jr. if there is something they wanted. Both wanted ice cream. "Ok," Penny said, "but do not get it on my car."

Penny paid for the groceries. Both James and Earlene told Penny they had the money to pay for them but Penny insisted. "I do not ever want any of us to be hungry again!" They understood that. They talked on the way home mostly about the horse show.

When they got home, Penny wrote Smith a letter telling him about the horse show. Then she got her Sunday clothes together for church. She asked if anybody wanted to attend church with her. Missy said she would go. Earlene said she didn't have any good clothes to wear to church. Penny said, "Mother, we will go shopping next week and get you some nice clothes." Earlene said, "Penny I didn't say that so you would go and buy me some clothes. I just wasn't thinking or I would not have said that."

"You need them mother, and you deserve to have them."

Penny told her mother and dad what Billy said about going to the state horse show. She said she would know more about it Monday. She said this is the State Cutting horse show and there would be cutters from all over the state as well as from other states.

The next morning Penny insisted James Jr. went to church with her and Missy. He didn't want to but Penny is not going to let him stay home. He needed to be in church. At Church she went to her Sunday School class. They had a good class. Penny went with James Jr. to find his class. It is his first time to be there. After Sunday School Penny found HB and Ruth. She thanked them for letting her have the money she won. They said it is part of the cutting horse business. Penny said they would put the money to good use. After church Penny filled the car up with gas and got them all a cold drink to drink on the way home. They all liked that.

Monday, Penny drove to school and is back in time to work the horses. Billy had a talk with Penny about the State Horse Show. He said, "Penny the state show is this Friday and Saturday. The events start early and we stay late each day. I need you to be out of school Thursday and Friday, we will need to clean the horses up and pack the trailer. You will stay in a motel room and I want to warn you, you will see things you never thought you would see. There will be some drinking and you may have young men flirting with you. If you have someone who is bothering you, let me or Shirley know. You need to pack your clothes and things as well your show clothes. Shirley is driving our car so we will have a way to get to and from the motel and to the restaurants. It will be good if you have some money for snacks and cold drinks and things like that. Other than that the farm pays for the motel and food."

Billy asked her if she had any questions. Penny said, "Billy I only have one show shirt. Do I just wear my everyday shirts?" Billy said, "I never thought about that. I will tell Shirley to stop by the western store in North Little Rock and pick you up as many shirts as you need." Penny said, "Thanks."

Penny asked if she could ask Suzy Pugh to stay in the motel room with her. Billy said, "I will be talking to her dad tomorrow and I will ask him. Anything else you want to ask? Penny asked, "Which horses and which classes will I be showing?" Billy said, "Three as of now but there might be another one. I haven't decided."

"Okay now, let's catch us a horse. Penny I might ask you to show Brown. We want to push them hard today and tomorrow then slack off Wednesday so they will be fresh for the show."

It is getting late when they quit for the day. Penny said, "I will see you tomorrow," then hurried over to Ms. Ruth's house; the lights were still on. She knocked at the back door and HB answered. He said, "Hello Penny, you are out late tonight." Penny said, "Mr. HB, I need to talk to Ms. Ruth. Is she still up?" "Yes, she sure is; she is in the living room." Ruth came into the kitchen. She could tell Penny had something important on her mind. She said, "What is it Penny?" "Ms. Ruth, Billy told me we would be at the horse show two days and I will be staying in a motel room two nights. Ms. Ruth I have never even been in a motel room. much less spent the night. Ms. Ruth I don't have a suitcase or anything to carry my clothes in."

"I did ask Billy if he would ask Suzy Pugh if she would share the room with me. I don't want her to know I have never stayed in a motel room. I only have one show shirt but Billy said Shirley would stop at the western store in North Little Rock and we would pick out two."

"Penny I assure you I do understand, and tomorrow when you get off work come by and we will talk about it. I will make sure you have everything you need and I will talk to you about staying in a motel room. I don't want you to stay by yourself and if Suzy can't stay with you I will come and stay."

Penny said, "Thank you Ms. Ruth. I owe you so much. If it weren't for you I would still be working in the field." Ruth said, "Penny you don't have to worry while I am still around. Now go home and get ready for school tomorrow. By the way, you tell the principal you will be out of school Thursday and Friday, and if he has anything to say then you tell me."

"Thank you again Ms. Ruth. Goodnight," Penny tenderly replied. She had grown quite close to Ms. Ruth.

Next afternoon Billy told Penny to saddle Brown and cut a few cows on him. He is still green but has lots of ability. All she needed to do is to keep his mind on his business. She cut two cows and made him pay attention to his work and he looked like a pro. Billy said, "I think you need to show Brown. She rode Peppy and Blaze and got into them both to make sure they didn't get lazy. Billy worked Pete and Roany and really got into them. They should be ready. When Penny left she drove to Ms. Ruth's. She asked if she came at the wrong time. Ruth said, "No your timing is good. Come in the bedroom, I have something to show you." She had a suitcase and a clothes bag for her hang up clothes like her shirts.

She showed Penny how to use the hanging bag and the compartments in the suitcase. She also had a small case for her makeup and a hair dryer. Ruth said, "Penny I have an extra hair dryer you can have. Have you ever used one?" Penny said, "No I have not." Ruth plugged it in and showed her how to use it. "You should have plenty of room to carry what you need. You will need a couple of changes of clothes besides your show clothes. This is for going out for supper. You will want to change out of your show clothes when you get in after the show." Penny understood that. "One more thing," Ms. Ruth went on to say. "I put a new bar of soap and shampoo in your cosmetic case. What they give you at the motel aren't any good."

Penny said, "That makes me feel so much more at ease." Ruth asked if Suzy was going to stay with her in the motel room. Penny said she will find out when she gets to work the next day. Ruth said to let her know one way or the other. Penny gathered up the suitcase and bags and loaded them in her car, thanking Ms. Ruth again.

When Penny got home, she showed her mother the suitcases and the hanging bag. Penny said, "I can put my jeans and underwear and a pair of shoes in the suitcase. I might take an extra pair of jeans if there is room." She showed her mother the hair dryer Ruth had given her. They talked about the hanging up clothes. Penny is all set and ready.

The next day she told her teachers she would be at the State Horseshow helping the Silver Leaf farm with the cutting horses. They only said she would have makeup work to do. That was fine with Penny. When she got to the horse barn, Shirley is there helping Billy. Penny asked Billy if he had heard from Suzy Pugh. "Yes, I did and Suzy is happy to share a room with you." That is a load off Penny's mind. They cleaned up the horses and packed the tack in the trailer and truck. She and Shirley talked. She is going to stop at the western store and buy Penny two more show shirts.

Penny is relieved about that. Shirley said, "Your and Suzy's room is next door to mine and Billy's, so if you need anything just knock on the door."

Chapter 16

✳ ✳ ✳ ✳ ✳

Now Penny is getting excited. Billy asked Penny if she is asked to put on an exhibition like she did at their show would she do it. Penny said, "I will if you ask me to." Billy said, "If the show people want you to do it I am going to tell them you will ride Peppy in the arena like you did at our show for $50.00. If you cut a cow it will be $100.00." Penny said, "Gosh do you think they will?" Billy said, "They might, so you tell them what it will cost in case I am not around. Don't do for free." She asked Billy what time should she be ready in the morning. Billy said, "Be ready by 6:30. Shirley will go with you and Suzy to the restaurant for breakfast. I will leave earlier and feed the horses then I will be back to pick you up. Suzy will probably go with her dad. Her dad and mother are staying at the same motel as we are."

Penny drove straight to Ms. Ruth's and told her Suzy is going to stay with her. Penny asked what she needed to know about staying in a Motel. Ruth said, "Keep your door locked at all times and if someone knocks on your door ask them who they are. If you don't know them don't let them in. Send them to Billy. There will be two beds in the room. You will have to share hanging up space and bathroom space for personal items. You and Suzy have a good time. Laugh and relax."

Penny and her mother packed her clothes. Earlene made sure her clothes were ironed and had her shirts in the hanging bag. Finally everything is packed. Penny laid out the clothes she is wearing to the show. She bathed and went to bed early. She had so many things on her mind it took a while to go to sleep. Next morning Penny loaded her things in her car while Earlene fixed breakfast. Earlene said, "Penny I think I should ride over to the barn and stay until you leave and bring your car back to the house." "You are so right. I had not thought of that." They drove to the barn and Billy and Shirley were already there. Penny introduced Shirley to her mother. Shirley said, "We will take good care of Penny, so don't worry."

They loaded Penny's clothes into Shirley's car. Penny helped Billy wrap the horses' pasterns. Finally they were all loaded. Billy told Penny to check and see if she had all of the tack she needed for Peppy. She took a look and said, "There is one saddle blanket short." Billy said, "I know it and we are getting a new one when you stop at the Western Store."

Finally Billy is loaded up and ready. He told Shirley to follow him until they got to the Western Store. The trailer is loaded with five horses. It is a load for the truck to pull but the truck was built for pulling trailers. Billy took the blacktop road to Carlisle then on to Little Rock. Everything went fine.

Once they got to North Little Rock, Shirley pulled into B F Smith's Western Store. She and Penny went in to look at the show shirts. They all were pretty. They found Penny's size and Shirley told Penny to pick out three. This is an order from Ms. Ruth. The sales lady showed horses too and she knew what to look for. They settled on three. They were so beautiful and would look so good on Penny. Shirley bought a new saddle blanket for Peppy. She would use it on the other horses too. Finally they were ready to go.

They arrived at the barn where the horses would be stalled. They found Billy; he was locating the stalls. Penny helped unload and take the wraps off the horses' feet. Finally they were all settled in and the tack is locked in the trailer. They would have night watchmen.

Penny couldn't believe there were so many horses there. All the State Fair rides were set up; it was amazing to Penny. She knew she had to keep her mind focused on the horses. Penny led the horses around some to let them stretch after their trip in the trailer.

She put them in the stall and gave them water. The first event will start at 11:00. It is Penny's event to show Blaze. Sure enough, the show people wanted Penny to do an exhibition on Peppy. This meant she would have to get dressed earlier than she wanted to. Shirley drove Penny back to the room to get dressed. Shirley helped Penny with her hair and made sure her clothes fit correctly. Penny looked so good. They drove back to the arena and Penny got Peppy out and brushed her. Shirley helped do Peppy's mane. They put some green ribbons in her mane and she looked so good.

Suzy rode up and they were so glad so see each other. She also helped get Peppy ready. Peppy seemed to know what she and Penny were going to do. HB and Ruth came by. The show management talked to HB about Penny showing Peppy in an exhibition. He told them if she wanted to do it and cut a cow it would cost them $150.00. They said they would pay it, and wanted her to do it again before the last event. Ruth found Billy and told him to have the photographer get lots of pictures of Penny and Peppy, and Suzy too. They didn't tell Penny or Suzy because they thought it might make them nervous.

Penny put on her chaps and hat; she had a halter on Peppy and would take it off before she rode into the arena. The tractor was raking the arena and smoothing it out. The cattle would be brought in and settled after the arena was ready. It took about thirty minutes to get that all done. Penny rode Peppy around outside with just a halter on until the cattle were settled. Finally the announcer welcomed all the participants to the Arkansas State Cutting Horse Show. He said, "Now I want to direct your attention to the north gate. We have a special treat for you. I want to introduce to you Penny Parks and her horse Peppy, representing the Silver Leaf Farm in Lonoke County."

Billy is with Penny and told her to relax and put them on a show. She would cut one cow for the audience. The gate opened and Penny and Peppy came in at a run and circled the arena. Penny was not holding on she is waving to the crowd. She brought Peppy to a sliding stop. She spun her around and ran to the other end and asked Peppy to come to a sliding stop. She rode her in a circle then a figure eight. The audience is clapping and yelling.

The announcer asked if they would like to see Penny cut a cow. Of course they did. Penny eased in the herd and got a cow out and Peppy locked up on it head to head. The audience is screaming. The cow stopped hard and turned. The photographer got a picture of Penny and Peppy. Peppy is almost on the ground and her ears were pinned back, dirt is flying up. In a minute Penny quit the cow and circled the arena. She took Peppy to the east bleachers and Peppy bowed down; then to the west stands and Peppy bowed to them.

It was a good show. She waved at the audience and rode Peppy out of the arena. Billy is there and put a halter on Peppy. He said, "Good job Penny! Guess what? You will get to keep the money they pay you to do this. And you know something else? They are paying you $150.00. They want you to do it again before the cutting is over." Penny is so pleased about that. That is money for her mother's clothes. Suzy came up and told Penny she looked so good.

Penny thanked her. She said, "I have to go get Blaze saddled and warmed up. I am showing in the first event. Suzy said "I will get my horse and we will ride around together if you want." Penny said, "Yes please ride with me." They rode around and talked. Penny is looking forward to her company in the motel room. Penny said, "Suzy you are the first good friend I have ever had." Suzy said "I am honored. We will be friends for life."

Billy came over and told Penny her event is coming up. He told her to go ahead and ride Blaze into the arena and ease him around on the opposite end of the arena where the cows are. He said just relax on Blaze but make him pay attention. This is a pretty big class so try to make him work hard. Shirley helped Penny with her hair and makeup and adjusted her chaps. She rode around for about an hour. They changed the cattle and dragged the arena where the horses worked. Finally they called, "The next horse to work is Blaze, owned by the Silver Leaf Farm and shown by Penny Parks." The crowd gave Penny a big applause. Billy had the turn-back men in place and told Penny which cow to cut.

Penny eased Blaze into the herd all the way to the back gate. She turned her horse, then stopped and let the cattle peel back to the fence; all except the one Billy told Penny to cut. The cow stopped and Penny positioned Blaze, then she dropped her rein hand down to Blaze's neck. The cow moved to Penny's right and Blaze headed the cow and made her go the other way. The cow tried again and Blaze locked up head to head on the cow. She quit that one and eased another one out front. This cow was just as good as the first one. They locked up head to head. Every time the cow would turn Blaze was right there.

Penny would cut one more cow. She took the one standing away from the herd. Not much time is left but the cow moved toward the herd and Blaze is right on the money. The horn blew and the crowd gave Penny and Blaze a standing ovation. Billy met Penny as she rode back toward the gate. Billy said, "Penny your score will be hard for any horse to beat. You had Blaze working like a champion." Penny said, "I could tell he was really trying." Billy said, "Cool your horse out and put him in the stall, then go see HB and Ms. Ruth. They are sitting on the east side down close to the front." Suzy rode up to Penny and told her, "I'll bet you win that class. You and Blaze did really good."

"Thank you Suzy, are you showing in the next class?" "Yes, I am and I hope I do as good as you." "You will Suzy; I just feel it in my bones." After a while she put Blaze in his stall and went to find Ms. Ruth and HB. Shirley is sitting with them. She walked up and spoke. The announcer came on and said, "Here are the results of the Novice class. In first place… Penny Parks riding Blaze. HB and Ruth gave Penny a big hug. They said they were proud of her for the exhibition and the way she showed her horse in the cutting. Penny thanked them for the kind words. She said, "I thank you for giving me the opportunity to ride your horses. That means more to me than you will ever know." "Penny, we are the ones that are honored. You have put Silver Leaf cutting horses on the map. We hope you ride our horses for a long time." Penny sat down between Ruth and HB.

Penny told Ms. Ruth, "Suzy and I are really good friends. The first good girl friend my own age I have ever had."

Ruth said, "I am so happy for you Penny." Penny told them Suzy is going to show in the next class. Penny waited around to watch. Finally they announced Suzy Pugh up next. As the turn-back men got in place, Penny asked Ms. Ruth which one is Suzy's dad. Ruth pointed him out to Penny. Ruth said, "He is a good trainer and a good person. He sure raised Suzy right."

Suzy eased into the herd and cut a cow right off. Her horse did a really good job of holding the cow. She quit that one and got another and the cow and her horse locked up head to head; it was a good show. She quit that one and got another that was just as good. When the horn blew Suzy's horse was locked up, really getting her horse showed. Penny jumped up and yelled, "Yea Suzy." She told Ms. Ruth. "I am so excited for her." "Me too, Penny," Ms. Ruth said.

Penny spoke to Shirley and said, "Shirley, I hope you don't think I am ignoring you. This is all so new; sometimes I just don't think straight. Shirley said, "Penny I would never think that. You have a job to do so just do it and don't worry about me." Penny said, "I want to go speak to Suzy, then I will find Billy to see if I need to saddle Brown." She met Suzy out back and gave her a big hug. "Suzy you did it. That was so good!" Suzy said, "Thanks Penny; he sure felt good." Ruth knew enough about Suzy to know that being friends with Penny would make her try harder. That showed in this class.

Penny found Billy and asked him if she is showing Brown. He said, "Penny, Peppy will show in the next class. Let's get her ready. Penny went to the stall and brought Peppy out. She is still pretty clean from the exhibition. Penny gave her a good brushing and combed her mane. Penny petted and rubbed on Peppy and talked to her. Peppy loved Penny. She felt so at ease around her. She wanted to please Penny. Penny saddled her up and went out to start warming her up. She found Suzy and they rode around together.

While they were riding, the class Suzy showed in is finishing up. They ran the cattle out to their pen and started running the tractor around scratching up the arena. Before long the announcer said, "Here are the results of the $300 Novice class. In first Place is Poco's Pride, owned and shown by Suzy Pugh." Suzy let out a big scream. That is her first win in a long time. She said, "Penny come meet my dad and mom." She found her dad and gave him a big hug. She said, "Dad, this is my friend Penny Parks. She won the class before mine. Penny, this is my dad, Roger Pugh." Penny said, "I am so glad to meet you." Roger said, "Penny you did a heck of a job showing your horse and in the exhibition. You are some kind of cutting horse rider." "Thank you," Penny said "I really love doing it."

Suzy asked her dad, "Where is mom?" "She is at the concession stand getting us something to eat." Suzy said, "We are going to find her." They did find her standing in line at the concession stand. She introduced her to Penny. "Penny, this is my mother Sissy." "Hello Ms. Sissy", Penny said. Suzy said, "Did you hear that I won the last class?" "No, I did not. Oh my goodness Suzy, I am so proud of you. Congratulations."

Suddenly Penny remembered she is supposed to get Peppy ready for the next class. She rode her around until the called for that class. Billy said, "Penny this is a real tough class. Just go and do your best. If you don't win it is okay." Penny just said, "Me and Peppy will do our best."

It seemed like forever until they called Penny's name to work. She is so ready and so is Peppy. Penny said, "Peppy, we are going after a high finish. Be ready." Penny, as always, made a deep cut in the cattle and set one up perfectly. Peppy locked on to it and went head to head. Penny quit that one and got another one close to the edge. Peppy locked on to that one and was down almost to the ground.

Just as the horn blew Peppy slipped down on her knees. Penny jumped off and walked Peppy around to see if she was limping. She seemed okay but HB wanted a veterinarian to check her. He did and said Peppy is just fine.

Penny is upset. She thought she had pushed Peppy too hard but Billy said, "Penny, things like that are just part of the game. Peppy is fine she just slipped on the loose dirt." That satisfied Penny. She rode her around and cooled her down. After a bit Billy rode up and said, "Put Peppy in her stall and give her some water. We are all through for the day."

It had been a long day. Penny asked Shirley if Suzy could come up to her room and get ready for supper. Shirley said, "Of course. Tell her to bring her luggage to room 221. I will have each of you a door key." Penny found Suzy and asked her to bring her clothes to her room and they would get ready for supper. She said she would be right up. "We are about to leave."

Billy and Penny got in the car with Shirley and drove to the motel. Shirley went by the motel office and got two keys for Penny's room. She unloaded her clothes and found the room. She unlocked the door and walked into the room. It is nice, two beds that looked comfortable, and an air conditioner. The bathroom is large: it had a shower and a tub and an area to put on makeup. Penny hung up her clothes and put the suitcase on a rack at the foot of her bed. She waited on Suzy. She came in about ten minutes later. They put their luggage up and Penny asked Suzy if she wanted in the bathroom first. "Yes, I do need to use the bathroom."

Penny sat down on the bed and then laid down on it. She is almost asleep when Suzy came out. Penny asked Suzy if she needed to use her hair dryer. Suzy said, "If you don't mind." Penny got it out for her then went into the shower. In about thirty minutes they were both ready to go to supper. Penny knocked on Billy and Shirley's door and told them they were ready to go. Shirley said, "We are about ready; give us ten more minutes." Penny and Suzy stood on the balcony and looked around, watching the people come and go. It is not dark yet; in fact the sun is just going down. In a few minutes Shirley and Billy came out of their room and said, "We are ready. Lock your door."

They walked to Shirley's car. Shirley drove, and Penny and Suzy sat in the back. Billy said, "Okay girls. What are you hungry for?" Penny said, "I could eat a snapping turtle." They all laughed. Shirley said, "How about seafood? There is a really good seafood restaurant just up the street." Penny and Suzy were all for it. Shirley said they also serve the best steaks in the country. Billy went for that. In a few minutes they were parking at the restaurant. Suzy told Billy and Shirley, "I have money for my supper so ask for a separate ticket if you don't mind."

The girls all ordered a big seafood platter. Billy ordered a big T-bone steak. They all ordered iced tea to drink. While they were waiting Billy said, "You girls did a super job today." They thanked him for the compliment. "Penny, I guess it will be tomorrow before we know if you and Peppy got a place." Penny said, "If Peppy hadn't slipped down I thought we would have a place." Billy said, "The horn blew just as Peppy slipped, and anything that happens after the horn blows doesn't count so maybe you got a place." "Penny, Brown is eligible for a Novice horse and Novice Rider class and I am out of the Novice classification so if you don't mind I would like for you to ride him. He will go in the first class in the morning."

That is ok with Penny. Billy said, "After that class they want you to do another exhibition on Peppy." "Good," Penny said. "I can use the money to buy my mother some Sunday clothes and my sister some more school clothes." Finally the food came and they all ate and ate. They were stuffed. Shirley paid for Penny's, Billy's and her bill. Suzy had a separate ticket. All enjoyed each other's company. Billy said, "I am going to let you girls out at the motel and I am going to check on the horses. Shirley will be up and ready at 6:30." Penny and Suzy said, "We will be ready." "Ok then, goodnight." "Goodnight" they all said. Penny and Suzy walked Shirley to her room, and then unlocked their door.

They both took their boots off and lay down on their bed. All of a sudden Suzy went "HONK' like she was snoring. Penny got tickled and couldn't stop laughing. They had such a good time just acting silly. Finally they both got in their pajamas. Suzy called her mother and told her to call her at six o'clock. She said she would. Penny would get up at that time too. They were two happy girls. Each had won a class and would get a trophy and maybe a belt buckle. Plus the classes paid good money. Penny said Suzy, "I have a question for you." Suzy said, "Sure Penny. What is it?" "Have you ever peed in a horse trailer?" This broke Suzy up. "Are you serious?" Suzy asked. Penny said, "I am serious." Suzy said "about a thousand times." They both laughed.

The next morning Suzy's mother called and woke Suzy and Penny up. They washed up and got dressed. Both were waiting for Shirley to come out of her room. She came out and asked if they had their door locked. Penny checked and it is locked. The restaurant is just off the motel lobby. It is crowded with horse show people. The waitress took them to their seat. All ordered coffee. They ate a good breakfast, but not too much; they didn't want to be stuffed when they were riding their horses. Both Penny and Suzy were showing in the first class. Penny got Brown out of his stall and walked him around some then tied him to the trailer and brushed him good. Shirley is helping. They got him looking good. He looked like a champion cutting horse. Penny is glad to be riding him.

Suzy is busy with her horse so Penny only saw her briefly before she showed Brown. She walked him around and kept him on his toes. The announcer called for the next class. It is the $500 Novice. Penny would work in the third set of cattle. It seemed like forever before Penny is up. Before she rode into the cattle, she stopped Brown and spun him to his left then to his right. He is ready. Penny did as always: made a deep cut and got the cow Billy told her to get. Brown set her up right in the middle and locked up head on with her.

On the next cow he locked up head to head and had her stopped at every turn. The cow turned and ran off. Penny got another good one and Brown worked her like a champion cutting horse. When the horn blew, Penny pulled Brown off the cow, he didn't want to quit. Penny knew she had done a good job. The crowd cheered. Billy rode out with her and said, "Penny that was a good job. Brown really got down and worked hard. He might win the class." Penny thanked him for the help. Penny rode Brown around and cooled him out. Suzy rode up and told her she really did do a good job.

Penny said, "Suzy remember when I asked you if you had ever peed in a horse trailer?" Suzy said, "Yes, Penny. Do you need to pee?" "Yes I do, bad." "Our trailer is right over here. Come on. I will hold your horse." Penny hurried in the trailer and closed the door. In a few minutes she came out and said, "Thank you Suzy." "Now you have peed in a horse trailer; nothing to it." They rode around until Brown was cooled out. Penny said goodbye to Suzy and unsaddled Brown, put him in his stall and gave him fresh water.

Penny went and found HB and Ruth. Shirley is sitting with them. Ruth saw Penny coming and asked her to sit by her. She said, "Penny have you seen today's paper?" "No I haven't." Ruth said, "I have something to show you." Right on the front page is a big picture of Penny and Peppy cutting a cow. It is from the exhibition Penny and Peppy did. It showed Peppy almost down on her knees and head to head with the cow with her ears pinned back. It showed Penny sitting on Peppy watching the cow. "Oh my goodness," Penny said. "That is so good of Peppy!"

HB said, "Penny I want your permission to use that picture as the logo of our cutting horse operation. We will have an artist paint a sign and have it at our barn." Penny said, "I am sure you don't need my permission, but I would be honored to have it for the cutting horses." HB said, "That is the best cutting horse picture I have ever seen. By the way in case you haven't heard, you and Peppy finished third in the class you were showing in last night. That was a tough class and third is a real good finish." Penny said, "I don't know what to say. Peppy did all the hard work. She was really trying hard."

Chapter 17

Penny asked Shirley if she would take her back to the motel so she could change for the exhibition. Shirley said, "Sure, Penny let's go." Penny said, "I think I will shower and get really clean." Shirley said, "I will help you do your hair." Penny bathed and washed her hair and used the new dryer to get it dry. She put on a pair of her new jeans and her last show shirt. She looked so good. When she got back, Ruth waved her over to where she and HB were sitting. A photographer walked up and asked if she could get a picture of her and the Hacketts. Penny said, "I will be so glad to."

The photographer got them around and against a good background and took three pictures. Penny asked if she could have one of the pictures. Ruth said, "Yes, you can."

Penny sat with them until the class was over and the tractor came in and dragged the arena. When that was done a fresh set of cattle is let in, and one of the riders settled them down. By then Penny was riding Peppy with a halter. In a bit the announcer said, "We have a special event coming up. Let me call your attention to the North Gate. We want to present Penny Parks and her horse Peppy. They represent the Silver Leaf Farm in Lonoke County."

Billy said, "Penny, just relax." The gate opened and Peppy came in at a run going around the arena. Penny is waving with both hands.

She brought Peppy to a sliding stop, then spun her around to the left and then to the right. Penny rode her in a small circle, then a larger one, then a figure eight, and came to a sliding stop. The announcer said, "How many would like to see Penny and Peppy cut a cow?" Everyone in the stands stood up and clapped. Penny settled Peppy for a moment then rode her deep into the cattle and got one out. The cow is a good one and Peppy and Penny really put on a good show. When the cow ran off, Penny rode Peppy out of the herd and around the arena.

She rode to the east stands and Peppy gave a bow, then the west stands and Peppy bowed. Penny then rode Peppy over to where the Hacketts were sitting and gave them a special bow. The crowd went wild. Penny rode out and Billy is waiting with a halter. There were people waiting on Penny to get an autograph. Suzy is there and Penny had to ask her what they meant. Suzy showed her and Penny must have sighed fifty pictures of her that was in the newspaper.

Penny then rode Peppy with a halter on and more people came up with their cameras and took pictures. Finally, Penny and Suzy were back together. Penny asked Suzy to come with her to see the Hacketts. Ruth waved them over and asked them to sit down. She had something to show them. Ruth opened a folder and it is full of pictures of Penny and Suzy. Most of the pictures were pictures of them cutting a cow, but others were pictures of them sitting together. One picture showed Penny and Suzy sitting on a fence holding their horses. They were so surprised they both had to wipe tears from their eyes. It meant so much to Penny and Suzy and made Ruth Hackett so happy. Shirley was sitting by them and she was tearing up too.

To make a perfect day more perfect they announced the winners of the class Penny and Suzy were in. The announcer said there is a tie for first place, "Suzy Pugh and Penny Parks your winners of the $500 Novice." They both just broke down and cried and held on to each other. Now they are bonded for life. Suzy's mother Sissy came running over and gave Suzy a big hug. When things settled down, they showed Sissy the pictures of Suzy and Penny. Now she is crying too.

The Hacketts came up and told Penny and Shirley they were going to have to go to get back to the farm. They thanked everybody for the good time. They told Shirley they were sorry to miss Billy ride in the Open Class. Shirley said, "Billy understands. It is going to be really late when he shows." They all said goodbye again and left. That left Penny and Suzy and Shirley. Before long it is time to go eat supper. They had missed lunch. Penny found Billy and asked if she could help with Pete. Billy said, "No thank you, I will take care of him. If you don't mind, tell Shirley to take you and Suzy to supper and bring me back a sandwich."

Shirley asked the girls what they were hungry for. "Anything," they both said. "We are hungry." "Know what?" Penny said, "I could eat a big fat hamburger with cheese on it and a plate full of french fries and a big glass of ice tea." Suzy said, "I will have the same." Shirley said, "Me too." Shirley said, "The best place for that is the restaurant at the motel. They have the best burgers. Let's go! I can get Billy a burger there too."

As they went in the restaurant some of the cutters recognized Penny and Suzy, and they gave them a big hand of applause. They were both surprised and embarrassed but they took off their hats and waved to the crowd and said, "thanks to you all. We had fun." They enjoyed their meal. Shirley got Billy a big cheeseburger and fries. It is going to be a long night. Billy is going to show Pete and Roany in the biggest event and had the most prize money of any event.

Penny didn't know what to make of all the attention. In fact she is somewhat embarrassed about it. As they ate they talked about the day and all the good things that happened to them. They were so happy they could hardly hold it in. Shirley kidded them saying, "What are you girls so sad about?" Penny and Suzy had a good laugh. Suzy said, "I bet we won't even go to sleep tonight." Shirley said, "Yes, you will when you hit the bed; both of you will pass out." Shirley asked if they were going to sit up and watch Billy ride Pete and Roany. Penny said, "I will stay up if it takes all night." Suzy said, "Me too."

After they ate Shirley said, "You two go to your room and rest. I know you are worn out. I will take Billy's supper to him and I will come back to get you close to the time Billy shows." They both thought that is a good idea, Suzy said, "I am going to shower and wash my dirty hair." Penny said me too. They went to their room and sat down for a while. They were so tired. Finally Penny asked Suzy if she wanted the bathroom first. She said, "I went first last night so you can go first tonight." Penny said, "I will be out in a few minutes. She got her under clothes and headed for the shower. Suzy sat in the easy chair and fell off to sleep.

Penny woke her up when she started the hair dryer. Penny said, "Okay sleepyhead! Wake up." Suzy got up and headed for the shower. They both had fresh clothes to put on. They felt so much better. They lay on their beds and talked for a while then both of them went sound asleep. In about two hours Shirley came to the door and woke them up. "Who is it?" Penny asked. "Shirley." Penny opened the door and asked her in. She could tell that they both had been asleep. Penny asked if Billy is close to showing. Shirley said, "By the time we get there he will be getting close. He is showing Roany first." They were ready to go.

They found a good place close to the cattle. Penny and Suzy asked if they could go find Billy and wish him good luck. When they found him he was talking to Suzy's dad. They wished both of them good luck. Suzy's dad is showing two horses also. Penny said, "Billy, make old Roany pay attention and he will cut a hole in the ground." Billy said, "Thanks Penny."

They walked around and spoke to some of the cutters, then went back and sat by Shirley. Shirley is a little nervous for Billy. So was Penny. Roany was the last to work in that set of cattle. He had Roany spinning and stopping before he rode into the cattle. Both looked very good. Billy rode deep into the herd and cut a good cow. Roany worked the cow to a standstill. Billy cut another and Roany really held the cow in front of the herd. Billy peeled another off and Roany is locked up on it when the horn blew. Penny, Shirley and Suzy all stood up and applauded. Penny said, "I will go and see if Billy needs help." She found him out back and asked if she could cool Roany out. Billy said, "You sure can and thanks." I will go find Shirley and sit by her for a while then I will saddle Pete."

When they announced Roany's score Billy is happy. He thought Roany had done his best job of cutting cattle. He hoped Pete would be as good. Penny cooled Roany out, put him in his stall, and gave him some water. Penny went and sat by Suzy, who was next to Shirley and Billy. Penny said she thought Roany might get a good place. Billy said he did good. Finally it is time to saddle Pete and get him ready. Penny knew Billy was not going to need her help warming Pete up. It was getting late and the crowd had thinned out.

Billy had Pete ready when they called his name. Billy had his turn-back men all ready. Pete eased into the herd and cut a really good cow. Pete really put on a show. Billy quit that one and got another that was just as good. Pete is surely going to be in the money. Suzy's dad had shown while Penny was cooling out Roany. Suzy said, "He did real good." After Billy finished he asked the girls if they were ready to go back to the motel. They were ready. It wasn't long before Billy came over and told the girls to go to the room. He would catch a ride with Suzy's dad. Penny and Suzy were ready for the bed. They asked Shirley what time they should be up.

Shirley said, "Penny you stay in bed until I call you. I am sure Suzy's mother will call for her. Anyway you two have a good night." They both said, "Thanks." Once they were in bed Penny and Suzy said good night and they were asleep. Both slept hard. They slept until eight o'clock the next morning. Suzy's mother called, and then Shirley called for Penny. She asked them if they could be ready for breakfast in thirty minutes. Both said they would be ready. Suzy's mother joined them for breakfast. She told Penny she enjoyed her performance with Peppy as well as her cutting. She also thanked her for being Suzy's friend.

At breakfast Shirley told them that Roany finished fourth and Pete finished third in the Open Cutting class. Shirley said that is good. Suzy's dad finished second but didn't place on the other horse. All were happy with the results.

After they ate, Suzy went with her mother. She told Penny she might not see her at the barn so she would say goodbye. "Penny, this has been the best time of my life! I love you and can't wait until we meet again." Penny hugged her and said, "I love you too! I hope we can visit soon. I want to be your friend for life." They swapped mailing addresses and both promised to write.

At the barn, both Suzy and Penny got a call over the loudspeaker asking them to come to the arena for the presentation of awards. Both were surprised. They hurried to the arena and contestants were gathered. The state Cutting Horse president handed out the awards. Both Penny and Suzy won trophy buckles and two trophies, plus prize money. Penny got a check for three hundred dollars for her exhibition. Penny had finished first in a class then third in a big class and she and Suzy tied for first in one class. The president handed Penny another check for $749.00. That was over a thousand dollars for the two days. Billy was also awarded checks for his finish in the open cutting.

She found Billy and asked if she needed to give him the checks. Billy said, "Penny, I have an agreement with HB on how prize money is to be split. HB told me whatever money you win is yours to keep. You can thank him. You deserve it. Another thing, you will be paid for attending and working at the show." Penny was stunned.

Finally they were loaded and on the way home. Penny rode with Shirley and they had a good visit on the way home. Penny dozed off to sleep and had a short nap. She told Shirley she was sorry for falling asleep. Shirley said, "Penny you are still tired." They pulled into the horse barn about five o'clock and unloaded the horses, took the wraps off and put them in the stalls and gave them fresh hay and water. The unloaded the tack box and put all the equipment away. Shirley said, "Come on Penny, and I will drive you home.

She thanked Billy and Shirley and told them how much she enjoyed the show and how much she learned.

When Penny got home she unloaded her suitcase and hanging clothes. James Jr. and Missy came out to help her carry it in the house. Penny thanked Shirley again and gave her a big hug. Finally Penny was home. Penny went in and hugged her mother. She said, "Penny how did you do?" Penny answered her, "Good enough to take you and Missy shopping and get a new refrigerator and stove and maybe some more furniture." Earlene said, "Penny, did you rob a bank?" They laughed. "Mother, I have so much to tell you I don't know where to start. But I will start with my new friend Suzy. We shared a room at the motel and were together most of the time. I put on two exhibitions and got paid three hundred dollars for that. They took my picture while I was showing Peppy cut a cow and they put the picture in the newspaper."

"Mother, I won two trophy belt buckles and two trophies and over seven hundred dollars plus the three hundred they paid for the two exhibitions. I have over a thousand dollars. We are going shopping Saturday afternoon right after I get through riding. You and Missy are going to try on clothes. We will bring something back for James Jr. Don't try to get out of it because I won't let you." Missy heard the good news and clapped her hands and yelled, "YEA FOR PENNY!"

Penny had bought three copies of the Arkansas Gazette to give a picture to Smith and for her mom and dad.

Penny showered and got ready for bed early. She laid out her clothes for church. She informed James Jr. that he is going to church with her and Missy. She would write to Smith tomorrow night. In the morning Penny got up and helped her mother fix breakfast. They talked as they were cooking. Penny said, "Mother, we have enough money to upgrade our kitchen appliances. Be thinking about what we would like to have." "Penny, you don't have to spend your money on us." Penny interrupted and said, "Mother I watched you and daddy starve yourself so we kids could eat. The Lord has blessed me; I know it is his will for me to help this family. Please let me help and let's get the right things for the house and clothes for you. I want you to be proud of yourself and look nice when you go to church and to town."

Penny told James Jr. to get ready for church. She didn't have to tell Missy. At church there were several members who had seen Penny's picture in the newspaper. They were surprised to know what Penny could do on a horse. The pastor in his announcements held up the picture of Penny and Peppy that were in the newspaper and said, "We congratulate you." Penny nodded in acknowledgement. Penny's life would be a little different from then on.

After church Penny had several people to come up and congratulate her for the horseshow. After they left the church she filled her car up with gas and had the oil checked and the pressure in the tires. She bought them cold drinks to drink on the way home. That afternoon, Penny and Missy picked up limbs that had fallen in the yard. They were making plans to plant flowers and shrubs. Missy and Penny are good friends as well as sisters.

Penny remembered she had school work to catch up. Most of all she is going to write Smith a nice long letter. She also remembered she needed to return Ms. Ruth's luggage. She put it in the car and drove to her house. She and Ruth had a long talk about the show and Penny couldn't thank her enough for her help. Ms. Ruth said, "Penny you learned a lot the past few days. That is a good thing. You will continue to learn the more you get out and do things." Penny asked if she had sent Smith a picture. Ruth said, "That is the first thing I did when I got home." Penny said, "Thank you."

Monday, Penny drove to school. James Jr. and Missy were up and ready at 7:30. Penny had several comments about the horseshow. She thanked them but did not dwell on it. After school Larry rode to the gin with Penny. She went in and spoke to Mr. Quick and asked how things were going. He said, "Just fine." He thanked her for letting Larry ride with her. She went home and changed into her horse riding clothes and drove to the horse barn. Billy is already riding.

Penny asked, "Which horse do you want me to ride first?" He said, "We need to ride all the new horses. Catch any one you want and take it to the round pen." Penny could tell the horses were fresh. They hadn't been ridden in a while. After they finished riding, Billy came over and told Penny he appreciated her help at the cutting. He congratulated her on her winnings. Penny said, "Billy if it hadn't been for you I would still be trying just to stay on a horse. All the success I had is because of you and I know it." Billy said, "Thanks but you have something inside you that I have never seen in anybody else." Penny said, "Thanks! I feel comfortable on the horses and I think I have more determination in me than most people. All my life we worked hard just to put food on the table. Now I want more than that. I know I have lots to learn but I am learning every time I saddle a horse."

Billy said, "That is the way to do it. We have more cutting events in fact we have one every month. Penny, I know you know this, but my business is training horses. If I don't have horses to train I don't get paid. What you might not know is, because of the success we both had at the State Horse Show, I have had several horse owners ask me to take their horses and train them. In fact we will be full up when they get here this week. That would not have happened if you didn't do as well as you did. I know the exhibition you and Peppy did helped more than anything. I thank you for working so hard. HB is tickled to death about how the show went. He and Ruth love you and want you to do good. I do too."

"When the weather cools off I will start riding earlier in the afternoon and save some work for you when you come in after school. You will always have something to do with cutting horses." Penny felt more like she is a part of the cutting horse operation. She proved she can pull her own weight. The school week was good. Penny had some studying to do but is keeping a good grade in all her classes. She didn't have much time for school activities because of the horses. She didn't mind, the horses and Smith came first. Penny got three letters from Smith this week. She was happy to get them.

Smith is doing well in school but has to work hard. He will have a week out of school during Thanksgiving week. Penny can't wait.

Friday after school, Penny drove by the farm office to get her paycheck. Sue told her that Thursday and Friday were included. That is for the horse show. The check was over a hundred dollars. Penny signed the check and Sue cashed it. Sue and Martha wanted to know more about the horseshow. They had a picture of Penny and Peppy hanging on the office wall. Penny told them she enjoyed the trip and the horses, and told them Suzy Pugh stayed with her at the motel. She said, "I peed in a horse trailer. That was my first time." They all got a big laugh over that. Penny said goodbye and drove home and changed clothes. They rode until dark. There were more horses to ride. Three came in this week. One more is due Sunday and that will be as many as they can ride.

Friday night Penny told her mother and Missy they would go to Stuttgart to Mansours department store to buy clothes and they would look at kitchen appliances. Penny finished riding about eleven Saturday morning, hurried home and cleaned up. They drove to Mansours and asked for McKenzie's sister-in-law. They said, "We remember you three. You work for the Silver Leaf farm." Penny said, "That is right. My mother needs some good clothes for church and for going to town as well as everyday clothes. Missy needs some too."

Penny said, "Start with mother. Don't forget she needs shoes too." The sales lady took Earlene back to the ladies' department and they looked at several outfits. Earlene tried on several different ones. They settled on five different nice outfits and three everyday outfits plus underwear and a good pair of shoes. This is the first new clothes Earlene had bought in years. Before they finished, Penny insisted on her mother getting some makeup. The sales girl took plenty of time getting the right shades and colors.

Missy is next; she picked out three pretty outfits for school plus some underwear and some cologne, and a pretty ring and bracelet. When they were finished Penny paid for the clothes with cash.

Chapter 18

They walked over to the appliance store and looked at kitchen stoves and refrigerators. They needed both. Their appliances are old and ugly to look at. Earlene and Penny picked out a good stove and refrigerator and a few more things for the kitchen. Penny asked, "Do you give a discount to the Silver Leaf farm?" The salesman said, "As a matter of fact we do." Penny asked, "Do you deliver them to their house?" "Yes, we will, free of charge in fact. We have a truck going there on Monday. Will there be anybody home?" Earlene said, "I will be there all day. Penny paid for the appliances in cash. They bought a good stove and a larger refrigerator with a freezer compartment in the top.

That is a big load off Penny's mind. Her mother and sister had good clothes and they had a new stove and fridge. "Mother, we still have one more thing to do for you and Missy. Next week, you two are going to the beauty shop for a haircut and shampoo."

Early in the year when Earlene moved on the Silver Leaf, her facial features looked hard and rough. She is underweight and under a heavy strain wondering if they would ever get out of the hole they were in. Now she has gained some weight, her face has softened and was not strained. She looks comfortable. She has become an attractive lady. She finally feels good about herself.

When they got home she modeled the clothes for her husband. James was glad and appreciated what Penny had done. They told him about the new appliances and he was really surprised. He told Penny she didn't need to do that. Penny said, "I did it because I wanted to and we will enjoy using them." James said, "I will take the old ones out so the new ones can be installed."

"Okay mother, in the morning you are going to church with us. Dad, can you go?" Penny asked. "I wish I could but I have to work; this is the busiest time of the year. I do get paid overtime so it is not bad," he said.

Penny, Missy, James Jr., and their mother dressed for church. Earlene looked so nice. Penny helped her apply her makeup. Earlene looked like a different person. She is relaxed and at ease. Penny is so proud. At church Penny took her mother to her class and introduced her to the teacher. Earlene carried her mother's bible and the teacher gave her a new Sunday school book. After Sunday School, Penny got her and they all sat together for the church services. After church Penny took them to the restaurant and they had a good lunch. They took James a sandwich and a large drink. On the way out of town Penny stopped for gas and had the oil and tires checked.

Penny had homework and needed to write Smith a letter. She changed out of her Sunday clothes and put on an old pair of jeans and her cowboy boots, the pair with the spurs. Penny wrote Smith another letter. Penny knows Smith looks forward to getting them. The new stove and refrigerator were delivered just like the salesman said they would. They looked so nice in the new kitchen.

School and horse riding went well all week; the new horses were good ones. They will win lots of money. After work on Monday Penny went by Ms. Ruth's and asked her if she could help get her mother and Missy an appointment at the beauty shop for Saturday afternoon. They need a haircut and a good shampoo and something to cover up mothers gray hair that is creeping in. Ruth said, "Come see me tomorrow. I will let you know if they have an opening." Ruth said, "How about you Penny?" Penny said, "I am going to wait until Smith comes home I want to look really special for him."

"Thanks Ms. Ruth. I will check with you tomorrow before work." Next day Penny stopped at Ms. Ruth's on the way to the horse barn. Ruth told Penny Earlene and Missy had appointments in Lonoke Saturday afternoon at 2:00. The shop is located next to the Ford Auto Dealership right on main street. "You can't miss it." Penny gave Ms. Ruth a hug and said, "Thank you so very much." "My pleasure Penny," Ms. Ruth replied.

Billy had two horses tied to the fence for Penny to ride around the big field after a workout in the round pen. "These horses have a lot of fire in them. They will be good ones."

All the farm operations were busy with the harvest. Weather is good and crops are excellent. The gin is busy. They are ginning later and running seven days a week trying to catch up. The soybeans are about ready. The farm bought two new combines this year. James is servicing them and getting them ready for harvest. Penny stops at the farm office about twice a week and speaks to Sue and Martha, and to McKenzie if he is in. The new horses are coming around; Billy is going to start them on cattle soon. The next cutting is in Pine Bluff in two weeks and they are getting ready for that. The horse barn is a busy place. Penny is glad she can help Billy make him and Shirley some money.

When Penny got home she told her mother and Missy about their appointment at the beauty shop on Saturday afternoon. Missy would get a haircut and shampoo. Her mother would get the same but with something to cover up the gray that is creeping in. Missy is so excited. Earlene is too. She is really touched by her daughter's generosity. She did say she had never been to a beauty shop in her life. Penny said, "Come to think of it, I haven't either. We will be ok. Ms. Ruth said they would take good care of us."

The week went by fast. Saturday morning Penny and Billy worked horses on cattle. They took turns cutting and turning back. Billy said he is pleased at the progress. Penny went home and showered and dressed. Missy and Earlene were dressed. Penny said, "Let's go, it is a little early but we can get a sandwich or something before the appointment." They thought this is a good idea. They ate lunch at Ketchum's café just up the street from the beauty shop. Missy and Earlene were both nervous and felt anxious about getting their hair worked on. They walked down the street to the Beauty Shoppe and went in. There is a beautician who met them at the door.

She told them, "You are next but it will be a few minutes yet." They sat down in the waiting area. The beautician came out and said her name is Sandy. "I will be helping you. Who wants to go first?" Penny said, "I think Missy is ready. Is it ok if I come back too?" Sandy said, "Sure you can, but Missy will be just fine." I just want to be there when you start on her then I will leave. Sandy got Missy in the chair and explained what she was going to do. "Now, how do you want your hair to be cut?" Penny and Sandy discussed Missy's hair and asked Missy what she thought? Sandy showed her some pictures. Missy saw one and said, "I want mine to look like that." "Good choice," Sandy said. "That will be so cute on you." "Ok," Penny said, "I will get back to the waiting area." In about thirty minutes Missy came walking out. She looked so pretty. Missy is just beaming she is so proud of herself.

Sandy said, "Earlene come on back." "Penny, come with me please," Earlene said. "Sure I will." Sandy got Earlene in the chair and they discussed what Earlene wanted her to do. Penny said, "She wants her hair cut and washed and the gray covered up." Sandy asked her to look in the mirror and told her based on her facial features and shape she recommended a certain style of cut. She show her some pictures like she did Missy, and Earlene decided on a certain cut. Penny said, "That is my favorite too." When Sandy was finished she called Penny back. She gave Earlene a mirror and asked, "What do you think?" Earlene looked at Penny and smiled. She said, "Penny, thank you so much! This is the best gift I have ever had."

Penny said, "Mom you are so beautiful." For the first time in her life

Earlene felt beautiful. Earlene and Missy would look so good in church.

Penny is so proud and so thankful she could make it all possible.

Sunday, they all looked so good. Penny drove to church and they sat together during the worship service. Ruth came by and spoke and told Missy and Earlene they looked so pretty. Ruth gave Penny a hug. Ruth couldn't be happier that Penny would take her money and spend it on her family. Ruth loves Penny as much as a daughter.

Billy and Penny are getting ready for the cutting show in Pine Bluff. Penny is going to show Blaze, Brown and Peppy. Billy is showing two of the new horses plus Roany. They are not showing Pete. The trailer would be full. On Friday before the Saturday show they bathed all the horses and trimmed them up. Billy is good with electric clippers. The horses looked so good.

Show day and they were loaded and ready. Shirley is coming along to be with Billy and help with the horses. Penny is wearing one of her everyday shirts but will change into one of her show shirts just before she rides.

They pulled into the show grounds. They have a very nice arena; they have a big rodeo there every fall. Billy parked in a good shady place that was not crowded. Penny is looking around for Suzy but would put her duties with the horses first. She knew Suzy would be doing the same. Blaze would show first, so Penny had him tied to the trailer brushing him and getting him ready. When she was finished she saddled him, and Billy said to ride in the arena. Several horses were already there. As she rode in she spotted Suzy. They spoke but they both had to ride their horses and get them ready.

Billy came up and told Penny the show management people wanted to know if Penny would show Peppy and cut one cow for a hundred dollars? Penny said, "Sure, when do they want to do it? Billy said, "I told them I would like to do it just before the first event." That is fine with Penny. Penny asked Billy if he could ride Blaze and let her get Peppy out and get her ready. "Yes, I will." Billy said. Penny brushed and cleaned Peppy up real good. Shirley helped.

They had some ribbon left over from the State show so they used that in Peppy's mane. Penny got in the trailer and changed into her show clothes.

She is ready; she put her chaps on and Shirley fixed her hair. Peppy is looking good. The announcer asked the audience to direct their attention to the west gate. He introduced Penny and Peppy. Billy is at the gate and told Penny to relax and have fun. He opened the gate and Peppy came in at a run around the arena. She did some sliding stops and spins and figure eights. The announcer asked the crowd, "Would you like to see Peppy cut a cow?" They applauded really loud. Penny eased Peppy into the herd and got a good cow. Penny worked a little longer than she wanted, but Peppy was locked up head to head with the cow and the crowd is screaming. Finally the cow ran off and Penny quit the cow. The did their bows to the audience and rode around once more, but a slow gallop this time waving to the audience.

Penny thought that was an easy hundred dollars. Billy took Peppy and let Penny get on Blaze. Billy said, "Penny you are getting better at that. You will make lots of money." Penny replied, "I can use all the money I can make. I love doing that." Nobody knows how Penny gets Peppy to do all the things she does. Penny won't tell. That is between her and Peppy.

In a while, it was Blaze's time to work in the lowest class, the Novice. He won that class easily. Penny rode Blaze outside and she looked for Suzy. Finally they spotted each other. Both dismounted from their horses and hugged each other. They had lots to talk about. Suzy is getting ready for the next class and had to leave Penny, but said she would look for her when she finished. Before she left she asked Penny, "Could you hold my horse while I go into the horse trailer." Penny said, "Sure."

After Blaze is cooled out Brown would be next to show, but it is too early to saddle him up. Penny went and found Shirley and sat by her. Penny is waiting for Suzy to show. She didn't have long to wait. Suzy is up next. She is riding a horse her dad is training. She did a really good job of showing the horse but the cows she cut weren't that good. After she cooled her horse out, she came and sat by Penny and Shirley. They all had a good visit.

Penny had to go and saddle Brown and get him warmed up really good. Sometimes he gets lazy and Penny won't allow that. Billy came around and said Penny would show first in the second group of cattle. That would be over an hour before she showed. She took her time riding Brown around but kept him on his toes. Finally they called for Penny and Brown. They were already in the arena. Penny spun Brown hard both ways and really got his attention. Brown is ready to do a professional job of cutting. Billy had the turn-back men ready. Suzy's dad is helping.

Penny eased Brown into the cows and made a deep cut all the way to the gate. She eased out the cow Billy told her to get, same as always. She had it set up perfect, right in the middle of the arena. When she was ready she lowered her reins in her left hand. The cow broke hard to Penny's right and Brown made a long jump and headed the cow. Brown put on a cutting horse clinic. Every move was the exact right one and Penny had him thinking ahead of the cows.

When the horn blew, Brown was locked head to head with the cow. Penny had to pull him off the cow. The crowd is clapping and yelling. As Penny rode out, Billy rode up and said "Penny, Brown might turn out to be the best horse we have." Penny said, "He was trying. He is so strong. I know that helped him." Penny won that class too. She cooled Brown out and went to find Suzy. Suzy was riding and didn't get to see Penny's ride. Penny said. "Brown did really good. I believe he will get a good place."

Suzy and Penny weren't getting to spend enough time together. Penny asked Suzy when could she come and spend the night with her. Suzy said, "I sure would like to, but with school and the horses I don't have time to do anything. Penny said, "I know, but I miss you so much." Suzy said, "Penny, I miss you too. Maybe some Sunday you could come over and spend the afternoon with me." Penny said, "I will do that."

One more class to go for Penny; it would be Peppy's turn. It is a big class and a tough one too. That didn't bother Penny and she knew Peppy would do her very best.

It is a long wait until Peppy would show. Penny sat by Shirley and Shirley said, "Penny, I am hungry are you?" Penny said, "I haven't even thought about it, but I am starved." Shirley said let's go find the concession stand and get something to eat. Penny got a foot long hot dog and a large drink. Shirley got a burger and fries. They sat at a table and ate their lunch. Shirley got Billy a big burger and fries and a large drink. When they left, they found Billy and gave him his lunch. He went to the bleachers with Shirley and Penny and ate his lunch. Billy said he had two more owners who wanted Billy to train their horses. Billy said, "I won't have a place for them until next month. I will call you when I get an opening." That was okay with the owners.

Penny said, "I think I will get Peppy and give her a good grooming. I want her to do really good in this class." Penny knew it would be a hard class. Penny also knew Peppy is a good horse that can cut cattle with the best of them. Being a tough class never crossed Penny's mind. Her mindset is winning. Penny took her time getting Peppy ready. She saddled her and Penny just led her around for a while. They saw Suzy eating her lunch. She is by herself. Penny walked over and sat by her until she finished. They were talking about Penny coming for a visit, and when Smith came home Penny would have Suzy spend the night and they would have a double date; actually a blind date for Suzy. Penny would have someone nice and good looking for her.

It would be another hour before Penny and Peppy showed. Suzy was through for the day. She won her class too. She would be watching Penny. Billy came around and they talked about the class. Penny said she is not worried. He said HB and Ruth will be here in time to watch you show Peppy. Penny is glad. She stayed busy getting Peppy ready. Penny is working hard to get her to relax; herself too. She did a lot of talking and rubbing on Peppy. Peppy will be ready.

Before they knew it, they were calling Peppy and Penny's name. They rode into the arena and the crowd gave them a big applause. Penny did as she always does; she eased Peppy into the cattle very slow and steady. The herd broke around just as Penny had planned. There is one cow set up just perfect.

Penny dropped her rein hand and Peppy took over. The cow tried to go left then right, and then tried to run. Peppy was ahead of the cow at every turn. Penny quit that one and got another that was just as good. Peppy was ahead of the cow at every turn. She peeled another off the herd and Peppy locked down on her. The horn blew and the crowd gave Penny and Peppy a standing ovation.

Billy said, "Peppy may win that class too." He told Penny to cool Peppy off and go find HB and Ruth. "They are sitting with Shirley."

After a while Peppy had cooled down Penny put the halter on her and tied her to the trailer. Peppy is done for the day. So is Penny. Billy had two horses to show in the Open event. She found HB and Ruth. They both gave her a bug hug and HB said, "Penny we heard you are winning everything. You did a super job in this event that was a great ride" "I was riding some good horses and they were really trying." HB said, "I heard you did a fantastic job in the exhibition too." "Yes we did, Peppy is getting better at it every time we do it." "Oh Mr. HB I wanted to ask you if I could put the trophies I won in Little Rock in your office. I don't really have a good place for them. I will keep the belt buckles though." "Penny I would be honored to have the trophies and show them off to my friends." Penny said she would bring them by Monday afternoon before she goes to the barn.

They sit back and watched the rest of the cutting; so far Penny had the highest score. There were only three to go and they were good horses. The first one had a good first cow. They scattered the herd because he was in too big a hurry. The next one did a great job but placed one point behind Penny. The last one to show just couldn't get it together and Penny won the class. It would pay big money. Penny said, "Mr. HB do you want me to split my winnings with the Silver Leaf?" HB said, "Penny you keep every "penny" you win. I hope you win a million dollars. We love to watch you and Billy show cutting horses. You two have made the Silver Leaf horse operation the best in the country. We love it."

Ruth motioned for Penny to come sit by her. She asked if Suzy was there. Penny said she is but she is busy helping her dad. Ruth said, "Penny we are so proud of you. HB thinks you are the best cutting horse rider in the country." Penny said, "I love the horses and I am just beginning to understand them." Penny told Ruth she had planned a double date with Suzy. She said she and Smith have to find someone nice that Suzy will like. Ruth said, "I am sure you will find just the right one."

Penny and Ruth talked about other things. Ruth asked Penny to drive her to Stuttgart after she finished with the horses on Saturday. Penny said, "I sure will." Ruth said, "I need to get groceries and a few other things. We can eat lunch at the same place we ate at before." Penny said, "Oh I will like that."

Billy showed Roany and one of the new horses in the Open Class. Both horses got a good place. Billy was pleased. When they finished Billy brought Penny the money she won, plus the exhibition money. It is over six hundred dollars. Penny couldn't believe it and couldn't wait to tell her family. It seemed like a long trip home. Shirley helped with the unloading and stalling the horses. Each horse got fresh hay and fresh water. Penny hugged Shirley and told her she enjoyed visiting with her. Billy bragged on Penny and said that he had more owners wanting them to ride their horses. "I told them as soon as we had an opening he would let them know."

Penny hurried home and showed her mother the money she won. Penny asked her mother if there is anything she needed for herself and the house. Earlene said, "No we have enough. Penny said she was going to put the money in her own private "bank" and save it for Christmas and this winter." Penny said, "I already have over five hundred dollars saved." Earlene said, "Penny, you are so good to us."

Chapter 19

Saturday when Penny got off work she went straight home and bathed and put on clean jeans and a western shirt. She took one of the trophy buckles she won and snapped it on her new belt that Smith bought for her. Penny looked like a real cowgirl. The buckle is big and shined like silver. It read "Champion Cutting Horse Arkansas State Fair 1951."

She drove over to Ms. Ruth's and they got in Ruth's Cadillac; Penny is driving. They had a good time talking on the way to Stuttgart. They stopped for lunch at the same place they ate before. It is hard for Penny to decide what to eat. "Ms. Ruth, what do you think I would like?" Ruth asked. "Penny, they serve the best shrimp plate. I think you will like it. It comes with a good fresh salad and baked potato and a sauce that you dip the shrimp in. They serve you a generous amount of shrimp. Then we can have dessert." Penny said, "That sounds so good. That is what I will order." Ruth ordered the same thing.

The meal was so good. Ruth said, "Penny, this is more than I can eat; please finish the shrimp." Penny said, "Are you sure?" "I am full but they taste too good to waste," Ruth said. The waitress brought their dessert; it was delicious. Penny said, "Thank you so much. That was a great meal." Ruth asked Penny if she was ready to go to the grocery store. Penny said, "Yes I am. I want to get a few things for our Sunday dinner."

As Penny pulled out and was headed for the grocery store, Ruth said "Oh I forgot I was supposed to stop at the western store and pick up something." "Sure," Penny said. She parked the car and asked Ruth if she needed some help. Ruth said, "Come in with me. I might need some help." When they went inside they met up with the man that makes all the leather goods and the saddles came over to meet them. He said, "Hello Penny, do you remember me? I made your chaps; how do you like them?" Penny said "I love them; they feel so good." He said, "I have something else you will like."

Penny looked confused. He said, "Come with me." She and Ruth followed him around the counter. He has something covered up. He took the cover off and there is the most beautiful cutting horse saddle she had ever seen. She knew it was hers when she saw her name stamped on the back of it. Penny went to her knees and sobbed. She got up and lay across the saddle. She said, "It is the most beautiful saddle in the world! Ms. Ruth, you and Mr. HB shouldn't have done this." Ruth said, "HB and I want you to ride good horses and have good equipment. You deserve it Penny, enjoy it." "I will," Penny said.

The saddle maker showed some of the features of the saddle. It is all handmade and hand carved. This saddle will last you the rest of your life, and your kids' too. They loaded it in the trunk of the car. Penny was still crying. "Ms. Ruth you are too good to me." Ms. Ruth gave her a hug, "I care very much about you, and you are so welcomed. Do you feel like going to the grocery store Penny?"

Penny said. "Yes I do." Penny got a shopping cart and followed Ms. Ruth around the store. Ruth loaded the cart up to the top. She asked Penny what she wanted to get. Penny said, "I think I will get two chickens and a gallon of milk." Ruth led her over to the meat counter and got the chickens and then to the milk box. When they were finished, Penny loaded the groceries in the back seat. The saddle is in the trunk. Penny was still sniffing on the way home.

Ruth tried to change the subject. Ruth asked her how she is doing in school. Penny said, "I am doing just great. I have mostly all A's; I have one B in math." Ruth told Penny that next week Mary is going to drive her to the doctor in Little Rock. Penny said, "What is wrong, Ms. Ruth?" Ruth said she has some internal bleeding and it needs to be checked out. "Oh, no!" Penny said. "Ms. Ruth, will you tell me what the doctor has to say? I can miss school and take care of you if you need me." "That won't necessary. I am sure it can be fixed with medicine." "I can't stand to see you hurting. I will be ready to do anything to help," Penny told her.

By then they were at Ms. Ruth's. Penny unloaded the car she wouldn't let Ms. Ruth help. Penny helped put the groceries up. She put the chickens and milk in her car.

"Is Mr. HB is home?" Penny asked. Ruth said, "Check in the living room." HB is in his chair taking a nap. Penny said, "Mr. HB, I hate to wake you up but I have to thank you and Ms. Ruth for the saddle. She went over and gave him a hug and a kiss on his cheek. "Mr. HB, that is the prettiest saddle I have ever seen and it has my name stamped on it. I am so happy." HB said, "Penny you need a good saddle to show the horses in. It is good for us to show you off and we like doing it."

"Thank you so much." Penny loaded the saddle in her car and drove home. She unloaded the saddle and took it into the living room and set it on the couch. She called her mother and Missy in; James Jr. is with his dad. Penny said, "Look what Ms. Ruth and HB bought me. Isn't it beautiful?" "Oh it is Penny, I am so proud for you." Penny said, "I will only use it when I am showing."

"I bought two chickens for our Sunday dinner tomorrow." "Good," Earlene said. "I will put them on tonight and have them ready in the morning, then all we have to do is heat them up tomorrow."

The next morning Earlene, Missy, and James Jr. dressed for church. Earlene and Missy looked so pretty in their new clothes and the new hair do's. They enjoyed the service and felt comfortable that they looked as good as anyone in the church. After church, Penny did as always, filled her car with gas and had the oil and tires checked. She bought them all a cold drink to drink on the way home. She had empty bottles to use as deposit.

They all changed out of their church clothes and into their older clothes they just wore around the house. Earlene and Penny fixed Sunday dinner. James came home to eat. They were all glad to have him home. After they ate Penny showed him her new saddle.

James liked the saddle. He is glad to be working for someone that appreciates what his daughter can do. James is doing well in his job. The Silver Leaf management depends on James to keep the equipment in good running order. James is doing that. He knows how to prevent a lot of breakdowns. If he sees something wrong, he doesn't mind stopping that equipment and telling the driver. They all know James means business.

Things are going good. Penny is riding horses and is getting a lot out of them. Ms. Ruth got a good report from the doctor. Soon it would be Thanksgiving and Smith would be home. Penny and Suzy write to each other at least once a week. They both miss each other. Smith wrote Penny and gave her a date he would be home. He asked Penny for a date the night he got home. He wanted to see Penny; his folks could wait. Penny will be so glad so see Smith.

They will have one more cutting horse show before Smith comes home. It will be in Little Rock and Penny might have to spend the night in a motel.

The contest will be in the same arena where the State Show is held. Penny and Suzy were looking forward to that and would stay together in the motel. Penny and Billy were working new horses to show at the show. Peppy and Brown and Pete would show, along with the two new horses. Penny would show one and Billy would show one. They were busy getting ready. The show will be held the second Friday and Saturday in November.

Billy said to Penny, "I have some not so good news. On the outside horses the owner gets half the prize money and we get half.

That is just the way the business works. The owner pays the entry fee and mileage for hauling his horse. On the Silver Leaf horses you get to keep what you win. I am sorry I didn't tell you sooner. You have the right to refuse to ride any of the outside horses." Penny said, "That is not a problem. If that is the usual way I can live with it."

They will work the horses hard until the day before the show and then let them rest.

On Monday before the show they made the final "tune-ups" on the horses. Billy is obligated to take the two new horses. That is part of his deal with the owner. Billy thinks they will do well. They hammered at the horses, and on Wednesday they quit them early to let them rest.

They bathed the horses and clipped the long hair and made them look good. Penny would ride with Shirley, same as last time. Penny asked Shirley if she had room for her new saddle. She did and asked Penny if she would like to stop at the western store and get new saddle blankets. Penny thought that is a good idea. Billy went ahead and unloaded the horses and tied them to the trailer. When Penny and Shirley got there, they helped brush them and get them looking good. Penny is still eligible for the Novice class and would show one of the new horses first.

She and Shirley got the new horse ready and put Penny's new saddle and blankets on him. Penny named him "Billy Bob." She changed her shirt in the ladies' restroom. Shirley helped with her hair and makeup and got her hat on just right, and her chaps adjusted. Penny looked good and her new saddle made her look even better. The horse is a little nervous; this is his first time to show. He is looking around and not paying attention. Penny stopped him and spun him around hard and made him back up. Now he is paying attention. Penny didn't know it but Billy Bob's owner is in the stands. When the cattle were settled, Penny would show last on that group of cattle. This gave her time to get the horse settled down and get his attention on what he is there for. The first horses weren't that good. Penny thought she had a chance of winning.

She eased Billy Bob into the cattle and made him stop and not get excited. She kept him calm and let the cattle ease by. She eased him forward and set a cow up in the center. The cattle stayed calm and Penny dropped her rein hand and squeezed Billy Bob with her knees to let him know to move. He made a little lunge at the cow to make her move and the show is on. Billy Bob got down low and kept the cow moving to the left and to the right. Penny quit that one and got another that tried to run toward the fence and Billy Bob headed the cow before she could get close to the fence.

Penny peeled another off and Billy Bob headed that one and kept her in the middle of the arena. The horn blew and Billy Bob is still working. Penny had to pull him off. No doubt about that class; Billy Bob won it by a wide margin. Billy rode out of the arena with Penny and said, "Penny that was a great ride. You are riding as good as any Pro I know, including myself." Penny thanked Billy. Penny rode Billy Bob around and cooled him out. When he was ready Penny took him back to the trailer and took her saddle off.

A man approached and introduced himself as the owner of Billy Bob. His name is Charles Wilson. Penny shook his hand and said, "Mr. Wilson I think you have a really nice cutting horse." He thanked Penny for riding him and said he is sending two more horses when Billy has an opening. He said, "I like the way you handled him and kept him calm and his mind on his business." Penny thanked him again and said, "That is what I try to do on every horse I ride." Mr. Wilson said, "Billy is a good trainer, but I like the way you handle horses." Penny thanked him again.

As soon as she could, Penny went looking for Suzy. Suzy was at her trailer saddling a horse. Penny walked up and spoke. Suzy is so glad to see Penny. Penny asked if she could stay at the motel with her. Suzy said, "I am not sure we are going to stay, but if we do I will be glad to stay with you."

"Penny I have missed you so much. I wished we lived closer to each other." Penny said, "So do I." Suzy is only going to show in one class and it is coming up. Penny said, "I hope you win." "Thanks

Penny." Suzy did a good job showing, but didn't place. It is a tough class. When Suzy is finished cooling the horse out, she came and found Penny. They sat with Shirley until Penny had to get ready for the next class. She is showing Brown. Penny asked Suzy to come with her and see her new saddle. "Penny that is beautiful! It has your name carved in it. I love it." Penny said, "I do too."

Suzy helped Penny give Brown a good brushing and cleaning. Penny said, "I will see you when I get through showing." Suzy said, "I will be sitting with Shirley." With that, Penny got on Brown and they rode to the riding area. This is a tougher class than the first one but Brown is a better horse than the first one. Finally it is Penny's turn. Billy had the turn-back riders ready. Penny did her usual thing and set the cow up in the middle. Brown locked on to the cow and Penny won that class too. Since Brown belonged to Mr. HB, Penny gets to keep all the prize money. She is looking forward to riding Peppy. She cooled Brown out and tied him to the trailer.

Suzy came over and told Penny that was a winning ride. "Thanks Suzy!" "Have you eaten?" Penny asked. Suzy said, "No I haven't." Penny said, "Let's go find Shirley and get something to eat. Shirley is all for it. She said, "We have time to go to the motel restaurant to get a good meal and not eat at the concession stand here."

Shirley drove her car to the restaurant. They all had a good meal and a good visit. After a while Penny asked Suzy to walk to the trailer with her. They wanted to visit more. Penny cleaned Peppy up and she and Suzy made plans to see each other when Smith comes home. Suzy said, "I will see you when you get through." "Thanks Suzy." Penny rode over to the riding area to get Peppy warmed up and ready.

As usual Peppy shows in the bigger classes so she has to be ready. She is. Penny has a knack of getting horses in the right frame of mind and ready to cut. Peppy wants to work hard for Penny. When it was Penny's turn she did as always, rode deep into the herd. She could sense that Peppy is a little over-anxious. Penny pulled her back and settled her down. When she got the cow that she wanted she let Peppy have at it. Peppy is all over the cow; down in the dirt with her ears pinned back. Penny won that class too. Penny has won three in a row. Fans of cutting, cutting horse trainers and owners were paying attention to Penny. HB and Ruth were there in time to watch Penny and Peppy.

A rich horse owner found Penny and asked her to work for his barn. Penny said, "I am sorry but I won't leave the Silver Leaf Farm at any price. That is my home." The owner said, "Penny you are one of the best riders I have ever seen. You will do well." She thanked him for the offer. He and HB were friends, and he told HB that he couldn't hire Penny at any price. "She said the Silver Leaf Farm is her home." This pleased HB and Ruth.

Penny is through for the day. She went and sat with HB, Ruth and Shirley. Suzy came up and sat by Penny. She said, "Congratulations Penny! It must have been the new saddle that helped you win everything you entered." Penny laughed and said, "I am sure it helped."

Penny asked Ms. Ruth about what the Doctor had to say about her. Ruth said, "He gave me some medicine and said if that didn't help I might have an operation." "Oh, Ms. Ruth I sure hope not, but if you do I will be there to take care of you. "Thanks Penny," Ruth said. "I will be all right." Penny could sense some concern in Ruth's voice.

It is Billy's turn to show. He is showing Roany first he would be up soon. Pete would not be far behind. Both horses showed good and both placed in the Open. That is a good day for the Silver Leaf. HB came over and sat by Penny. He said, "Penny I have something to discuss with you. I want you to move up in the classes you are showing in. You are too good for the lower classes. You need better competition. I am going to see what it takes for you to show in the Non Pro class. You may have to own the horse you show. If that is right I will sell you Peppy for one dollar and have the papers transferred in your name. Later on when Peppy is ready to breed you can sell her back. It is all perfectly legal. If it weren't I wouldn't think of doing it."

"The Non Pro means you're not a professional horse trainer. You work for the Silver Leaf so we will be ok there. The non Pro is a very though class. Big time horses and big time money and big name riders compete in that event. Then you can show one of my horses in the open class. You will have some very tough competition but if you win or even place the money is good. I know you are ready for it." Penny said, "yes I am ready, any time you say but I don't know if Peppy can beat the really tough horses. HB said she may not and if she can't we will breed her and find another one. Penny said, "I believe Brown has the best potential of any horse in the barn." HB said, "Let's work on him and have him ready by the next cutting show in December. In January or February there is a Regional Cutting horse show in Jackson Mississippi. It will last a week. We will work something out with your school so you won't be penalized for missing school."

"I will be looking forward to it. Mr. HB I think you already know I will be doing my very best to win." "I do Penny. I ought to add that in the bigger shows you can show in the Novice classes you are eligible for, that might be the best place for Peppy. We want you to win all the money you can." Penny said, "I hope I can do more exhibitions. I have taught Peppy to side pass that makes her look better showing."

When they were all through showing. Billy suggested they load up and go home. "It will be a little late getting home but I hate to spend the night and then have to drive home." They were all for it. They quickly loaded the horses and all the tack. Penny put her new saddle in Shirley's car. They followed Billy home. They pulled in about eleven o'clock and unloaded. They gave the horse's fresh water and fresh hay. Penny got her saddle and luggage out of Shirley's car and headed home. She had a key to the house but her mother heard her drive in the yard and heard her at the door. She said, "Penny, is that you?" "Yes mother." Earlene opened the door and they visited a while before Penny hit the shower. She said, "I am too nasty to go to bed like this. I have to shower."

She told her mother she won over $400.00. "That is more money to go in "my bank," Penny said. Plus she still had the money coming for her work at the barn and the time she spent at the horse show. "Mother we will have a good Christmas and we won't be hungry this winter. By the way Thanksgiving is coming up and Smith will be home. I wonder if we can invite Smith for Thanksgiving dinner we can get a turkey or ham or both and have a great dinner." Earlene said, "That is a good idea." Tomorrow is Sunday and they will be getting up and ready for church. Time is getting closer to when Smith will be home. In fact, next week. Penny made an appointment at the beauty shop to get her hair cut and washed. She is so anxious to see him. She wrote him a long letter and asked him about Thanksgiving dinner. He wrote back and said he would be there. He is due in on a Saturday afternoon and he told Penny he would be at her house at 6:30. They would go out and eat and then just be together. That makes Penny so happy.

She couldn't wait she is so anxious. Finally Saturday arrived. Penny was at the beauty shop Saturday morning. She missed the Saturday riding but she had already made it ok with Billy. Penny's hair looked so pretty and she had makeup on and a pretty dress. She is a beautiful girl. Smith was there promptly at 6:30. He came to the door and knocked. Penny opened the door and Smith said, "Penny just let me look at you. You are beautiful." Penny hugged him and gave him a big kiss. Smith visited with Penny's family then they left for Stuttgart for supper.

Smith is so grateful for Penny. He said, "Penny I want to marry you. I love you and I need you to be with me." Penny said, "I feel the same way Smith but we both know that is not going to happen anytime soon but I pray that someday it will happen." They had a good dinner and had a good visit. Smith told Penny what his days and nights are like. He wanted to know about the horse showing. Penny is excited to tell about that. She said, "I am very happy with the money I am winning but Mr. HB and Billy thinks I should show in the better classes. I am confident I will do ok."

Penny said, "Smith, I don't want to share you with anyone but my friend. Suzy Pugh and I have talked. She is coming to spend the night and I want to have a double date with her and someone who would like to date her. She is a very pretty girl with a good personality." Smith said, "I know her, I will ask Andy, my roommate, he is home and is not dating anyone. He is nice looking and a barrel of fun." "Good," Penny said. "When can you ask him? Smith said, "I will try and set it up for Saturday night." "That will be perfect." Smith said, "He can spend the night with me."

Chapter 20

Things had never been better with Penny she still had to ride horses after school and Smith would be coming by almost every night. Smith told Penny he had contacted Andy and he is all for the double date with Suzy. "We need to get the word to her." "I know she has a phone and Billy knows her phone number he calls her dad often." That afternoon Penny asked Billy for Suzy's phone number. Billy said, "I have a business card from her dad. I think I have it in my billfold. Let me look. I have a phone in my office if you want to you can call from there." Penny said, "I really need to talk to her." Billy showed her where the phone is and how to use it.

Penny called and Suzy answered. Suzy is surprised but glad Penny called. Penny said, "we have our double date set up for Saturday night. Can you come over Saturday afternoon and spend the night. Smith has you fixed up with his room mate. He is from Stuttgart. Smith says he is nice looking and a barrel of fun. His name is Andy." Suzy said, "I don't know how I will get there. We only have one car." Penny said, "don't worry I will come and get you, Smith might come with me and we will take you home on Sunday." Suzy said, "Penny I hate for you to have to do that but I really need to get out with friends.' Penny said, "I will be at your house at 2:00. Smith and I are looking forward to it."

Penny rode horses Saturday morning and she contacted Smith by phone and he would be a Penny's house at 1:00 they would take his car. Penny finished riding about 12:00 and hurried home and cleaned up. She ate a quick lunch and is ready when Smith got there. She met Smith at the door and gave him a big hug and a kiss and an "I love you."

They had a good visit on the way to Suzy's house. Her house is just outside of Stuttgart. They drove into Suzy's right at 2:00. Suzy is ready. Suzy spoke to Smith and wanted them to speak to her mother, Sissy. They visited with her for while and promised to take good care of Suzy and have her home Sunday afternoon. Sissy said, "you all have a good time and be careful." Smith told her about Andy being his roommate at school. He said, "we will have a good time. We are planning on going to Little Rock and eating a good meal and going to see a good movie. It may be a little late when we get back to Penny's house but they can sleep late in the morning." Sissy said that sounds like fun.

On the way back they all had a good conversation. When they arrived at Penny's house Smith helped carry her clothes in. Smith said, "I need to go and we will see you two at six o'clock." "We will be ready."

Penny introduced Suzy to her mother and Missy, her dad is working and James Jr. is with him. Suzy said, "Penny you have a nice house." "It is almost brand new. You should have seen our old house it wasn't too good." Suzy had heard how poor her family was when they moved on to the Silver Leaf. She knew Penny is proud of her new house and her new life. Penny and Suzy walked around the headquarters, she showed her the farm office where she works some and they walked over to the farm shop where her dad and James Jr. were working. She introduced Suzy to them. Penny's dad said, "Suzy I have heard lots of good things about you. Thank you for being Penny's friend. She loves you very much. Suzy said, "I love Penny very much."

They walked to the gin and went in the office. Larry is there working his dad had the day off. They visited about school and Larry told them what he was doing. Penny said, "she would see him after school Monday." Suzy said, "Larry seems like a nice person." Penny said he is nice and smart too. I think Smith is a little jealous but he has nothing to worry about.

They walked around some more Penny walked her by Ms. Ruth's and they went in and said hello and told her what their plans are. Ruth spoke to Suzy and said, "Suzy it is good to see you." You all have fun and be careful."

"We will and thank you" Suzy said. Penny said lets walk over to the store and get us a cold drink. They walked in and Mr. Beavers said, "Hello Penny who is your pretty friend?" Her name is Suzy Pugh from Stuttgart. She is spending the night and she and I are double dating with Smith and a friend of his. "Good for Smith and his friend I know they will be happy to show you two off." "Aw Mr. Beavers you are too kind" they got their drinks and went outside in the shade and drank them. There is a good breeze and they enjoyed being outside in the shade.

Soon it was time to walk back to Penny's house and get ready. Penny let Suzy shower first and use her hair dryer. Penny said, "Suzy do you have everything you need?" Suzy said, "I will know in a few minutes." They took their time getting dressed they both were in their underwear. They put their makeup on, they helped each other get it on. Then the perfume and finally the finishing touches to their hair. Then their clothes. Penny had been saving one of her outfits just for this special occasion. Suzy had a new outfit too she looked gorgeous. Andy is going to be surprised.

They were almost ready when Smith and Andy drove up and knocked on the door. Missy answered the door. She spoke to Smith and Smith introduced Andy to her. Missy said, "I will check on the girls I know they are about ready. Finally they came out. Smith introduced Suzy to Andy. Andy's first words were "will you marry me?" Suzy got a laugh and said "only if you are rich." They all laughed. They visited a minute or two and Smith asked if 'they were ready?" "We are." Suzy and Andy got in the back seat. Andy said Suzy, "do you remember me?" Suzy said, "I do not." Andy said, "remember when we all went to the movies on Saturday afternoon and there was a kid that had braces on his teeth and talked with a stutter and bugged you every time he saw you?"

Suzy said, "don't tell me that was you." "Yes it was and I told everybody I knew that you were my girlfriend." "My goodness Andy you really turned out good." She got a laugh out of that. "It is so good to see you. Now we have things to talk about." Andy said, "I won't even mention your freckles." "Oh no" Suzy said. Penny asked Smith why he is going this way. He said we are going by Granny Ruth's house. She wants to see us and take a picture. They parked near the back door and Ruth's motioned for them to come in. she said "you girls look darling" I have to have a picture of you all. She took three pictures. Penny looked so good with her new haircut. She hopes things work out for Penny and Smith. Ruth thought she just couldn't bear losing Penny as a friend.

They left for Little Rock and Smith knew just the place or them to eat. It is a little pricy but they all deserved it. It was such a good meal. They got to the movie just in time and it was one that made the girls cry. In the middle of the movie Penny whispered in Suzy's ear. "Suzy, I need to find a horse trailer." Suzy burst out laughing. She said, 'Come on Penny I will hold your horse. Then Penny burst out laughing. It was such a good time everything seemed perfect.

They drove back to Penny's house and the boys walked them to the door.

Smith gave Penny a big kiss and hug. Suzy told Andy, "you get one shot at a good night kiss so don't screw it up." Andy said, "I won't." He gave Suzy a long passionate kiss. Suzy knew he likes her. She said "good night Andy, I really enjoyed the evening it was fun. Call me sometime." Andy said, "hey wait a minute. I am going back to Stuttgart tomorrow, would you ride with me and I will take you home?" Suzy said, "well it would save Smith and Penny a trip. She said what time are you going? Andy said, "how about eleven o'clock and we can eat lunch before I take you home?"

Suzy said "Andy, you got a deal. Be here at eleven" Andy said you can count on it. Penny and Smith were glad they liked each other. Smith and Penny said goodnight. Smith asked if he could come over when Andy picked Suzy up. Penny said, "you know you are welcome here anytime." "Good. I will see you at eleven and we will go to Lonoke for lunch."

Penny and Suzy were two happy girls when they came inside. Everyone in the house is asleep so Penny and Suzy went in Penny's room and closed the door. They talked a long time before going to bed. They were sleeping together. When they laid down they gave each other a big hug and a kiss. They both slept soundly. It was after nine o'clock when the got out of bed. Earlene had them some breakfast fixed. They told Earlene about their dates. Earlene said, "It sounds like fun." Both said, "it was." Penny told her mother that Andy is coming by for Suzy they both live in Stuttgart and Smith is coming by we are going to Lonoke to eat lunch.

Sure enough Andy is on time he put Suzy's luggage in his car. He opened the door for her. Suzy got in and sat close to Andy. Andy liked that.

Smith is right behind he and Penny were on their way to Lonoke. Smith and Penny were together the rest of the day and Smith stayed at Penny's house and kept her company. Earlene had a good supper.

Penny hated to go to school but they only had two days this week then they would be out for Thanksgiving. Next day Penny is working a horse when Smith drives up. He gets out and sits on the arena fence. Penny rode by and spoke. She said, "I will be through in about an hour." Smith is impressed with the way Penny sits a horse and the way she handles it. Penny is a little anxious about what HB had told her about showing in the more competitive classes. Peppy is good but not good enough for the bigger classes. Penny is working on doing more on the exhibitions. She might get a place in some of the shows and that will help.

She asked Billy if she could ride Brown and give him more work. Penny believes he is a winner. He is so strong and agile. Billy is not sure. Mainly he thinks he could win on him but he has Roany and Pete and Blaze. That will have to be worked out. Penny needs a good horse for the non pro and open classes. She can show Peppy in the Novice classes which she can win. The monthly shows are good but nothing like the show in Jackson, Mississippi is going to be. If she does good there HB might let her go to more of the big shows especially this summer.

That part will have to wait; Penny's focus is on Smith. She wants as much time with him as she can get. So far things are good Smith will spend the day with her on Thanksgiving Day. After he goes back to school she won't see him any more until the Christmas holidays. That is a long time away from him.

After she was done working the horses Penny invited him home with her and waits while she showers and dresses. Smith wants Penny to go with him to visit his parents and when he brings her home he will spend the night with Granny Ruth. Penny is out of school and they can be together the next day until Penny has to go ride. Penny is looking forward to that. While Penny was dressing Smith visited with Missy and Earlene. They had a good time visiting. Smith found out Earlene has a good sense of humor. He noticed how pretty she is with the new haircut and some of the stress off her mind. Smith is happy for her and Penny. Missy is a cute girl and will break some boy's heart. She likes Smith mainly because Penny has talked about him so much.

Penny enjoyed the visit with Smith's mother and dad. Mary had fixed a good supper. They stayed until almost 10:00 then headed for Granny Ruth's. Smith stopped at their favorite parking place. They hugged and kissed. Penny is somewhat aroused. So is Smith. Penny said, "Smith, when we do it the first time it won't be in a car." By then Smith had lost it in his pants. He said, Penny I just went off.

I am sorry. Penny said, "That might be a good thing. At least you won't go to bed hurting."

That cooled things off. Smith said, "I will see you tomorrow at the barn." Penny said, "Good, I am planning on working Peppy on cows and on our exhibition. She is getting really good." Smith said, "I have to see that. I have never seen anyone do that before."

Smith took Penny home and told her again and again how much he loves her. Penny returned the compliment. She said, "Smith I pray for you every day, I do hope someday we will be married and have kids and raise them here on the Silver Leaf." Smith said, "That is my plan."

After school Penny dropped Larry by the gin and went home to change into her riding clothes. When she got to the barn Smith was already there. They visited and Penny got Peppy out of her stall and brushed her off. She had the halter on her and rode her in the arena a while to warm her up. Then she reached up her neck and pulled the halter off. Penny worked her slow and worked on the side passing. Peppy caught on quick. Penny then put her in a canter and rode around the arena and did some sliding stops and spins. Then she rode in circles and figure eights. Smith could not believe what he was seeing. He had never seen that and Penny rode by and asked if he would like to see her cut a cow.

"Of course," Smith said. Penny did as always she eased Peppy in the herd and cut one out. It worked really well. Finally it ran off. Penny came riding over to Smith and said, "I think that is enough for today. I need to work her on cattle." Billy rode up and asked Smith what he thought. Smith said, "If I had not seen it I would not have believed it." Smith said, "Wonder how she controls the horse?" Billy said, "I have no idea and Penny won't tell me."

Billy asked Penny to saddle Peppy and work her on a few head of cattle.

She did and Peppy did well. Peppy will do anything Penny asks her to do.

Smith is very impressed with Penny.

Work went on until dark, Penny asked Smith to come by her house for supper. He said, "Are you sure it will be ok with your folks?" "Sure it will." After Penny was finished Smith followed her home. Penny went in and told her mother Smith would be eating with them for supper. Earlene said that is good I just cooked lots of fried chicken. Earlene can really cook and the meal was delicious. Smith had plenty to eat. They sat at the table and visited with Penny's family then went and sat in the living room.

Smith said, "Penny you are out of school tomorrow why don't we call Andy and see if he and Suzy can meet us for lunch?" "That would a fun thing, can you call tonight? Smith said I sure can I will call from Granny Ruth's house and let you know in the morning." Penny walked Smith to his car and they hugged and kissed and told each other how much they loved each other.

Penny went in and showered and went to bed early. Next morning Smith came by and told Penny, Andy and Suzy, "meet us in Stuttgart for lunch."

"That is good Smith we will have a good time. Remember I have to be back in time to get the horses rode."

"Penny, we can leave here at 10:00 and meet Andy and Suzy at 11:00 and visit a while before we eat lunch." Penny agreed with that. Smith was at Penny's right at ten they took their time driving to Stuttgart. They met Andy and drove to Suzy's to pick her up. On the way Andy said he is falling for Suzy, "She is so sweet and a caring person, pretty too, and a personality to top it all." Penny said, "You are right about that, she is my friend and I love her too."

They drove up to Suzy's house and Andy went to the door. She came out and gave Andy a hug. They held hands as they walked to the car. Penny whispered to Smith, "Do you see that? Smith said "yes I do I believe Andy is in love." Penny said, "I am glad for Suzy she deserves a good person." Andy opened the door for Suzy, she liked that. Once in the car Suzy spoke to Penny and Smith. Smith asked, "Where do you guys want to eat lunch?" Andy said, "You pick the place Smith, you are driving," Smith said, "Let's drive over to

Clarendon and eat catfish at the fish restaurant on the White River." They all agreed. Penny and Smith noticed Suzy and Andy sat close together on the way over. They were talking about Andy's family. Andy said, "My dad is a Doctor and Suzy's mother used to work for him. Now she is a Registered Nurse and works at the hospital. So we have something in common." Andy said, "I might become a doctor but I haven't made up my mind yet.

Smith drove onto the parking lot at the fish place. It is a little crowded but they were in no hurry. They got a table overlooking the river it is a pretty view. They all had the catfish with French fries and slaw and hushpuppies. A typical southern dish. It was good and they all ate all they could hold. They had a good visit while they ate. Andy invited them to his house to play some pool. It is a big nice house and a good play room. Smith and Andy played pool and Penny and Suzy talked, privately. Suzy said, "Andy is so sweet and thoughtful, I really do like him but he will be going back to school next week with Smith. I won't see him again until Christmas. I don't think I can wait." Penny said, "I know what you mean but I have committed myself to waiting on Smith."

Suzy said, "Andy did mention that he might leave school at semester and come back home if he and Suzy were to start going steady. I wouldn't push him into that I know he will go off to college and be gone a long time. I know I could fall in love with him and maybe I already have but I need someone who is close and not gone all the time."

Penny said, "Suzy I understand but you will be out of school soon and maybe something will work out." "I know, maybe I am just being selfish but I do not want a long distance romance," Suzy replied. At least Suzy knew what she wanted. Maybe things will work out for her and Andy.

Smith and Penny left in time for Penny to ride her horses. Smith dropped her off at her house. Penny kissed him good bye. Tomorrow is Thanksgiving Day and Smith asked what time should he come. Penny said, "Around mid morning if that is ok." Smith said, "See you then."

Penny drove her car to the horse barn. Billy said, "Penny why don't you bring Brown out and give him a workout in the round pen then you can cut a few head of cattle." "Fine", Penny said. She got him out of his stall and saddled him up. She brushed him off then took him to the round pen. He is fresh and had a lot of buck in him. After while he settled down and Penny rode him into the arena. She turned him around and made him back up and spin. He is so athletic Penny thought.

She worked three cows on him and he did an excellent job. Penny had to stay after him a couple of times with her spurs to keep him from loafing. Billy was watching and said, "Good job" Penny. After that Billy worked Pete and Roany and Penny worked Blaze. They all did well. They talked about the next monthly cutting; it would be at Suzy's dad's barn and arena. Penny is looking forward to that.

They rode the new horses in the arena and Penny rode one around the big field. They rode until dark and Billy said, "No riding tomorrow, enjoy the day with your family and friends." "Thanks," Penny said. "See you Friday."

Penny and her mother were up early preparing the Thanksgiving meal. They enjoyed working together in the kitchen. Penny said to her mother, "Guess we will get to tryout the new stove today." Earlene said, "I know it cooks just fine. This will be a good meal. Penny and Earlene stopped and cleaned up and changed into some good clothes before Smith arrived. Earlene told Missy and James Jr. to put on good clothes. James did the same. Smith arrived right on time he sat in the kitchen while Penny and Earlene put the finishing touches on the Thanksgiving dinner. After a while Earlene told Penny to stop and visit with Smith. She is happy to do that. They walked outside and walked around the neighborhood. They held hands as they walked.

Thanksgiving dinner is at the Parks family's home. Earlene and Penny cooked up one of the best thanksgiving meals Smiths said he has ever eaten. Earlene's turkey and dressing is out of this world.

She learned to cook it from her mother from a very old recipe. It is Penny who delivered the Thanksgiving Blessing it was touching. She said this family has so much to be thankful for. Smith stayed until the middle of the afternoon. He is headed back home. His folks were having friends over for supper. He told Penny he would see her tomorrow on Friday. Smith told her how he had to go back to school on Saturday because he had some studying to do before Monday.

Penny and Suzy were two happy girls when they came inside. Everyone in the house is asleep so Penny and Suzy went in Penny's room and closed the door. They talked a long time before going to bed. They were sleeping together. When they lay down they gave each other a big hug and a kiss. They both slept soundly. It was after nine o'clock when they got out of bed. Earlene had them some breakfast fixed. They told Earlene about their dates. Earlene said, "It sounds like fun." Both said, "It was." Penny told her mother that Andy is coming by for Suzy; they both live in Stuttgart, and Smith is coming by we are going to Lonoke to eat lunch.

Sure enough Andy is on time. He put Suzy's luggage in his car. He opened the door for her. Suzy got in and sat close to Andy. Andy liked that. Smith is right behind. He and Penny were on their way to Lonoke. Smith and Penny were together the rest of the day and Smith stayed at Penny's house and kept her company. Earlene had a good supper.

Chapter 21

Penny helped her mother clean up the kitchen and put the leftovers in their new refrigerator. She and Missy got out and rode around the neighborhood and stopped and visited some of the neighbors. Missy had a good friend living on the farm and they stopped there to visit.

Next day, Friday, Smith came in the early afternoon. He asked Penny to go riding around. They just drove and talked after while Smith drove to one of the secluded places on the farm. He and Penny held on to each other. She could tell Smith is getting aroused. Penny said, "STOP!" Smith is shocked. He said "What's wrong, Penny?" She said, "You know what is wrong. I love you and I would like to go all the way with you, but I won't. I am sorry. If I have to do that to keep you then I will have to let you go. That would break my heart but I am saving myself for the man I marry." Smith said, "Penny, I just can't help it." Penny said, "You arouse me too, but I am determined. It is the right thing to do. I know there are other girls that would gladly give themselves to you, but I am sorry I just can't." Smith said, "Penny I love you and I don't mean to offend you, but I do need more."

Penny said, "Smith, I am sorry but I guess you need to do what you think is best for you. Just remember you are the love of my life and I want to be the one who marries you." Smith said, "Penny, I guess I should leave." "Don't do that Smith, please." They talked some more but Smith took Penny home and left for town. Penny is hurt but knew she had to stop it. Penny closed the door to her room and cried most of the night. This is going to be hard to get over but being the determined person she is she will get through it.

Penny is at the barn early next morning riding Peppy and practicing on her exhibition. She didn't see Smith drive up. He got out of the car and waved to her. She rode over and got off of Peppy. Smith said, "Penny, I know you are right and I am so sorry I acted like I did." Penny said, "I hope you can see it from my side. How would you feel if you married someone that had slept with every boyfriend she has ever had? Would you trust her? Smith, you can trust me every day as long as I live." Smith said, "Penny I apologize and I will do my best to behave myself but sometimes I just can't help myself."

He walked over to Penny and handed her a small box. "Open it Penny." She opened it and it is the most beautiful ring she has ever seen. Smith said, "It is a friendship ring. I hope I can replace it with an engagement ring someday." "Oh Smith I am honored, I love you more than anything. You have made me so happy." They held on to each other, Penny is sniffling. After a while Smith said, "Penny I need to go; just remember you can trust me too."

When Penny finished riding she drove to Ms. Ruth's and knocked on the back door. Ruth invited her in. Penny said, "I just had to stop by and show you the ring Smith gave me. He said it is a friendship ring." Ruth said, "Penny it is beautiful; congratulations." Penny said, "Ms. Ruth I thought I had lost him forever." She went on to tell her what happened, every word. Ruth said, "Penny you did the right thing. I know it will be hard for you two to be away from each other but hopefully things will work out. I am proud of Smith for apologizing. That was the right thing for him to do too."

"Thank you, Ms. Ruth. I am going home to show the ring to mother and Missy." Her mother and Missy were so surprised at the ring. Penny did not tell them what had happened. Penny ate lunch and went by the farm office to get her pay. She visited with Sue and Martha. They said things had been very busy but is slowing down. Penny likes to visit with Sue and Martha; they are fun to talk to. Sue gave Penny her check; it is for almost a hundred dollars. Penny signed it and Sue cashed it. They said good bye and Penny drove to the horse barn.

Billy would be there. Penny left the ring at home; she didn't want to take a chance on losing it. Billy told Penny to saddle up Brown and he said, "I am going to do something different and see how it works. Once we get through riding a horse I want to put a halter on and turn him loose in the round pen and be sure to close the gate. That will allow the horse to lie down and wallow. It is a natural thing for horses to do. They enjoy that. That will keep them from wallowing in the stall."

Penny gave Brown a hard workout. He wasn't paying attention and Penny is not going to let him get away with that. Billy said he is going to let Penny show Brown in the Non Pro and the Open classes at the December show. Penny would still get to show Peppy in a lower class. Billy said, "I want to start pointing him toward the Jackson, Mississippi show. He should be at his best by then." She is happy about that. She thinks Brown is going to be a winner. He just needs a winning rider. Good thing about it, Penny will get to keep all the money she wins on him.

Brown is a tall horse and has the look of a thoroughbred and has a beautiful head. He really looks good under saddle. Penny left the horse barn and drove by the gin. Cotton is still coming in but is slowing down. She spoke to Mr. Quick and Larry. They said everything is going well; they have ginned a lot of cotton. The cotton on the Silver Leaf is making a bumper crop. The price is good too. Maybe the yearly bonus will be good also.

Penny went home and looked around the yard; it needed some tending to. She and Missy picked up limbs and raked leaves and carried them to the burn pile. The yard is beginning to shape up.

Penny and Missy went in and cleaned up and put on their PJ's and house shoes. Both were tired.

Now everything is going good. Penny is working hard with the horses, and school will start back Monday. She has some studying to do. Time is passing. It is only a week until the December horse show. They will be ready.

The week passed fast and now it is show day. The weather is getting colder and harvest is coming to an end. Billy and Penny got the horses ready for the cutting show. They would leave about 8:00 the next morning. Shirley would go with them in the truck. Penny went to bed a little early. Next morning she is at the barn on time. She had her new saddle in her car. It would look good on the horses she is showing.

Shirley and Penny get along good, they are friends and Penny can trust what Shirley tells her. They loaded up the tack and the horses. It is not far to the show. As they drove into the parking area, Penny saw Suzy and waved at her. They would be together soon and talk. They tied the horses to the trailer and started brushing them. It would be a while before Peppy showed, and Brown would go in the next class after that. Once they were finished they went to the arena to see what was going on. The beginners were showing and Suzy is turning back for some of them. When Suzy was finished she came over and sat by Penny and Shirley. Both Suzy and Penny had lots to talk about but this is not the place or the time. It would have to wait. They talked about their horses instead.

Later, Penny and Suzy saddled their horses and rode around and talked. Penny told Suzy about the ring and what she and Smith talked about. Suzy said Andy is getting serious. Suzy wasn't ready for a steady relationship, especially with someone who is far away at school.

It is getting close to Peppy's time to show. Penny warmed her up good before she showed her. Billy had the turn back men in place and told Penny which cow to cut out first. Penny rode in as always and got the right cow. Peppy held her out and did a good job. The second cow worked better and Peppy had to get down and really work to hold it back. That was good. Peppy did what a winning horse is supposed to do. The third cow was good too but the horn blew before they really got anything done. When Penny heard the score she didn't think Peppy would win but might get a good place.

She rode Peppy around and cooled her out. Suzy thought she might win. Penny said, "It is going to be close." Peppy won by one point; which made Penny feel much better. She tied Peppy to the trailer and took the saddle off her and put it on Brown. She left him tied to the trailer until it was time to warm him up. Penny and Suzy continued their talk. Suzy said, "Penny I am proud of you for doing what you did with Smith. Sometimes it is hard not to give in." That is one reason I don't have a steady boyfriend. I am not giving in to them either. We are too young to be sleeping with every horny boy we go out with." Penny said, "Thanks, my feelings too."

Penny had to get her mind back to cutting. She got on Brown and rode him around until it is his time to show. Penny changed from one show shirt to another. Shirley helped her get her hair fixed and her hat on correctly. She looked so good on the horse. She didn't know it but HB and Ruth had arrived and were sitting by Shirley. Billy had the turn back helpers lined up and the announcer called Penny's name and Brown's registered name. She entered the herd the same way she always did. Brown is paying attention' his ears were perked forward watching the cows and waiting for Penny to tell him which one to cut.

Penny set the cow up in the center of the arena and dropped her rein hand. Brown went to work. He really felt good under Penny. He stopped the cow at every turn. The second cow was even better. The cow and Brown were head to head; in fact Penny couldn't quit the cow while it was working. The horn sounded and the crowd applauded. Billy rode out of the arena with Penny. He said, "Penny, you and Brown looked like a million dollars. I am sure you will win that class too. That is a tough class and the money will be good even if you just place." Penny said, "Thanks Billy; I could tell he was trying hard." Penny cooled Brown off and unsaddled him and put her new saddle in the truck so it wouldn't get stolen. She went to find Shirley, and saw Mr. HB and Ms. Ruth. She walked up and spoke to them. HB said, "Penny, you are the best cutting horse rider I have ever seen." Penny said, "Thanks! I am proud of myself. Three months ago I had never even petted a horse. Billy says I have more cow in me than the horses have."

Penny sat by Ms. Ruth. Ruth asked her if she is feeling better about her and Smith. Penny said, "Yes I am. In fact, I feel relieved to have that behind us. I don't care if Smith dates other girls. I might go to a party or somewhere where there are boys and Smith knows he can trust me if I do." Ruth said, "Good. I feel better too."

Penny stayed and watched the rest of the Non Pro class which she was in. It is a big class with some good horses. Penny is listening for the scores; so far she is in first. Billy came by and they waited for the class to be over. Billy said, "Penny, I think you are going to win it." Penny won by two points. HB went over and gave Penny a big hug. Penny said, "Mr. HB, I thank you for giving me a chance to ride and prove myself." HB said, "You have done more than prove yourself. In fact, you can legally show Brown in the non pro class and the open. You are going to make a lot of money." That sounded good to Penny.

The next class is the Open class. Billy is showing Pete and Roany. Penny is showing Brown. Penny wants to win but does not want to compete against Billy and HB's best horses. She told Billy she didn't feel right showing against him. Billy said, "Penny, forget that. Competition is good for us all. Get out there and do your best to win." "Ok I will." Penny said. Penny and Brown were showing in the first set of cattle. Ten horses show, then they will drag the arena and bring out a fresh batch of cattle. A rider will ride through them slow and get them settled before they show 10 more horses. She and Brown did a great job. Penny is well pleased with Brown but the cows were a little wild. She did not think she would place. Billy showed Pete and did a really good job. He thought he might get a place. Then he showed Roany and Roany did a super job. Billy thought he would place, too. Suzy's dad also showed and he and Billy were tied for first place on Roany. Pete was right behind them. This is a big class and has some of the best horses in Arkansas, Mississippi and Louisiana. Penny sat with the Hacketts and Shirley and watched all the class. Roany and Pete placed third and fourth in their class. Brown finished sixth and out of the money. Penny is happy with that. Suzy came over and told Penny goodbye and said, "I love you Penny." "Love you too," Penny told Suzy.

HB congratulated Billy and said, "We had a good day today. I am well pleased." Billy thanked him. Penny and Ms. Ruth were still talking when HB said, "Ruth let's go." Penny helped load the horses and the tack. They would be happy going home. Penny had almost $400 dollars in her jeans. Good money for a Sharecroppers Daughter she thought.

When the horses and tack were unloaded and put away, Penny left for home. It is dark by then. She went in and told her family how much she won. They were happy for Penny. Penny said, 'I promise you we will not go hungry this winter."

Things would get back to normal, church tomorrow then school and Penny is trying to keep her grades high. The gin will run probably for another two weeks then only gin a couple of days a week as long as there is enough cotton. Billy would work all the new horses while Penny is in school, but he would leave Peppy and Brown and maybe another that needs some attention. This would keep Penny sharp as well as her horses. She is still working Peppy on the exhibition. Peppy is improving every day.

It is not long until Smith will be coming home for Christmas. Penny is making her a Christmas list. She would buy for her family, Smith and something special for Ms. Ruth. She is already thinking about what she will buy. Maybe not clothes for her mother and Missy; Missy likes jewelry and makeup, although she is a little young for that. She will go see Mrs. Russell and ask her to make a special apron for Smith's mother and her mother. She will get her mother special soaps and shampoos to keep her hair looking nice. As for Smith, well, she doesn't know just yet.

She writes Smith every day and Smith writes to Penny every chance he gets. The days move forward; soon it is time for the Christmas decorations. The Parks family had never had a pretty decorated Christmas tree. They would go out and cut a tree and put what decorations they could make but never any Christmas tree lights. It would be different this year. Saturday Penny and Missy would go to town and buy Christmas decorations. Penny could have asked Ruth for some of her old ones but Penny wanted to have brand new decorations; something for the Parks family. They would buy some decorations for the living room and the front and back door.

Missy was so excited when Penny told her of her plan. They would go to Stuttgart where there is a big selection. Penny and Missy would have lunch at the seafood restaurant. Missy had never eaten this kind of seafood. Penny wanted her to enjoy herself. Penny told her mother of her plan and she thought it was a good idea if that is what Penny wanted to do.

Saturday morning Penny and Missy drove to Stuttgart and to a large store that sold Christmas decorations. Penny got a shopping cart and she and Missy took their time and bought Christmas tree lights, glass bulbs and small Christmas ornaments. They bought a beautiful angel to go on top of the tree. They were so pleased. They looked at wreaths for the front door and found a beautiful one that would be perfect.

They checked out and Penny paid in cash. She felt so good that she could afford it. They headed for the seafood restaurant. Missy had the best time trying to pick out what she wanted to order. Finally she settled on the seafood platter, mainly because that is what Penny ordered. Penny said, "I have had this before and it is really good. Save room for dessert; they have the best pie here you ever ate." When they were finished they were so full. Missy said, "That is the best meal I have ever had." Penny tried to show Missy about good table manners and said, "Missy, if you are with a boy you wouldn't order the highest price item on the menu. Find out what he is having and you get something about the same price or less. She gave her a good lesson and Missy appreciated that. It gave her confidence.

They drove home and unloaded the car and showed their mother what they bought. Earlene is getting into the Christmas season. They would get a tree next week and start their decorating.

The next week Penny, Missy, James Jr., and Earlene headed for town to pick out a Christmas tree. They were for sale on the square in Lonoke. The family looked at every tree and finally bought what they thought is the perfect one. Penny had bought a stand for it, one they could put water in to keep the tree fresh. After a while they were loaded and ready to head for home. They all sang Christmas songs on their way home; they felt good and were into the Christmas season. Once they were home they unloaded the tree. James put the tree in the stand and set it up. He is happy too. It made him happy to see his family so happy.

They couldn't wait until it is time to decorate it. James Jr. was a little sloppy with the icicles; Earlene had to show him the correct way to put icicles on a tree. Missy and Penny strung the lights. Penny wanted them to be just right. They turned on the radio and listened to Christmas carols as they decorated the tree. Finally it is time to put the angel on the top. They got James to do that, and it was just right. Earlene and Penny got a sheet, and made a very nice skirt for the tree. Now they were ready for the presents.

Ruth asked Penny to drive her to Little Rock to do her Christmas shopping. She told Penny she could shop too. Penny is happy about that. They went early Saturday morning and got there in time to get a parking place. Ruth knew they would all be full if they waited. This is the first time Penny had seen the "hustle and bustle" of Christmas. The stores and streets were so beautiful with all the decorations and lights. They bought so much in fact, they had to stop and make a trip to the car to unload what they had bought. Then they stopped at McClellan's and had lunch and rested a while.

It was getting late when Ms. Ruth said, "Penny I am so tired, are you about finished?" Penny said, "Yes, I just bought the last gift on my list." "Good," Ms. Ruth said, "Let's go home." They did stop at the barbeque place to load up on supper for their families. Ms. Ruth paid for all that. Penny protested, but Ruth would not be denied. When they arrived at Ms. Ruth's, Penny unloaded the car. She had her presents separate so they would not get mixed up. She thanked Ms. Ruth for the day and Ruth said, "Penny I appreciate you so much. We always have fun when we go out together." Penny said, "Yes we do; thank you." She gave Ms. Ruth a hug and said, "I love you, Ms. Ruth." Ruth said, "Penny, I love you too."

Penny loaded her presents in her car then drove home. Missy and James Jr. helped Penny unload the car. Penny gave them strict orders not to look in the sacks. Penny took all the presents into her room and locked the door. She was tired and wanted to rest some. Missy and James Jr. tried to get Penny to tell what she got them. Penny said, "I am not falling for that, you two will have to wait until Christmas." Penny got the barbeque out and fixed all their plates. They had cold drinks in the fridge. They all liked their supper.

Smith would be home soon and Penny wanted to get things ready for him. With Ms. Ruth's suggestions Penny bought his gift, actually three. She wanted him to be happy with his Christmas from her.

Next day was Sunday and church day. This Sunday the entire family went to church in the Parks car. It was a good Sunday. Penny treated them to lunch at the local restaurant that caters to the church crowd. Penny had spent a lot of money; at least for her it was a lot, but thankfully she had it to spend. She still had plenty left and would earn more. School is going to dismiss for Christmas this coming Friday. They would be out two full weeks. Penny is looking for time with Smith and her horses. There would not be any more cutting shows until the Jackson, Mississippi show.

School went fast. Penny is working the horses; every afternoon she is concentrating on Peppy and Brown. Penny is hoping to get asked to do an exhibition on Peppy. That would be some money she could count on. Penny got a letter from Smith saying he would be home Saturday. He had classes on Friday. He also said his mother and dad insisted he spend Saturday night with them. He would see her at church on Sunday and invited Penny to eat Sunday lunch with him and his family. That is good news for Penny! She would sit with him during the morning service. Earlene would drive the kid's home after church if James didn't go.

Saturday, Penny and Billy worked all the horses hard. They knew they would have some days off and didn't want the horses to lose any ground. Penny concentrated mainly on Brown. She knew if she won any money it would most likely be on Brown, but she is not counting Peppy out.

On Sunday, Penny couldn't wait to get to church. When they arrived, Smith is waiting. Penny got out and gave him a big hug and said, "Smith, I am so glad to see you." "Same here Penny." Penny walked in the church with Smith; they are in the same Sunday school class. Penny sat close to him. When Sunday school was over they only had a short time to talk. Smith told her about his trip home. Penny asked Smith if it is okay to ask Missy to sit with them. "Sure Penny; you don't have to even ask." Penny went and asked Missy to sit with them. Missy was sitting by herself so she was happy to join them.

When church was over Penny walked her family to the car and told them she would see them later on this afternoon. Penny enjoyed the meal with Smith's parents. They asked her about the horses and the picture that was in the paper. Penny said, "It seems to come natural to me. However, falling off a horse eight times in one afternoon might have had something to do with it, too." They all laughed.

They stayed at Smith's house until mid afternoon, and then Penny suggested she needed to go home. Smith said, "I am ready when you are." Smith and Penny were happy. Now, they had an understanding. Penny is not going to have sex with Smith. Now

Smith knows that. Penny is still the same girl that rode onto the Silver Leaf Farm in the back of an old truck. If he didn't have the respect he should have for Penny then, he does now. He knows she is independent and can sure get by without him. Other boys would love to go out with Penny. Penny thinks Smith's parents also have new respect for her now.

Chapter 22

On the way home they talked about their plans for Christmas. Smith said they are having a Christmas party at the Country Club on Wednesday night starting at 6:30. He asked Penny to go with him. "That will be fun," Penny said. Smith did stop at their favorite parking place and they sat and talked and hugged and kissed but Smith did not try to touch Penny. Penny appreciated that. Hopefully she had gotten her point across. Penny said Smith, "Let's go to my house." Smith, "That is a good idea."

"Penny, I almost forgot they are inviting 13 and 14 year old teens to the dance. Do you think Missy would like to go? I have a cousin that is 14 and I would like to ask him to come if Missy will go. It is not a date, but they can sit together." Penny said, "Oh what fun that would be, lets both ask her." They went in and asked Earlene if it is okay to ask Missy to go to the party. Earlene said, "If you two will watch after her. Penny said, "Mother, you know we will."

Penny called Missy from her room and Smith asked her if she would like to go. He told her about his cousin he said he is a nice young man, and cute too. Missy's face turned a little red; she is embarrassed. She said, "can I talk to Penny in private?' "Sure you can. Let's go in my room." Missy said, 'Penny what do I do? I don't know anything about going to parties and boys and dancing. What would I wear?" Penny said, "Leave all that to me. I went through the same thing and I went and asked Ms. Ruth about it. I will teach you all you need to know. I will teach you how to dance too. I want to see you on the dance floor having a good time." Missy said, "Okay Penny, if you will teach me." "Good" Penny said. "Let's go talk to Smith."

Missy is excited, but a little concerned about meeting Smith's cousin. They went in and Missy said, "I will be happy to go with you to the dance. Tell your cousin he had better be nice. What is his name?" "His name is Tanner Smith. He will be a good boy. If he is not, just tell me and I will take him home." Now Missy is happy, but still a little nervous about it. Smith said we will pick you two up at six o'clock Wednesday night. Missy said, "So soon?"

"Yep, Missy you will have a real good time."

After Smith left Missy said, "Penny what am I going to do?" Penny said, "I tell you what you are going to do. Just be yourself and speak to the other kids and introduce yourself. Here let me show you." They practiced on that for a while. Penny schooled her on how to approach the punch table where all the snacks would be. Missy is a little more comfortable. Penny said, "I want to see you talking to the others, especially Smith's cousin. I want to see you laughing and I want to see you dancing, even if you have to ask Tanner to dance with you. It is just a party. If anybody makes fun of you or is not nice to you, I want you to come get me immediately. Nobody will do that but you never know. Don't you worry one bit about that." "Okay," Missy said. "Now teach me how to dance. Slow dancing and fast dancing."

They got their old record player out and worked on dancing. They would do more the next day. Penny said, "Missy, talk to Mama and get your clothes ready. We will do your hair on Wednesday you will be the cutest one there. Promise me you will have fun."

"Missy, get out that old jig record we used to dance to. You know the jig dance grandma taught us." "Yeah," Missy said, "I had forgotten about that. Do you think we will do that at the dance?"

Penny said, "Maybe not, but I did it once and everybody went crazy for it. Somebody might ask me to do it again and if they do, you and I will do it for them. It will be fun. We are good at it. Smith and I will introduce you and Tanner around to the guests."

Penny felt so good about Missy getting to go somewhere like the Country Club. It would be good for her. She is so pretty and when she is dressed and fixed up she is a beautiful young lady.

Missy followed Penny around asking questions. Penny said, "Missy you know all you need to know. You just make up your mind that you are going to have fun. You will be the prettiest girl there so be confident. If you make a mistake, like spill your punch, just laugh about it. Do not take it seriously."

Penny is busy riding, but told Billy she would be taking Wednesday afternoon off to get ready for a party. Of course Billy did not mind. Wednesday morning Penny rode hard and got done most of what she needed to. She went home to get ready. Missy is so nervous. Penny said, "Missy let me see what you are wearing tonight." Missy had it all laid out. Penny said, "Missy that will look so good on you. Later on this afternoon we will wash and fix your hair. Check your shoes do they need polishing?" Missy said, "I did that this morning. They look fine." "Good," Penny said. "This is going to be a night we will talk about for years to come."

By the time Smith and Tanner were to arrive, Penny and Missy were ready. They both were so pretty. Smith and Tanner came to the door and Smith introduced Tanner to Missy. Tanner had on a new suit and looked good in it. Missy thought Tanner is a very cute boy. She already liked him. Tanner opened the door for Missy. "That is so nice of him," Missy thought. As they left, Smith said, "We have to go by Granny Ruth's and get our picture taken. It won't take long." "Good," Penny thought. She wanted Ms. Ruth to see Missy all dressed up. Ruth said, "Oh. All of you look so pretty and handsome. You girls will be the prettiest girls at the dance." Missy and Penny both thanked her.

Ruth took several pictures. By the time they reached the Country Club, Missy and Tanner were talking and laughing. Penny thought they would be just fine.

When they walked in, several of their friends to came over and spoke. Penny introduced them to Missy and Tanner. Someone asked Penny if she was going to do the jig dance again. Penny said, "I will if anyone wants me to. Missy might even help me." The party has a live band. It was a good band; they could play any style of music. Smith and Penny took Missy and Tanner over to the punch table and got them some punch. It was delicious. Tanner and Missy got settled in at a table with some kids she didn't know, and she did what Penny told her to do—introduce herself. It didn't take long before they were all laughing and talking.

After a bit the band started playing. It is the first live band Missy had ever seen or heard. The first song, no one got up to dance. Then about the fourth or fifth song, the dance floor is full. Missy could see Tanner is shy so she said. "Get up Tanner; you are going to dance with me." Tanner jumped up and said, "Let's go!" They got started off on the wrong foot but they both laughed and Missy said, "Let's try it again." In a bit they were dancing away. They didn't miss a dance.

When the party was nearing an end, the band leader announced he had gotten a special request for Penny Parks to do her jig dance. Everybody yelled and clapped and backed up around the dance floor. One of the band members got out a fiddle. Penny waved at Missy to come over. Missy did. Penny introduced her, "This is my sister. She is going to dance with me." The fiddle started playing and Penny and Missy put on a show. The crowd was so loud they could hardly hear the music. Penny and Missy were tired when the song ended. The crowd loved it. Missy couldn't believe she had done that. Now Missy had lots of friends.

On the way home, Missy and Tanner talked all the way home. Penny and Smith just listened. Penny did manage to give Smith one big kiss and hug. She thought she saw Missy giving Tanner a kiss. That is okay. When Penny and Missy got ready for bed, Missy asked Penny if she could sleep with her. Penny said, "Of course, I know you have a lot you want to talk about." Missy said, "Yes I do." Missy couldn't stop talking, she was so wound up. Finally Penny said, "Missy, it is time to go to sleep. We will talk more tomorrow."

"Ok, I am tired now. Thank you for the lovely evening, Penny. I will never forget it," Missy said, and drifted off to sleep.

Next morning Penny is at the barn early. She and Billy talked about what they wanted to do about getting the horses ready for Jackson. Billy asked Penny to ride Roany and Peppy. He is a little leery of letting Penny on a stud horse, so he would ride Pete. Billy and Penny are riding the outside horses. Penny is getting along very well with them. If they do well enough and the owner is willing to pay, they might show one of them at Jackson in the Novice class. However, the trailer will only hold six horses. It will be a load to pull. It might work out that the owner will pull his horse to Jackson.

Penny is also working on the exhibition with Peppy. HB called the Jackson show people and asked them about Penny and Peppy doing an exhibition. They had seen the picture of Penny and Peppy cutting a cow with no tack on the horse at all. They said they would if they could agree on a price. HB said it is $150 per performance, and she will cut a cow with no tack on the horse.

The show management later called HB and asked if Penny would do two exhibitions; one at the beginning of the show and one on the final night. HB asked Penny and she said, "I would gladly do it." That is money she can count on. They rode hard all day and quit about four o'clock. Penny asked Billy if it is ok for her to call Suzy. "Sure," Billy said. Penny called and spoke to Suzy and asked her if they might go on a double date again. Suzy is all for it, if Andy is. They didn't make any specific plans.

Penny is tired. She went home and showered and changed into her "dating" clothes. Smith would be coming by. Smith came about 6:00. Penny had not eaten supper yet. Smith said he hadn't either. They would go to Lonoke and eat. They had a good time talking.

Penny told him how excited Missy was to get to go to the party. She had a great time. Smith said Tanner really had a good time and hoped he could see Missy again.

They talked about their Christmas plans. He and his mother and dad would have a supper with HB and Ruth on Christmas Eve, and they would exchange their presents then. Penny said she wanted to spend Christmas Eve with her family. On Christmas Day Smith would eat Christmas dinner with Penny and after that they would go by Ruth and HB's to visit. Penny said, "Good! I have presents for them I can give them to them then."

Christmas is going to be on Monday this year. There will be Christmas programs at the church on Sunday. In the meantime Penny is obligated to ride the horses and get them ready for Jackson. Smith spent his days with his family and friends. He would come by the horse barn and watch Penny and Billy work the horses. Afterwards, Smith would come by after Penny got off work. Penny and Smith are getting along so well. She loves him and she knows he loves her.

One evening, Penny told Smith she would buy him supper if he would take her to Stuttgart. Smith said "Hey that sounds good! Why don't we call Andy and Suzy and see if they would meet us?" Penny is all for that. Smith called Andy who said he had a date with Suzy so they would meet Smith and Penny at the steak house. "All set. See you at six o'clock," Smith told Andy. This made Penny happy because she misses Suzy. They all had a good time eating and visiting. They sat in the restaurant until it is almost time to close. Penny told Smith she is paying for his supper. He protested, but Penny ignored him and paid for it. She is glad she could do it. It made her feel like she wasn't depending on someone else.

Penny sat close to Smith going home. Smith turned the radio on and they listened to Christmas music. Smith did stop before they got to Penny's house he held her close and told her he loved her. Penny told Smith she loved him too. Smith took Penny home and walked her to the door and kissed her good night. He said I will see you tomorrow, either at the barn or here. Penny said, "Smith, I can't wait."

Penny and Billy worked all the horses hard. They would not ride Christmas Eve or Christmas Day. Penny also worked on her exhibition with Peppy. When Penny arrived home there were two trucks parked in the driveway. They had Bell Telephone written on the door. Penny went in and found they were installing a telephone in their house. Earlene told Penny it is to be used for work. The farm needed a way to get in contact with her and her dad in emergencies. The family could use it in an emergency but needed to keep the line open for work. McKenzie is there watching the workers. It is a private line and that is good. The telephone is a dial phone.

McKenzie spoke to Penny and asked her how she liked working with the horses. Penny said, "Oh, I love doing it! We are doing good with them." She told him about going to the Jackson, Mississippi show in February. McKenzie said, "I saw your picture in the paper. Everybody was surprised but me. I knew you could do it." Penny thanked him for his confidence in her.

On Friday Penny baked a big batch of cookies for the gin crew and some for the farm office. She delivered them when she went by and got her pay check. It is close to a hundred dollars again. She took some of the cookies to the gin and told the old guys loafing there she brought them something. She sat the cookies down in front of them and hugged each one, wishing them a Merry Christmas. They all thanked her and began to eat them. She said, "Save some for Mr. Quick and Larry." Friday afternoon, McKenzie showed up at the Parks home with a cured ham. He said, "HB and Ruth do this every year. They give one to each family."

McKenzie also handed Penny a check and one to her dad. He said, "This is the Christmas bonus we promised if we made a good crop." Penny asked if she could open hers. McKenzie said, "Sure you can." Penny opened the envelope and there is a check made out to her for five hundred dollars. She let out a big yelp. She showed it to her mother and dad. She said, "Dad, open yours." James was reluctant to but he did. His is for $1,500. He almost fainted. He wasn't expecting anything close to that. He shook McKenzie's hand and thanked him. So many good things are happening to the Parks family. They are so thankful.

Saturday is the day before Christmas Eve. Penny would ride horses Saturday morning, and then Saturday afternoon her family, except James, would go to town and buy groceries for Christmas. Earlene had been baking pies and cakes for the family. She baked one for the Russell family and took it to them. They are still so sad about their son, especially this first Christmas season without him. It made Earlene cry.

Billy let Penny off early on Saturday so they could get to town. They had a good time shopping. Earlene gave Missy and James Jr. money for Christmas presents. They were good shoppers. They found some good presents for their parents and Penny. They bought lots of groceries for Christmas; they would last for a good while. Penny said, "I almost forgot, we need wrapping paper—pretty wrapping paper." Earlene said, "Yes, we do; where can we get it?" "I'll bet Sterling's will have some." They went by and they bought several patterns. It was beautiful.

Smith is coming by for a while. Penny had told him she needed to wrap presents. She and Smith talked while Penny wrapped her presents. They made plans for Sunday. They would go to church with their families and be with them on Christmas Eve as they had planned. Missy helped with the wrapping, except for their own presents. Missy is artistic. She made the presents she wrapped look so good. Penny is finding things out about Missy, all of them good. Missy is growing up.

The church service was so good. It was about the Christmas story. Penny sat by Smith and when no one was looking she would hold his hand. After church Penny lingered and visited with their church friends, wishing each one a Merry Christmas. Penny's family is ready to go home. She reached up and gave Smith a kiss on the cheek. Smith said, "I Love You". "You too; see you tomorrow for dinner."

They all were in a good mood going home. They were glad they went to church. For lunch they ate sandwiches with cake for dessert. They didn't mind; it was good. After the table was cleared Penny had more presents to wrap. They turned on the Christmas tree lights. It looked so good, and there were lots of presents under the tree. They all rested a while then cleaned the house getting ready for Christmas day. The radio is on. The Christmas music filled the house. It is one happy family.

Missy and James Jr. wanted to open the gifts that night but Penny had already talked to her mom and they agreed there would be no presents opened until Christmas morning.

It is finally Christmas Eve night. Penny and Earlene made punch and they had homemade candy and cookies set out on the table. They had scented cinnamon sticks on the stove. It made the whole house smell good. They finished the wrapping, and all the presents were under the tree. James Jr. and Missy were so excited; Penny and Earlene too. Earlene and James told them stories about their Christmases growing up. They only got an apple or orange, and maybe a little candy. Penny remembered those days, too.

Sometimes she didn't get anything. She is not going to let that happen to her family, never again.

Finally, Penny said, "I am going to bed, Mother wake us up early." "I will," Earlene said. Missy said, "Penny can I sleep with you again please?" "Yes, you can Missy," Penny kindly replied.

Missy and Penny talked. Missy is anxious to find out things she thinks she needs to know about boys. Penny talked to her very straight forward about letting boys get fresh with her. Penny said, "Do not let them touch you. I am saving myself for the man I marry. I hope you do the same." Missy said, "I will, Penny. I promise."

Finally Missy dropped off to sleep. Earlene had gotten up early and made coffee and hot chocolate and had fresh cinnamon rolls for them. James Jr. said, "Okay! It is time for the presents!" Earlene said, "James Jr., you can play Santa Claus and hand out the presents. Remember, when you hand one out you can't give another one out until that person opens the gift."

James Jr. is so excited. There were lots of presents and it took about an hour to get them all opened. Everybody is so thankful for what they got. James Jr. didn't want clothes; he wanted fishing and hunting stuff, which is what he got. Missy wanted clothes and jewelry, and that is what she got. Penny got blue jeans and shirts, which she is thankful for. She needs them to wear to school and work. Earlene got makeup and clothes. She is glad of that, too. She also got a fancy apron from Penny. James bought her a beautiful wedding ring; something she never had. She was so happy she cried. She got James some things he needed for work, which James appreciated. It is the best Christmas the Parks family ever had.

They picked up all the wrapping paper and put it in a sack. James Jr. carried it out to the trash barrel and burned it. They all put their presents away, and Earlene and Penny started fixing the Christmas lunch. Penny is anxious for Smith to get there.

As dinner was being finished, Smith came in and spoke to everyone. He asked James Jr. and Missy what they got for Christmas. They were anxious to show him their presents. Penny came in and gave Smith a hug and asked him if he is hungry. Smith said, "As a matter of fact, I was waiting until I got here to eat." Penny is pleased.

Later, Penny called them all to the table. She blessed the meal and delivered a passionate blessing. She prayed for all and for a safe trip for Smith. The meal was out of this world. Earlene had baked the ham the Hacketts gave them. It was so good. The table was loaded with meats and vegetables and homemade bread cranberry sauce and jellies and fresh butter. James Jr. had killed some ducks and Earlene fixed those with her special dressing. Everybody ate all they could hold. Smith said, "I thought the Thanksgiving meal was the best I have ever had, but I believe this meal is right up there with it." Earlene told everybody, "Save room for dessert." She had made two pies, one a pecan pie and the other a delicious pumpkin pie with topping. They were so good.

As the afternoon began to wear down, Smith asked Penny if she was ready to go to Granny Ruth's house. "Yes I am. I have presents to take. Will you help me get them in the car?" Smith helped load them; there were quite a few presents. When they arrived at the Hacketts, Penny and Smith took the presents in. Ruth and HB were glad to see them. They visited, and Ruth offered some Christmas goodies. "Oh, I am so full! But I have to try some." Smith said, "Me too." Ruth is a very good cook.

They sat and visited about an hour. Ruth said, "Smith, go in the bedroom and get the presents that are on the bed." He came back with an arm load. Penny said, "I will go get the ones in the car." They got them all together and placed them around the tree. Smith would play Santa. Penny had done a very good job shopping for the Hacketts. She gave Ms. Ruth a very nice pair of house shoes and a pretty gown. She had an artist friend of Suzy's to paint the picture that was in the newspaper of her and Peppy. She had a nice frame for it too. The painting was autographed by Penny with a message that read. "Thank you, Mr. HB, for letting me be a part of the Silver Leaf Cutting Horse Operation. Penny Parks."

When Mr. HB saw the painting he almost teared up. The painting is very good. It didn't cost all that much either. He said, "Penny, you have made me very happy. God bless you." Penny said, "You are very welcome."

Then it is Penny's turn to give Smith his gift. Smith is surprised that Penny had done so well shopping for him. She bought matching western shirts for herself and Smith, and she had gotten Smith a very nice tie, and a friendship ring much like the one Smith had bought her made for a man. This made Smith very happy.

Finally it is Smith's turn. He handed Penny a large package that is a little heavy. Inside was a beautiful western jacket. Smith said, "Penny this will come in handy this winter when you are riding." She said, "Smith, it is beautiful, thank you so much." She gave him a big hug. There were two more presents from Smith. They were not western clothes but something she could wear to school and to Church. Smith said, "Mother picked these out." "Smith they are so beautiful. I will enjoy wearing them. Tell your mother thanks."

Finally Ruth came out with one more present for Penny. When Penny opened the gift she found a brand new pair of dress cowboy boots. Penny could tell they were not cheap. "Oh, Ms. Ruth and Mr. HB! You are too good to me I love you both. I promise you someday you will be proud of me." "We already are Penny," Ruth said.

Chapter 23

Smith said, "Penny I think we should be going." "Ok," Penny said. "Good night Ms. Ruth and Mr. HB. Thank you for the presents they are so nice." "Thank you, Penny," HB and Ruth replied. Penny and Smith left for Penny's house, but stopped at their regular parking place. Penny is so happy. Smith is too. They held each other for a long time. Penny said, "Smith, I should be home." She gave him a big hug and a kiss and said, "I love you more than you will ever know." "I love you Penny."

Smith drove Penny home and helped her unload the car. Smith stayed a while then headed for home. Penny walked him to the car. Smith said, "Penny, I will see you tomorrow. Are you going to ride?" Penny said, "I will ride in the morning, but I will take tomorrow afternoon off if you will come by." Smith said, "I will; I want to see you." "See you tomorrow," Penny said.

Penny told Billy she was taking off in the afternoon. Billy said, "We will be finished by then." They rode hard and pushed the horses, and got a lot done. Smith came by and Penny said, "Follow me to the house if you don't mind." Smith said, "Penny, don't change clothes. I want to show you off just the way you are. Leave your boots and spurs on." They drove to Lonoke and had lunch, then back to Penny's house. Penny did shower and changed clothes. They sat together on the couch and Penny snuggled up to him. She did not want Smith to go back to school.

They stayed at Penny's until time for Smith to go home. They enjoyed just being together. Next day Penny is back on the horses. After work, Smith came over and they drove to Stuttgart to eat. They called Suzy and Andy. They met them at the seafood place. They had fun talking. Suzy is falling in love with Andy, Penny could tell. Andy is already in love with Suzy. It is going to be hard when Andy went back to school too.

The Country Club had a New Year's Eve dance planned, and Smith asked Andy and Suzy to come with them. Suzy would spend the night with Penny and Andy would stay with Smith. That sounds like a good time. It is only a few days away. Penny is working on the dress she is going to wear. She drove by Mrs. Russell's house and asked her if she could do some sewing on the dress. Mrs. Russell is happy to. It is going to be a knockout of a dress; a little shorter than it needs to be. It would show off Penny's beautiful legs and butt. Smith would probably be jealous. She made an appointment at the beauty shop to get her hair done in a style to fit the dress.

Suzy is going to wear something similar. She will be a knockout too. Penny went by and modeled the dress for Ms. Ruth and asked her if it is too short. Ruth said, "It might be on some girls but definitely not on you Penny. You look darling." Penny thanked her and gave her a hug.

Saturday after riding, she drove to Lonoke to the beauty shop. She asked her mother and Missy to go. They did. The hairdresser is the same one she had before, and she fixed Penny's hair. It is beautiful. The party is on Sunday night, New Year's Eve. Suzy and Andy showed up about 7:00 at Penny's house. Penny would ride with them to town and meet Smith at his house. This time it is Smith's mother who took pictures of them. She said she liked Penny's and Suzy's dresses. Both looked beautiful. Smith and Andy were proud of their dates. The Country Club would be packed. They had friends waiting on them and saved them seats at their table. Smith introduced Andy and Suzy. They were all laughing and talking and having a good time. In a bit the band started playing; it is a very good band. They all headed for the punch bowl. It is really good. Smith said, "Don't drink too much; it might be spiked."

They stood around visiting and sipping their punch. In a minute, Smith and Andy said, "Let's hit the dance floor." They danced almost every song. Suzy eased up to Penny and said, "Penny, I need to use the horse trailer." They both laughed. "I will go with you," Penny said. Suzy told Penny, "I like Andy so much! What am I going to do when he leaves for school?" Penny said, "I know how you feel, Suzy."

The dancing went on. It is almost New Year's Day. They all stood on the dance floor waiting for the count down. They wanted to be kissing when the clock hit midnight. Smith and Penny, and Suzy and Andy were all hugged up and kissing when the band started playing Auld Lang Sang. It had been a good night. Smith and Andy and the girls got in Smith's car and drove back to Penny's house. They sat in the car for a while and finally Smith and Andy walked them to the door.

Only one more day until Smith and Andy left for school. Penny and Suzy stayed awake talking. Finally they went to sleep and slept until 10:00 the next morning. Andy and Smith drove up in separate cars about 11:00. Earlene had coffee and homemade bread for them; it was all so good.

They had a good time talking about the party. They all were happy. Missy didn't miss a word. After a while, Andy and Suzy left for Stuttgart. Penny was sad to see them go. Smith stayed at Penny's until it was time for him to go get ready to go back to school. He and Penny walked out in the yard and holding hands. Penny told Smith she didn't want to see him go. Smith said, "I don't want to go but I have to. When school is out we will have all summer together." She is sad to see him go, but Penny didn't want to make it any harder on Smith. She kissed him and told him she loved him and always would. Finally Smith left for home and wouldn't see Penny until Spring break.

Penny sat on the porch and cried. She finally cried it all out. Next day she is back riding horses. It is cold and Penny wore the new jacket Smith gave her. Billy and Penny are getting serious about the Jackson, Mississippi show. Penny intends to win the Non-Pro class. She has two exhibitions to do there too. She is thinking she will not wear chaps, spurs or a hat. She thinks that will be better. She does want to wear one of her good show shirts.

School starts Wednesday. Penny will only get to ride after she gets home from school. The gin only operates when there is enough cotton to run a full day. All the other crops are out. It has been a very good year on the Silver Leaf farm. The pecan orchard has a bumper crop too and the price is high. The Lord has blessed the Hackett family.

Back into the routine, Penny had a feeling something is wrong with Ms. Ruth. After she got through riding, she drove by and told Ms. Ruth she has a feeling about her health. Ruth asked, "What makes you think that Penny?" "I don't know, but I do. Are you having problems again Ms. Ruth?" "Penny since you asked I am. I am going in the hospital for an operation to stop the internal bleeding I have, but you don't need to worry about me."

"I knew something was wrong. I could just feel it. I will be there with you and help take care of you." Ruth said, "I will be all right Penny. I will have plenty of help." "I know Ms. Ruth, but they won't take care of you like I will." "Penny you are so kind. Let's don't worry about it now." "Ms. Ruth, I will worry about you every minute, and I will be praying for you every day." The next week McKenzie called Penny into his office and said they took Ruth to the hospital last night. We haven't heard anything yet but I will let you know as soon as we hear." Penny tried to be strong. She asked McKenzie, "Which hospital is she in? McKenzie said, "She is in the Baptist hospital in Little Rock. My wife and I will be going up there, would you like to come along?" "Yes, I would," Penny replied. McKenzie said, "I will call your house and let you know. I will leave word with your mother if you are not there."

"Thank you." Penny replied.

The next morning early McKenzie said "they are going to operate on Ms. Ruth this morning. My wife and I are going up to the hospital. You are welcome to come along." Penny asked "when are you leaving, McKenzie said within an hour." Penny said, "I will be ready."

McKenzie and his wife came by to get Penny. McKenzie's wife's name is Carroll Ann. She is a big lady but very pretty. Penny sat in the back seat and was very quite on the trip to Little Rock. McKenzie and Carroll Ann tried to cheer Penny up. Penny appreciated it but just wasn't in the mood for talk. Once they got to the hospital McKenzie led them to the elevator. Penny didn't say but this is the first time she ever rode an elevator. She wasn't nervous about it.

They found Ms Ruth's room and Mckenzie knocked on the door. Mary came to the door and invited them in. Ms Ruth is sleeping, she was given pain medicine. HB and Mark were there. HB explained what happened. He said Ruth started hemorrhaging real bad. HB called the ambulance and the doctor. They came and brought her to the hospital. The Doctor will operate this morning. The nurses came and prepared Ruth for the operation. HB said the doctor told him he is going in and find where the bleeding is coming from. Once he finds it he will find a way to stop the bleeding.

It was about an hour before they came to get Ms Ruth. That was about mid morning. It is noon before the doctor came out and talked to the family. He told them he found the source of the bleeding and had to remove some tissue. He said Ms Ruth should be fine. This is a relief to all including Penny. Penny told Mr. HB she could come stay with Ms Ruth and take care of her. HB said, "I know you can Penny but we have a nurse coming to stay with her but you can come by anytime you want to and stay as long as you want. Ruth will be glad to see you. This made Penny feel better. The Doctor said there is no need in everybody staying Ms Hackett will not be awake for several hours and she won't feel like talking then.

Carroll Ann said let's go to the cafeteria and eat then check back. If she is still asleep we should go home and not be in the way. McKenzie and Penny agreed with that. Penny felt better going home and was in more of a talking mood.

Next day, Penny got up early and dressed for school. First thing after school she drove by the farm office and asked Sue if they had heard anything about Ms Ruth. Sue said I just talked to HB and he said she is awake and is doing fine. She will be home in a few days. Penny felt better. She went home and dressed for the horse riding. Billy asked if she had heard anything from Ms Ruth and she told him what Sue had told her. Penny got her mind back on the horses. She reminds herself each day she is going to win the Non Pro class in Jackson and maybe another one on Peppy. She is working on her exhibition too. Penny is in a zone, now she is determined.

Ms Ruth will be home in a few days. Penny will be there when she comes home. She will visit her every day until she is well, even if she misses school. Smith is not coming home unless Ruth gets worse. The Doctor says Ruth will get over this and be 100 percent well.

Penny writes Smith every day and is keeping up with her school work. She gets most of it done during the school day and does not have to bring much of it home. She still worries about Ms Ruth though.

In a few days Ms Ruth was home. Penny is there to meet her. She helped unload the car and get her clothes washed and put up. Ruth is glad to see Penny. Ruth knew she could count on Penny to tend to her needs. Penny is there but not in the way. Slowly Ruth got her strength back. She and Penny would go riding and do a little shopping. Penny would get the groceries she needed.

January is about gone and February is the show in Jackson. Penny is working hard. She has dedicated the show to Ms Ruth and Mr. HB especially the exhibition. The weather is cold but not cold enough to stop Penny from riding. They put blankets on the show horses to keep the long hair from growing. Peppy especially. Penny wanted her to look her very best. Penny is trying to pick out music to be played over the loud speaker as she is doing her exhibition.

Penny and Billy are at it everyday, one of the owners is thinking he will pull his horse to Jackson. There is not enough room in the Silver Leaf horse trailer. The horse is a good one, a mare, and might get a place in the beginners class. Penny will ride her if the owner doesn't object.

Ms Ruth is almost well by now and she and HB are planning to go to the show. Penny called Suzy and asked if she is going. She said probably not she doesn't have a horse good enough to compete but she is going to ask her dad if she can go and support Penny. Suzy's dad is taking two horses to show and he said Suzy could go and help him with the horses and support Penny too. Penny asked her to stay in the motel with her.

Penny is riding Brown in the Non Pro and Peppy in the Novice and maybe one of the new horses. Brown is doing good. He is getting stronger and is very athletic. He and Penny get along well. He is a beautiful horse and with the new saddle on he looks even better. Billy has Roany and Pete doing good too. They are looking to make some big money at the show.

As time for the show came closer Penny and Billy fine tuned the horses but didn't push them too hard. They wanted them fresh. Penny asked Billy what the plans were about leaving and when would they be back home. Billy said we will leave early Monday morning on the 24th of February and come home on the 1st or 2nd of March. Be sure and take plenty of clothes plus your show clothes. Shirley will follow me down in the car like we did going to Little Rock. If Suzy goes she can stay in the motel room with you. It is a long trip and we will be watching lots of cutting and riding our horses. You have two exhibitions to do. Penny said "I have been meaning to talk to you about that. I don't want to wear my chaps or a hat. I will put my hair in a ponytail and wear a show shirt. I am going to ask if they will play music over the loud speaker while I am doing my exhibition. I think that will be better. Since Peppy won't have any tack I don't think I should have any either." Billy said, "Talk to Shirley about that." She already did and Shirley agreed with her.

"Penny, you will get tired of being away from home but remember this is a job and we want to do our best and make some money if we can. Penny said, "Brown and I are going to win the Non Pro you can write that down. Peppy might get lucky and win her class too."

Penny asked her mother and Missy to ride to town with her. Penny needed a few things, mostly a large suitcase and a cosmetic bag big enough to carry her hair dryer, makeup and other necessities and a hanging bag. They went to the local department store and found exactly what she is looking for. She bought extra underwear, just in case, and two blouses. She found a bag for her boots and shoes. She thought she had everything she needed.

Earlene got everything ready for Penny. She would have enough clothes to last a week. All the clothes were good clothes and looked nice. On Sunday, Penny and her mother packed everything up. Penny is to be at the barn at 7:00 in the morning. They would load the trailer with all the tack they needed. They would only take enough feed for a few days. They can buy feed at the show. They don't have enough room to take a lot of feed. Earlene will drive Penny's car back home from the barn. She visited with Shirley while Penny and Billy were loading the trailer and wrapping the horses' legs.

Finally they were ready. Penny is a little nervous. She hugged her mother and said she would call her and let her know how she is doing. Earlene hated to see her daughter drive off and leave her. She knew HB and Ruth would be there and she knows Ruth will see after Penny. Penny waved as they drove off. It would take all day to get to Jackson. She and Shirley had a good time visiting on the way down. It will be the first time Penny will be out of the state. When Billy stopped to get gas, Penny and Shirley visited the restroom and stocked up on snacks. Finally, just before dark they pulled into the show grounds and found the barn where they would stall their horses. The horses were thirsty and hungry. She saw Suzy's truck and trailer, and would see her later. Shirley told Penny the motel is within walking distance to the coliseum where the show will be held. The motel has a nice large restaurant, so eating would not be a problem. Finally Penny found Suzy and she loaded her things in Shirley's car. They would go check in then eat supper.

Shirley went with Penny and Suzy to check in; she wanted to make sure the rooms were charged to the Silver Leaf Farm. Shirley got two keys to Penny's and Suzy's room. They were all tired and went to bed early. Shirley said she would meet them at 7:00 in the morning in the lobby of the motel. They would eat then go to the arena. Penny and Suzy didn't talk much except to say they loved each other. Penny asked Shirley to wake them up when she got up.

Next morning after breakfast they headed for the barn to help Billy. Suzy would help her dad. Penny didn't know what to expect. She went with Shirley to the check in desk and got a schedule of the events. She learned the show is to start at 1:00. That is when she and Peppy would do their exhibition. Penny got Peppy out and cleaned her up really good. She and Shirley dressed her up with ribbon in her mane. Penny put on one of her good shirts and shoes, no boots and no spurs. She had a good song picked out. It is a patriotic song dedicated to those fighting the Korean War. There is a good crowd, mostly cutting horse people. The announcer called attention the far end of the arena. He announced that Penny Park and her horse Peppy would do an exhibition.

As the music started Penny and Peppy entered the arena. Peppy came in at a gallop and Penny is waving both hands to the crowd. No tack on Peppy whatsoever. She looked so good running around the arena. Penny brought her to a sliding stop then did some side passes to the music. Peppy did not switch her tail. She acted like she enjoyed showing off. Penny looked so beautiful on Peppy. The crowd loved it. Peppy did some figure eights and some stops and backups. Fast spins to the left, then right.

The announcer asked if the crowd would like to see Peppy cut a cow with no tack on. Of course they did. Penny rode Peppy into the herd slowly and cut a good cow. No turn-back help; just her and Penny. Peppy pushed the cow out and locked up head to head. The crowd is screaming. Finally, Penny pulled Peppy off the cow then rode to the middle of the arena and, without getting off Peppy, bowed to the crowd.

Penny got off Peppy and trotted out of the arena, with Peppy trotting right behind her. The announcer asked the crowd how they like Penny Parks and her horse Peppy. They got a standing ovation. The announcer gave Penny's name and said they were representing Silver Leaf Farms from Lonoke County, Arkansas. HB and Ruth were in the crowd.

Billy was waiting at the gate with Peppy's halter. Billy said, "Penny, you just keep getting better at this. Peppy acts like she likes doing it. You are through showing for the day, except I want you to get the new horse out and ride him around and get him used to the crowd. First, go see HB and Ms. Ruth." Suzy was waiting for Penny. They put Peppy in her stall and went and found the Hacketts. Suzy said, "Penny, you did so good." "Thanks Suzy," Penny said. "Let's go find Ms. Ruth and Mr. HB." Suzy said, "Okay." They found them sitting by Shirley and the Hacketts congratulated Penny on her performance. HB is tickled.

They sat by them for a while and Suzy said, "I should go find my dad and see if he needs help." Penny said, "I will see you at supper." Penny also left to ride one of the new horses. She rode him for almost two hours.

Chapter 24

Penny is liking the new horse. She is pushing him to get better and not be lazy. She thinks she can win on him. She has his attention. He will do whatever Penny asks him to. She mentioned to Billy she thinks she can win the Novice class on him. Billy is all for Penny riding him but he will have to ask the owner. Billy did say that if she won she would only get half of the winnings. Penny left all that up to Billy. That night Billy called the owner and asked if he would like Penny to ride his horse. He wasn't sure. Billy said he needed to make up his mind soon as he had to sign him up tomorrow. He said, "Billy, why don't you go ahead and ride him. You have more experience." Billy said, "Okay."

Billy entered the horse and would ride him that afternoon. Billy had him ready when his time came. Billy rode him in the herd and pushed a cow out. The cow ran toward the fence and ran under the horses' neck and back to the herd. That ended that. The horse is done for the show. Billy hated it and the owner hated it. Penny never said, but she could see that coming.

Peppy is next to show. They would only take the top ten horses with the highest scores and they would compete in the finals. Penny had Peppy wound up and ready. She eased Peppy in the herd as always and pushed a cow to the center of the arena and dropped her rein hand. The cow started for the fence but Peppy stopped it before it could take two steps. It went the other way and Peppy headed it and the locked head to head. Penny quit that one and got another one just as good. When the horn blew Penny knew she would be in the top ten. She is leading the class. She cooled Peppy off and went back to sit with Billy and Mr. HB. HB called her down and asked her to sit by him.

"Penny, you have a good chance of getting a high place in this class. Good for you. What do you think your chances are in the Non Pro?" Penny said, "I am going to win it. There is no doubt about it. I have been pushing Brown for this a long time. He is ready." HB said, "Good for you Penny. You will have lots of money if you win." "I will, In fact, I will buy you a present when I win," Penny said.

The preliminaries will be held Wednesday and Thursday and the finals will be held on Saturday. Penny is set to ride on Wednesday. She kept Brown ready until time for him to show. Penny and Brown are ready. Ms. Ruth and HB are in the stands waiting. Finally they called Penny and Brown's names. The announcer said "next horse to work is Brown's Little Man, owned and shown by Penny Parks from Lonoke County, Arkansas." To be eligible Penny has to own the horse. HB took care of that detail two months ago.

Penny woke Brown up and rode into the herd, talking to him as they went. Brown eased a cow out and wasted no time in moving her away from the herd. Brown worked very fast and had the cow running in circles. Penny quit that one and got another just as good. Brown put the pressure on that cow and kept adding pressure. Brown is leading the class when the horn blew. No doubt in Penny's mind she would be in the top ten and in the finals. She cooled Brown off and put him in his stall and gave him water and hay. He went and sat by Ruth and HB. HB said "Penny what kind of present are you going to buy me?" He was joking of course. "Mr. HB, I am going to win the Non Pro. I know I have told you many times before."

HB said, "Penny do you want to ride him in the Open Class?" Penny said, "I would like to, but I do not want to compete against Billy." HB said, "I understand that."

Penny had two days before the finals. Both Peppy and Brown would be in them; Peppy in the Novice, and Brown in the Non Pro, and maybe the open. Billy would be in the Open with Roany and Pete. Billy hated he lost the Novice with the new horse. The owner wished Penny had ridden his horse. Penny still had the exhibition to do with Peppy, but her class would be over before she did the exhibition.

Suzy is helping her dad keep his horses ready. He is showing two horses in the Open Class. They are good, and with some luck they might win. Penny spent lots of time at the barn brushing Brown and Peppy and working them. It seemed like forever but finally it is time for Peppy to show in the finals. Penny looked good in her new riding outfit Ms. Ruth had bought her. She got Peppy ready and the announcer called their names. Penny took her time and cut a good cow. Peppy went to work. Peppy squatted down and held the cow to a standstill. The crowd is screaming. Penny got another and Peppy did the same. Peppy had dirt all over her when she was finished. No doubt Peppy is in the lead.

Now there is nothing to do but wait. Billy and HB thought Peppy might win. They had four more horses to show before the winner is announced. Penny had her fingers crossed. So did Ruth. With three more to go, Peppy is still in the lead; two more, then one more. This horse lost a cow, and Peppy is the winner. They all screamed and yelled, including Ruth and HB. They all hugged. They were all so happy. Penny is going to collect lots of money.

Saturday afternoon came and time for the Non Pro finals. Penny had Brown pumped up and ready. She is the last to go in the class. She had to beat 173 to win. She is ready. Brown rode in the cattle and got a good one. He pushed the cow into moving; when she did, Brown was on top of her. Brown was squatting down low just like Peppy did and didn't let the cow go anywhere. Penny got another, and Brown is working with all he had in him. The judges saw that too. When the horn blew Penny stopped Brown and they waited for the score. The announcer said, "Here is the winner of the Non Pro, Miss Penny Parks and her horse Brown's Little Man with a score of 175."

HB, Ruth, Billy and Shirley were so happy, they were yelling for Penny. Billy ran out and got Penny. It is time for the awards for the Non Pro. Penny won a big belt buckle and a brand new saddle plus a big check. The photographers took lots of pictures. Penny asked HB and Ruth and Billy to be in the pictures with her. They did. Penny asked HB if she could put the saddle with the trophies in his office. I already have a beautiful saddle and I would like to put this with our other trophies in your office. HB said, "Sure you can, but if you keep winning we might have to add on to the office." Penny laughed and said "I hope you do."

Since Billy is showing two horses in the Open Class Penny decided not to show Brown. She would sit back and pull for Billy.

The arena crew dragged the arena and got it ready for Penny's exhibition on Peppy. Suzy helped Penny and Shirley bathe Peppy, to get her all cleaned up for the exhibition. Peppy looked so good and shiny. Penny looked so pretty. She wore no boots or hat, just clothes that looked so good on Peppy.

The announcer called everybody's attention to the far end of the arena and introduced Penny and Peppy. He said they were representing the Silver Leaf Farm from Lonoke County, Arkansas. The coliseum is packed. Penny rode in on Peppy waving to the crowd with both hands. She stopped in the middle of the arena and did some side passes. The music is playing patriotic music in honor of the boys fighting in Korea. Peppy did some spins and sliding stops. She looked so beautiful. Peppy looked like she is doing some dances.

The announcer asked if anyone wanted to see Peppy cut a cow with no tack on her. Of course the crowd clapped and yelled. Penny eased her in the herd and got a good one and locked up head to head with it. There were photographers placed all around and they got plenty of pictures. Penny quit the cow and rode around the arena with Penny pointing to Peppy and encouraging the crowd to give Peppy a standing ovation. They did. Penny rode to the center of the arena and Peppy did a bow. Peppy never once switched or wrung her tail, which is amazing.

Penny then jumped off Peppy and asked her for a kiss. Peppy kissed Penny on the mouth. Penny then turned and trotted out of the arena, with Peppy trotting right behind her. The crowd is wild. So were HB and Ruth; Shirley and Suzy, too. So far, it is the best show the Hacketts have ever been to. Billy is waiting with a halter. He said, "Penny, I don't know how you do it." Penny smiled and said, "I am not telling."

Suzy and Shirley went to help Penny clean Peppy up, stall her and give her feed and water. Shirley and Suzy gave Penny a hug. They were so proud of her. Penny thanked them and hugged them back. They went and found HB and Ruth. Penny went straight to Ms. Ruth and gave her a big hug and said "I love you Ms. Ruth." "I love you too Penny." She gave HB a big hug and said, "I owe you a present Mr. HB." HB said "Penny, you have already given me the best present in the world."

Penny is glad to be through with her part of showing. Now it is up to Billy. He has two horses to get ready. Penny hopes he doesn't ask her to ride them. She doesn't want to get the blame if he loses. HB told Billy to get his own horses ready. Suzy is helping her dad. The show is winding down one more day. Finals of the Open would be Saturday, with semifinals on Friday. Billy had to make the top ten to qualify for the finals. The entire Silver Leaf staff hoped he would make it. Suzy hoped her dad would make it too.

Once the semifinals started, Roany would work in the morning and Pete in the late afternoon. HB and Ruth took Shirley, Penny and Suzy to lunch downtown at a very good restaurant. It is the best meal they had all week. They all had a good time. They went back to the arena and waited for Billy.

Suzy's dad is going early in the round. Suzy and Penny sat down in the first row so her dad could hear them. Her dad, Roger, is riding a very nice looking horse. He pushed a cow out and really did a good job cutting it, then another good job. Suzy and Penny thought he would make it to the finals.

Finally Roany was up and did a very good job. He might make the finals too. Pete's turn: He did a fantastic job and for a while was leading the round. When the preliminaries were over, Suzy's dad was leading, and Pete and Roany were in the finals.

The finals would not start until 7:00 o'clock. Everybody went back to their room and got ready for the finals. Penny wanted Billy to win but she also wanted Suzy's dad to do good too. They ate supper in the motel restaurant. They walked over to the arena and waited for the show to start. There is a lot of excitement in the air, and lots of good horses. Roany did a good job. Pete was a little better, but Suzy's dad was the best. He won the Open Class and won a saddle and a trophy and a big belt buckle and lots of money. Suzy is so excited. Roany finished fourth and Pete finished third. It was a good payday for all. HB and Ruth took them all out for supper in one of the finest restaurants in Jackson. They invited Suzy and her dad. They were their friends.

Next day they got up early, loaded up and left for home. It is dark when they got home and got unloaded. Penny couldn't wait until she got home and saw her family. Shirley drove Penny home. She is so glad to see them. She told them what she won and about her exhibitions. She showed them the checks she won. She got $300 for the exhibitions and $600 for winning on Peppy and $1200 for the Non Pro and she told them about the saddle and trophy and belt buckle she won. Over $2,000; and it is all Penny's and her family's. Plus, Penny would get paid for attending the show in Jackson which is over a hundred dollars.

Earlene and James were so proud of Penny. All that money went in Penny's "bank." Penny couldn't wait to write to Smith although she knew his family had already called him with the news. She knew

Smith would be proud of her. Monday, Penny is back at school. Her picture was in the state and local paper for winning the cutting horse show. No more shows until spring. Penny was sure HB would let Penny show in some of the bigger shows in the nearby states.

There is still a lot of riding to be done. New horses were coming in to be trained and Penny would get to help with them. Billy would do most of the training. Penny could ride and make some money. Penny is getting better all the time. Spring is coming and HB is thinking of breeding Peppy to Pete. If he did, that might limit Peppy's exhibitions and cutting. Penny would still have Brown, and maybe Mr. HB would buy a new horse.

The horse business has to change. If Peppy is bred, then there would be more mares to be bred to Pete. Brown is going to be the money horse for Penny. He is still young and getting better and stronger. This summer Penny might get to get on the road with Brown and show him for the National Championship. The problem is he is a gelding. Maybe they could sell him for a lot of money. Penny still is in love with Smith and that is important.

Penny still needs to make money and the horses can earn her the most money. Penny needs to go to school. Smith will be home for Spring Break, and Penny and Suzy are the best of friends. Every chance she gets, Penny drives to Stuttgart and has lunch with Suzy. They love each other too. Things will work out.

Penny is growing up. She is older than her years; she is in her last year of high school. Smith will be going off to college. Penny is not sure if she can hold on to Smith or not. She has a life to live and she cannot let Smith own her. She might go off to college herself. She will discuss this with Ruth and HB. She would like to go to an Agricultural College and work for the Silver Leaf Farm. Penny knows the farm and knows what has to be done to make it successful.

She will continue with the horses and make lots of money with them. Her family is getting older too. Missy and James Jr.

are growing up. That is nothing to be sad about. Missy is an honor student at school. James Jr. wants to be a farmer. "God is good."

Time is moving along Penny is in a routine now: school, horses, family, church, friends and Suzy. Suzy is in the same zone too. She is growing up, same as Penny. Smith and Andy will be home soon. They will date. They are in love, but Smith and Andy do not own Penny and Suzy. Penny and Suzy will date two friends they met at a party. In fact, Suzy has a birthday coming up soon and her mother is going to have a party for her at the Country Club in Stuttgart. They both know they will be meeting boys. Penny and Suzy will double date if the meet the right boys.

Penny knows Smith is dating and has not questioned him about that. Andy knows it and told Suzy. Penny is riding the new horses that are arriving. In fact, Penny is the reason some of them are there. The owners like the way she handles them. Penny still gets paid every Friday same as always. She is a very hard worker.

Penny's pay is coming from the Hacketts although the horse owners are paying Billy to ride their horses. When the owners found this out, they contacted HB and told him they had rather be paying Penny to ride their horses. HB needed to work this out with Billy. Penny works hard, and her dad works harder than anybody on the Silver Leaf Farm. Penny's "bank" account is growing every week. She might have enough money saved up when she finishes high school to pay her way through college. Penny is very smart; she hardly has to study to make the high school honor roll.

Spring is coming. It is early March and the tractors are in the fields getting ready for another crop. There is lots of land to be plowed. HB and McKenzie decided to buy all new tractors; tractors with lots of horsepower. This would cut down on the labor force and get rid of all the mules used on the farm and all the mule drawn equipment. The big barns would be torn down or used for storage.

All this meant more responsibility for Penny's dad, James. He asked for, and got, more shop equipment and built on the farm shop. James also hired two more mechanics to keep the equipment running. The John Deere dealership in Lonoke offered James much more money than the Silver Leaf is paying him to work for them. James talked to McKenzie and told him of the offer. McKenzie matched the offer, plus an increase in the annual bonus. James is a smart man that means business.

Billy is thinking of leaving the Silver Leaf as the horse trainer. He has been offered a good job but HB told him he ought to take the job if he thought it is better than the Silver Leaf Job. Penny likes Billy and Shirley but didn't care if he stayed or went somewhere else. As long as Ms. Ruth and HB are living, Penny will have them on her side. She loves them and they love her. Mary and Mark like Penny, but still do not think she is good enough for Smith. Smith could end up with someone not nearly as good as Penny.

Mr. Quick has been retained as the gin's office manager. He is a very bossy man that wants everybody to know he is in charge. He also knows not to boss Penny Parks around, at least if he wants to keep his job. McKenzie is a little older, and HB hired him a man to be his assistant but he will take orders from McKenzie. Whatever McKenzie says, is the way it is. He is the boss and everybody on the farm knows it.

This Saturday Penny is driving to Stuttgart to spend the night with Suzy. They will eat supper in town and go to a party at one of her friend's house. It will be a good time. Penny is still writing Smith but only about twice a week. Smith is not writing her as much either. Smith may be on his way out of Penny's life. She is independent and will do what she thinks is best for her. She still has no plans to marry a farm hand and be poor all her life. She will not marry Smith either, if she doesn't love him and if he doesn't love her.

The weather is warming and soon it will be planting time. Some corn is already being planted. Smith will be home in a month for the summer. Penny got the word that he will have to serve time in the military this summer, so she will not see much of him.

Missy is studying hard and is on the honor roll. She wants to earn a scholarship and go to college. Penny is sure she will.

Penny is working Brown really hard. She is getting him ready for some of the bigger cutting horse shows. Penny wants to win all the Non Pro classes she can. She might cover three states if HB will help pay the bills. Traveling with a horse is expensive. Penny will need a truck and horse trailer if she is going to travel. Cutting horses is an expensive hobby. However HB knows that, and has the money to play the game. It is a hobby for him and he doesn't mind spending the money.

After Suzy and Penny talk, Penny has decided to break up with Smith. Smith's mother and dad want Smith to have a rich girl friend. Penny has noticed, too, that Smith does not take up for her like she thinks she ought to.

Next morning Penny is over at Ms. Ruth's and tells her what she plans to do. Penny says she still loves Smith but he doesn't take up for her. She knows Smith is dating another girl. Ruth just said, "Penny you do what you think is best. Smith is our grandson and we love him but we want you to be happy too. We love you Penny. We won't be mad at you if you break up with Smith. We will love you just as much." Penny hugged Ms. Ruth and said "I will always love you and I will always do anything for you." Ruth thanked her.

That night Penny called Suzy and told her what she was going to do. She is sending Smith's ring back. She told Suzy she could no longer trust Smith and would tell him so. Suzy told Penny she thought she is doing the right thing.

Suzy said she thought Smith is just a mama's boy and a spoiled brat.

Penny wrote the letter and enclosed the ring he bought her. She told him she is breaking up with him. Smith already knew the reasons why. If he pushed for more answers Penny would tell him. Ruth told Smith's mother and dad, and also told them Penny never thought they thought she is good enough for Smith. Ruth told them if Smith could ever find a better girl than Penny he should marry her.

Chapter 25

1n a few days the phone rang at Penny's house. She figured it
was from Smith. Penny asked her dad to answer it and, if it as
from Smith, tell him she was unavailable to come to the phone.
"If you want to leave a number she will call you back," James said.
Smith replied, "No, I will call back later."

He never called back. Penny is moving on with her life. As it
turned out, Smith called Ms. Ruth. He asked if Penny had talked
to her. She said," Penny and I have no secrets." "What did she say?"
Smith asked. Ruth said, "Penny told her she is breaking up with
you." "Did she tell you why?" "Yes she did. She said you have another
girlfriend and you are a mama's boy and she needed a man in her
life and not a wimp." Ruth knew she is lying but she had wanted to
tell Smith that for a long time. She would tell Penny exactly what
she told Smith if she asked.

Penny is hurt, but tough enough to get over Smith. She is going
to school and riding horses. Tomorrow after riding, Penny will dress
up a bit and drive to Suzy's house. They will eat in town mainly
because Suzy's mother is working at the hospital. They will attend
a party at the church. Suzy's church does allow dancing and they
will have a good time. They got to the church just as the party is
starting. Suzy introduced Penny to her friends. All the boys were

coming around asking to be introduced to Penny. They all danced with her and every one of them asked Penny for a date.

Penny and Suzy were the life of the party. They had so much fun. When they got home to Suzy's house they fixed a snack and ate. They lay in bed and talked a long time. When it was time to sleep they gave each other a big hug and said "I love you." Next morning Penny drove home and got there in time for church. Missy went with her. After church Penny took Missy to lunch. They have a good time together.

Back to school the next day then, after school Penny rode Brown hard. She is planning on showing him at the big shows and he needs to try his best to win. Billy is riding most of the new horses during the day when Penny is in school.

It will be just a month until the first cutting horse show. They will show the new horses and HB has decided to breed Peppy to Pete. Penny can still show a few exhibitions on her. Penny agrees with breeding Peppy. Peppy doesn't have the physical strength to hold up in a long season. The exhibitions would be just right for Peppy. Penny is not getting in the hours she has been but with the Saturday hours she is still making some money. She is saving all she can.

James is really working hard keeping all the equipment running on the Silver Leaf. He is as big on preventing breakdowns as he is on fixing them. Some of the workers are rough on equipment. When James sees they are not taking good care of the equipment, he will let McKenzie know. McKenzie will give them a warning the first time, the second time he will fire them. So far James has lowered the repair bills by a bunch. James keeps accurate records on oil changes and lubes of all farm equipment. This saves lots of money.

It is time to select the prom queen for the high school prom. Penny had been nominated. Wednesday is coming up and during the assembly Penny is the prettiest one and her answers to the questions were funny. She is so at ease. The vote is in. The Prom Queen is Penny Parks. She is so happy. She couldn't help but think about how she came to the Silver Leaf Farm riding in the back of an old truck, then to being champion cutting horse rider, and now Prom queen for the high school.

Saturday Ms. Ruth and Penny drove to Little Rock and pick out some very nice outfits for the prom parade and then for prom night. Penny had plenty of money to pay for the outfits but Ms. Ruth would not let her spend her money. Ms. Ruth paid for all of it. Penny couldn't help but tear up and cry. Ms. Ruth bought some really good outfits too.

During the prom parade, the parade float looked so pretty and Penny looked so beautiful. Ms. Ruth hired a photographer to take pictures of Penny in her outfits and at the ceremony before the prom. At the crowning of prom queen, Penny looked so pretty. Earlene and James were so proud. Ruth Hackett is just as proud. She framed Penny's pictures and displayed them in her house. Penny had never been happier.

The local newspaper had pictures of Penny and the Queen's Court. After the prom activities, Penny became the most popular girl in school. She could date any boy she wanted but never dated any of them. She had other things on her mind. She and Suzy were still very close friends. They are together as much as they can be. Sometimes Ruth and Penny would drive to Stuttgart to buy groceries and they would eat at a good restaurant. Ms. Ruth always insisted Penny invite Suzy to meet them. They all had fun.

After they ate, Penny and Ruth would go buy groceries. Ruth and Penny always have fun when they are together. Even buying groceries is fun for them. When they got home Penny would not let Ruth help unload the groceries or let her help put them away. Penny knew where everything went.

Time moves on. In a week Smith will be home for Spring Break. Penny had not heard from him and he is no longer on her mind. If he asked her for a date she might go, but things are not the same.

Brown is getting better at cutting. Penny does not want Billy or anybody else to ride him. Penny knows what she wants him to do and does not want some else messing him up. Penny wants him in a highest zone for cutting.

HB has agreed to have a practice cutting at the Silver Leaf a week before the first monthly cutting. That is good; it will give Brown some good practice. It will also be the week that Smith will be home. Maybe he can see Penny ride. The workers are getting things cleaned up and the cattle pens fixed. The place will look good; grass will be mowed. There will be a concession stand for lunches and restrooms with running water. Penny is proud to be a part of the Silver Leaf. There are four new horses in training, and they will show in the beginners' classes. Penny is not sure which one or two she will show. It doesn't matter; she will go at it to win.

They were riding hard when a car drove up. Smith came walking to the fence. Penny was on the other side of the arena and didn't see him drive up. Billy came over and told her Smith was waiting on her. She didn't immediately stop what she was doing. She went on until she could find a good place to stop. She rode over to Smith and got off her horse. She spoke and asked how he was doing. Smith said he is doing okay. He asked if he could see her after work. Penny asked, "What for, Smith? You have another girlfriend now." Smith said, "I am so sorry about that. I am dating another girl, but that is what we agreed on."

Penny said, "Smith I have to get back on this horse. I will be through here in an hour if you want to talk. You can help me unsaddle the horses and take them to the round pen for a roll. That is the best I can do."

Smith was waiting when Penny got through. He helped with the horses and after they were put up and fed Penny said, "I have to go." Smith said "Penny, please don't go. Let me talk to you please?" "Smith, I loved you more than any boy in the world and you deceived me. I would have waited a lifetime for you, but no more. I have another life now. I came here in the back of a truck and I think you did your best to take advantage of an ignorant country girl and a Sharecropper's Daughter."

"Smith those days are over, I have my own life now. If you want a date with me you have to ask me for a date and don't expect me to automatically say yes."

"Penny, I am asking, in fact I am begging to see you." "Ok when do you want to go out? "Tonight" Smith said. "What are your plans?" Penny asked. "I want to take you out to eat and just talk. I promise I won't try to touch you in any way." "Okay," Penny said, "But I am going to go like I am. I am dirty and nasty but I don't want to go and clean up." Penny told him to follow her home so she could tell her mother and dad.

Earlene wasn't surprised that Smith wants to date Penny again. Penny did wash her face and hands and comb her hair but she left her boots on with the spurs on them. Penny did not sit close to Smith in fact she sat as far away as she could. Smith asked her why she didn't want to date him anymore. Penny said, "There are lots of reasons, but mainly you tried to deceive me. Your mother has never accepted me as your girlfriend, plus you never stood up for me when you could have. I guess you thought I knew my place and wouldn't say anything."

"Smith I am not the same girl that rode onto this farm in the back of an old truck holding on to an old milk cow. I don't need you now I can make it on my own. You go ahead and date any girl you want and if you want to have sex with them, then go for it. You have hurt me all I can be hurt." Smith was silent. They went in the restaurant and Penny ordered a hamburger and a coke, but only ate a few bites. Smith tried his best to cheer her up but failed miserably. She is hurt.

Smith said "Penny what if I quit school and came home and went back to school here? Would that make a difference?" "Smith, your mother and daddy are not going to allow that, and they would only blame me." "Penny if I came back it would be because I love you so much. I can't lie about that, but I can guarantee you nobody is going to blame you, especially my folks."

Penny was quite then. She said "if you do come back are you going to date other girls? It is not okay if you do as long as we are dating. I won't share you with anyone."

"Penny the only reason I would come back is because I love you so much." "Smith, it would make me so happy to have you here but I cannot make myself feel guilty that you came back for me. It isn't long before you will go off to college, then you will be gone again and we would be back in the same situation again."

Smith said, "I know it is hard to explain and I don't have all the answers yet. But I love you and I will do what I have to, to keep you." "Smith I don't know. I do not want to mess up your life. My life is here. I have to help my family and I am making good money with the horses." Smith said "Penny, let's not talk about it now. If you love me like I love you, I promise we will work it out. You know that someday I will own at least a part of the Silver Leaf, then maybe all of it. College is important but it will not impact my life if I don't go."

"Let's think about it Penny. All I want is for you to commit to me that you will one day be my wife and the mother of my children. We will make the rest of it work." Penny started crying again. She said, "Smith, all I ever wanted is to be your wife and the mother of your kids. I love you, but if I can't trust you I will never commit to anything with you, ever."

"Penny I can promise you my trust. I promise and swear that I will be faithful and honor our wedding vows for as long as I live." Penny said, "I want you start honoring them now. That is important to me."

Smith said, "Penny in the next few days I am going to sit down with my folks and tell them I am not going back to school. However, it is only two months before school is out. Can I ask you to wait that long? It would make things work better. There are colleges that are close to here I can attend and get the credits I will need the most to run the Silver Leaf. Please work with me and be my love for life." Penny held him close and said, "I love you and I will love you for life. But please don't let me get the blame."

"Penny, I guarantee my folks will accept you as a daughter and daughter in law."

When they got home they said good bye. Penny told Smith she is going to discuss it with Ms Ruth. Smith said, "That is fine."

Penny went in the house and called Ms Ruth on the phone and asked her if she would talk to her about something important. Ruth told Penny to "come on over I'll be waiting." Ruth knew Penny had been crying. "Come in here in my office Penny and close the door." Penny told her about Smith coming by and all about their conversation about Smith leaving school and coming home to be with Penny. He told me, "I am the love of his life and wants me for his wife and the mother of his kids."

She told her what Smith said about college. Going to one close to home. Ruth sat silent and let Penny finish. Penny said she didn't want to get any blame for Smith's decision but knew she probably would. In a minute Ruth said, "Penny, Smith is old enough to make his own decisions. It is time he grew up. He has been spoiled all his life and maybe this will force him to grow up. I hope so. Let's just sit back and see if he carries through with what he says. I hope for his sake he does but if he doesn't Penny, I would let him go. You can't take care of him all his life."

"Let me tell you this. There is no other person in the world I would rather have as a grand Daughter in law than you. I love you and you love me and that means more to me than you will ever know." "Thank you Ms Ruth. I do love you so much and you always give me good advice." Penny gave her a hug and said goodnight.

She drove home and got in the shower, after she got her night clothes on she talked to her mother and told her what Smith said and what Ms Ruth said. Earlene said, "I have to agree with Ms Ruth. Smith needs to prove he is growing up."

Smith had done lots of thinking and praying. He knew his grand dad would give him a job on the farm but he did not want that and he knew Penny would not accept any charity. If he married her he would have to make it on his own. Smith is ok with that but he wanted to talk to his grand dad and his dad. Smith asked HB for a time he could visit with him. HB said, "Come by first thing in the morning."

The next morning Smith is waiting when HB drove up to the office. HB said, "Come on in, what have you got on your mind? Grand Dad it is a long story but if you can I want you to hear me out." "Go ahead Smith, I got all day."

"Grand dad I know you know I love Penny. We are both young, maybe too young but I love her and I want to marry her. She loves me and will marry me but she says, "We have to make it on our own and not take a job on the farm because we know your grand Dad would give you a job and pay you well. That is unacceptable to me." "Grand Dad, can you look down the road about ten to twenty years from now and tell me something I can get into now that I can support my family? We want kids so we will need money."

HB said, "Smith I am so glad you and Penny see it that way. "What ever you do you will need some help and support. I am getting up in years and there are things that would be good to make money but I don't need money. Let's start here on the Silver Leaf. We buy lots of seed, fertilizer, equipment, insecticides and hardware. We are in the process of putting down irrigation wells power units and it is hard to find someone to do that. We could sell all those things from here but would be better to have a business located in a town."

"I know a seed dealership that is for sale. If I had to bet on any one thing I believe it would be in seed. If you bought the seed dealership all the other things can be added at the same time. You should do quite well. You know the Silver Leaf is probably the biggest user of seed and fertilizer along with the irrigation wells in the county. As long as your price is competitive we would buy from you. We need a supplier of good Foundation and Registered seed. You could rent some land from us to raise those seed, gin them at our gin and then resale. We both will make money. Now might be the best time to get into this. The Mule days are gone, farm mechanization is taking over and that is a whole new ball game," Grand Dad and added.

"That is an opportunity that very few young people will ever have. If this sounds like something you would like to do I will do all I can to help get you started. You talk to your dad, if he is agreeable we will get it done. If he does not agree we will do it any way. It is your life, not his. Smith said, "Grand Dad I thank you so much and I promise I will work harder than any body. HB said, "Wait Smith, working hard is one thing but you will have a family to see after and raise. I will not have you neglecting your family for a few dollars." Smith said, "Grand Dad, I agree and I promise my family and Penny will always come first."

"I will tell you Smith, Ruth and I both love Penny like a daughter. She is a good, kind person that is not afraid of work and she loves us and would do anything for us if we asked. We would be so greatly honored to have her as a Grand Daughter in law."

Chapter 26

Smith went home to talk to his dad and mom. He told them what he and his Grand Dad talked about. Smith told them he is going to marry Penny. "School will be out in a month and I can get business classes close to home to help me run a business. Grand Dad told me about a seed company that is for sale and he will help me get it and the Silver Leaf will buy from us if our prices are competitive. We can sell other things too like irrigation wells, hardware, insecticides and other things."

Smith's Dad said, "Smith you are not going to let some little trashy sharecropper girl talk you into anything." Smith said, "Dad you need to take that statement back and take it back now. Penny is the love of my life and I will not have you or anybody else talk about her like that. Do you understand that?" Further, you and mom are going to accept her as your daughter in law. Don't you ever talk about Penny that way as long as you live. Mom that goes for you too."

"Now you can help us or not it doesn't matter. Gran Dad is willing and wanting to help. I suspect you better not ever make a statement about Penny like you just did in front of him or Granny Ruth. I don't need your help. I was hoping for your blessing but I can see I am not going to get that." "I am going back to see Grand

Dad in the morning and get the ball rolling. I will tell him what you said. Now, do I have a place to stay until I can get things worked out and a place to live?" Mary said, "Yes, you do Smith and I would never think about Penny the way your Dad just spoke of her. I will accept her just as if she is my daughter." Thanks Mom, I appreciate that. One more thing Dad if you try to stop us from getting married I will join the army and volunteer to go to Korea. I am serious about this matter."

Smith's Dad didn't say anything, he regretted making a statement like that about Penny but Smith is not going to let him take it back. "It is my life and not yours." The next morning Smith was at his Grand Dads office. He asked Smith how it went. Smith told him exactly what his dad had said about Penny. HB picked up the phone and dialed Mark's office number. He told Mark to "be in my office today at one o'clock sharp."

If you can't be here I will call another lawyer to handle the paper work. Further more, if you ever make a statement about Penny being a "trashy sharecropper girl" again I will see to it you don't inherit one acre or one dime of Silver Leaf Land or money. Now take it or leave it. Smith and I are going to buy us a seed company. And I am praying that he and Penny become man and wife and have us lots of great grand kids."

All Smith's Dad could say was, "Yes sir, I am sorry I made that statement about Penny. It will never happen again." HB said, "I hope for your sake you never make that mistake again."

"I am sorry I was trying to control Smith's life. I will help do anything I can do to help Smith and Penny get a good start. I also agree about the seed business, it will make them a good living and give them a chance to have a happy life and marriage. I will start preparing the paper work." Smith couldn't wait to tell Penny. He found her at the barn and asked if she could take some time to talk to him first then talk to Grand Dad and Granny Ruth. After that they would talk to his mom and dad.

"Smith what is this all about? Why is it so important?" "It is Penny I assure you. First though I want to talk to your Dad and Mom. I want to do that first, tonight as a matter of fact."

"Smith I can leave now and go home and clean up. Dad will be home about six o'clock. Would you have supper with us?" Smith said, "I will but I am too excited to eat much." Penny called Billy over and told him she had to leave. Billy said, "That is ok just tie your horse to the fence." Penny said, "Ok Smith, follow me home." When Penny got home she went straight to the shower. She dressed in clean clothes and went in and sat by Smith. Smith said, "Penny let's walk outside."

"Penny, lots of things has happened today, important things. First thing I want to ask you if you would marry me and be the mother of our children." Before Penny could say anything Smith said, "I want you to hear me out before you speak. I need to finish out the year and graduate with my class; It is only two months away. You will be graduating about the same time. I have talked to Grand Dad. I asked him what business he thought we could get into that would make us a good living. I never asked him for a job only advice. Penny, we will make it on our own we will have to have some help and advice but only that. No charity. We can make lots of money if we handle it right. Grand Dad told me about a seed company that is for sale we can add feed, fertilizer, hardware and irrigation wells."

He explained to Penny what HB had told him about the "Silver Leaf is one of the biggest users of seed, fertilizer and the other things I mentioned. Grand Dad said they needed a good supply of good seed. He said he is getting on in years and didn't need more money. Penny this is our chance. Grand dad said there is no other person in the world he would rather see me marry than you. He loves you and knows you love him and Ruth the same way. I also talked to my mom and dad. Dad was against it at first but after Grand Dad talked to him he came over to our side."

About that time James came driving up. Penny said, "Dad, Smith wants to talk to you." James spoke and asked Smith if it could wait until he had a chance to clean up. "Sure" Finally everything calmed down and they were at the table eating supper. Smith said, "Mr. Parks I have something very important to ask you."

"Sure go ahead,"

"Mr. Parks I am asking for your daughters hand in marriage," Smith said. James got choked on some food he was so surprised. "Smith, I don't know what to say. If you love her and she loves you and you think you can make a living for your family you have my blessing."

"I have to ask though what about Mr. HB and Ms Ruth and your mother and dad?"

"We have their blessing but I want to say we really don't need their permission. Penny and I will make it on our own." Smith told James about the conversation he had with HB. "Mr. Parks. Grand Dad told me there are things that would make a lot of money but he didn't need more money."

He told him about the seed company that is for sale. He told him about renting land from the Silver Leaf Farm and raising foundation and registered seed and ginning it at the Silver Leaf Gin. "Grand Dad said we both would make money. I know all this needs to be worked out but Dad is already working on the papers. I won't have to drive off and leave Penny any more. Penny has not said she will marry me but I am praying that she will. Grand Dad said the mule days are over and the age of farm mechanization is here. It is a good time to get started." James said, "I agree with that."

"I guess Smith you and Penny need to talk if she says yes then you have our blessing." Smith said, "Penny will you marry me and be my wife forever?

Penny said, "Gee Smith can I think about it tonight and let you know tomorrow?" "Penny, I am not kidding." Penny screamed, "YES! YES! Smith, I am yours forever. Oh Smith you have made me so happy." By then tears were streaming down Penny's face. "Oh I need to tell Ms Ruth and Mr. HB." Smith says "they already know I am asking you and they are so excited they will have you for a Grand Daughter in law. They are so happy too."

"Smith I love you so much now you will be mine forever." "How many kids do you want?" "A bunch," Smith said. Penny said, "Smith don't get me pregnant on our wedding night. I want to spend some time with you before we start our family." Smith said, I want the same thing." "Oh Penny, I am so happy. You just don't know."

Smith stayed a long time he and Penny talked but didn't make any plans. It is too soon and Smith didn't how long the legal work would take then they both had to graduate from high school. Penny is still riding horses and wants to continue until they start their family. No wedding date is set. Ms Ruth and Smith's mom will have some say in that. That is fine with Penny.

Times had never been happier on the Silver Leaf Farm. Penny married the love of her life and HB and Ruth were getting the most precious granddaughter in law. Smith's folks were making the best of it. Smith's dad and mom wanted Smith to marry into some wealthy family however Smith's mom is making the best of it. All the Bridal Showers seemed like they went on forever. Penny made sure her mom had good clothes to wear and she is made up properly for the parties. Earlene had gotten away from the inferiority complex she came there with to a very fine moved onto the Silver Leaf Farm. James gave Penny away to Smith and HB was Smith's best man at the wedding.

Penny and Smith were married in the church that brought the Parks family food, clothes and curtains the first year they moved on to the Silver Leaf farm.

There were some legal hoops to be jumped through. Penny and Smith were too young to own a large business. HB and Ruth had to become the buyers of the Seed Company and hold it until Smith and Penny were of legal age. HB and Ruth did not want Smith's dad to have anything to do with it except some legal work. If Penny continues with the horses and the seed business she will help make the family wealthy. She is a great saleslady and all the farmers love her. She and Smith will be millionaires by the time they turn forty. Not counting any inheritance from the Hackett family. Smith's dad had a reputation as a bully around the farm. No one liked him growing up. So no one really cares what he thinks about anything.

Penny wants to keep riding and showing horses as long as she can and that is ok with HB and Ruth. They still want their cutting horse operation to be promoted. Smith and Penny decided to build a large house on the Silver Leaf Farm. That is where they wanted to live and raise their family. Suzy Pugh and Penny are still the best of friends and will always be. Suzy would go to Nurse's School and Andy would become a doctor. Both Suzy and Andy would go to the same college.

Ruth and HB couldn't wait until they have great grand children. Finally Smith and Penny took control of the Silver Leaf Seed Company and were able to add fertilizer, insecticides, hardware, irrigation supplies, fuel and other items to the inventory. Smith and Penny will made lots of money. Penny will keep on riding horses and tending to Smith's needs.

A few happy years passed, The Silver Leaf Farm built a new horse barn and two arenas one covered and one open. Penny became the National Cutting Horse Non Pro Champion. She was able to buy HB the present she promised him. It is a silver and gold belt buckle with a SILVER LEAF CUTTING HORSES engraved on it. It had an engraving of a girl riding a cutting horse without any tack. That is Penny of course.

Then one day Penny ran in Ms Ruth's house and announced, "I AM PREGNANT WITH TWIN BOYS!!!"

MS Ruth said, "Oh Penny I am so happy." "Can I tell Mr. HB? I think you just did Penny. He heard you."

Penny is still a beautiful girl. Now, no one calls Penny a "trashy sharecropper girl." Now they have to deal with the many maternity showers for Penny.

Missy is the Art Teacher at England High School. Her husband, Don Dyer, earned a Degree in Agriculture at the University of

Arkansas and works for the Seed farm. James Jr. is a big farmer. Earlene is busy with grandkids. She had grown up a lot over the years too. A pretty lady with a pleasing personality. Earlene still has the purse with the money her mother gave her. Although no one knows exactly where she hid it. James is still in charge of the farm shop and has had numerous raises. Actually, James invented and owns patents for various pieces of equipment he developed for the Silver Leaf Farm. If James cashed it all out he is probably a millionaire too. HB passed away in 1968 and Ruth in 1972 both are buried in the family cemetery.

None of the Parks family have ever been hungry a day since moving onto the Silver Leaf Farm. All the good things that have happened to the Parks family and the Hackett family can be attributed to hard work, plain living, sweat, wit, grit and spit. May they all live long and happy lives and may God continue to bless them.

THE END

Epilogue

Penny is pregnant with twin girls, not boys as the Doctor thought.
Penny and Smith had two more children, both boys.

9 781733 226547